OXFORD LEGAL PHILOSOPHY

Series editors: Timothy Endicott, John Gardner (1965–2019), and Leslie Green

Property Rights

OXFORD LEGAL PHILOSOPHY

Series editors: Timothy Endicott, John Gardner (1965–2019), and Leslie Green

Oxford Legal Philosophy publishes the best new work in philosophically-oriented legal theory. It commissions and solicits monographs in all branches of the subject, including works on philosophical issues in all areas of public and private law, and in the national, transnational, and international realms; studies of the nature of law, legal institutions, and legal reasoning; treatments of problems in political morality as they bear on law; and explorations in the nature and development of legal philosophy itself. The series represents diverse traditions of thought but always with an emphasis on rigour and originality. It sets the standard in contemporary jurisprudence.

In memory of John Gardner
1965–2019

ALSO AVAILABLE IN THE SERIES

Right of Redress
Andrew Gold

A Theory of Legal Personhood
Visa A. J. Kurki

Imposing Risk: A Normative Framework
John Oberdiek

Law and Morality at War
Adil Ahmad Haque

Ignorance of Law
A Philosophical Inquiry
Douglas Husak

Reason and Restitution
A Theory of Unjust Enrichment

Charlie Webb
Allowing for Exceptions

A Theory of Defences and Defeasibility in Law
Luís Duarte d'Almeida

The Ends of Harm
The Moral Foundations of Criminal Law
Victor Tadros

Corrective Justice
Ernest J. Weinrib

Conscience and Conviction
The Case for Civil Disobedience
Kimberley Brownlee

The Nature of Legislative Intent
Richard Ekins

Why Law Matters
Alon Harel

Property Rights

A Re-Examination

J. E. Penner

OXFORD
UNIVERSITY PRESS

OXFORD
UNIVERSITY PRESS

Great Clarendon Street, Oxford, OX2 6DP,
United Kingdom

Oxford University Press is a department of the University of Oxford.
It furthers the University's objective of excellence in research, scholarship,
and education by publishing worldwide. Oxford is a registered trade mark of
Oxford University Press in the UK and in certain other countries

First Edition published in 2020

Published in the United States of America by Oxford University Press
198 Madison Avenue, New York, NY 10016, United States of America

British Library Cataloguing in Publication Data
Data available

Library of Congress Control Number: 2019953164

ISBN 978–0–19–883012–2

To Elizabeth, Mae, and George, there at the beginning

Series Editors' Preface

In the two decades since the publication of James Penner's groundbreaking book, *The Idea of Property in Law* (Oxford: Clarendon Press, 1997), the theory of private law has undergone a terrific boom. Much exciting work has been done on the theory of the law of obligations, focusing on jural relations—personal relations of legal right. An elucidation of the law of property depends on aligning that perspective on what one person owes another person with a true perspective on the relation between an owner of property and the thing itself. In binocular vision, animals such as human beings achieve a brilliant feat of integration without even thinking about it. The alignment of perspectives in the theory of private law depends, by contrast, on extended critical thought and reflection.

Penner has been training his energy and agility on the problems and on the wealth of new thinking in the field for those two decades. Now—with his characteristic cogency and candour—he offers a fresh new integration of perspectives.

To explain property rights, the theorist needs to focus on the rules that create jural relations. Listing the jural relations that arise from ownership of property (which no one could do) would lack the explanatory power that can be unleashed by identifying the rules that generate the relations. The effects in personam of rights in rem can only be explained in impersonal terms. Jural relations do not explain property; they are what needs explaining.

The result of this extended reflection is the view that jural relations emerging from property arise from general rules conferring and imposing them on persons, and the explanation of the relations lies in the rationale for the rules. And the explanatory work is furthered by new reflections on the justifications for such general rules. Our relations of right towards each other are shaped by our relations to the earth and to things. Rights in land ought to be constrained in ways that reflect our common interest in the earth. And there is a natural right to property: a moral right that does not depend on the state, although states have correlative duties.

Along the way, Penner honours the brilliant Wesley Hohfeld by taking a critical approach to his focus on the logic of jural relations. That critical approach is also constructive, and reflects a dedication to the explanation of the potential justification of property rights. If not for his untimely death, perhaps Hohfeld himself might have gone on to make some of the same progress in the explanation of the law of property that James Penner presents in his new book.

Timothy Endicott
John Gardner (1965–2019)
Leslie Green

Preface

About twenty years ago I wrote a longish book[1] and a very long paper[2] setting out what I thought were the central contentious issues in the theory of property rights, and my proposed solutions for them, or at my least reactions to them. The less longish book you have before you is partly a reflection on the twenty years of literature that has arisen in the meantime, some bits of which arose in reaction to those publications. But it also reflects independent developments in my own thinking. Either way, I hope it breaks a little new ground.

The first part considers again the sense in which a property right is a bundle of rights. Chapter 1 is essentially an additive exercise, that is, it adds to what I have previously written to explain why the 'bundle of rights' picture of property (or BOR) is misguided. I hope never to have to write about this again, but only time will tell. Chapter 2 is entirely new. In it I consider a pair of 'nominalisms', each of which claims that the sort of conceptualization of property that I and other anti-bundle theorists offer is flawed; nominalists deny the normative 'reality' or 'efficacy' of legal concepts such as 'title' or 'fee simple', claiming instead that all the normative, that is, legal, action takes place with respect to more basic (e.g. Hohfeldian) jural relations. In reply I argue that any attempt to reduce abstract concepts like 'title' to jural relations amongst individuals would ensure that we suffer a loss of understanding, and that this will hold true of any actual 'Hohfeldian' reduction of legal

[1] Penner 1997.
[2] Penner 1996.

concepts to individual Hohfeldian jural relations. The fact that nobody ever undertakes such a reduction is fairly strong evidence of the truth of this claim.

Chapter 2 also sets out one of the principal themes of the book, embodied in the principle that I dub 'The Guidance Function Principle of Norms', GFPN for short. The principle is this: that which is irrelevant to the application of a norm is not part of that norm. So, for example, it is normally[3] irrelevant to the application of the law of negligence that the alleged tortfeasor tends to vote Tory. Or that his mother is a Methodist. Or that he once owned a cocker spaniel. As I will argue, much of the confusion that arises from the BOR and nominalism arises from not honouring this principle.

Which brings us to Part 2. Part 2 undertakes a fairly minute analysis of what the Hohfeldian perspective on property offers the student of the subject. In purely commemorative terms this is timely, since it is now a century since Hohfeld's untimely death. Remarkably, to my mind, I don't think this sort of exacting analysis has really been conducted to the extent one might have expected, given Hohfeld's undoubted stature. To cut to the ending, my examination leads to an almost entirely negative conclusion, namely that no version of 'Hohfeldian analysis' illuminates our understanding of property rights; indeed, it obscures much which is of vital importance to that understanding.

One of the lessons that this part reveals is that the law of property, perhaps 'private law' in general, has much more to do with general and impersonal rules than it has do with rights,[4] or at least rights as explained by Hohfeld. In particular one of my conclusions will be that to the extent that we wish to talk about private law claim rights and powers, and of course we should, we should understand that the relation of correlativity between rights vis-à-vis duties and powers vis-à-vis liabilities is more complex than Hohfeld envisaged it, and the correlativity can only be achieved through the mediating function of rules.

Part 3 advances the claim that there is sense to be made of the intuition that a right to property, conceived broadly as the right to

[3] One could concoct undergraduate exam hypotheticals or problem questions in which each of these features might indeed be relevant. All statements of legal norms implicitly or explicitly include a *ceteris paribus* clause. That is, legal norms are not understood to be exceptionless.

[4] Including all of the four Hohfeldian variations of rights: claim-rights, liberties, powers, and immunities.

make use of the external resources of the world, is a pre-political or natural (which is not to say asocial) right, that is, a right which does not depend upon the existence of a state. The claim turns upon three crucial issues. The first is the relationship between the right of exclusive possession of tangible property, land and chattels, and the right to use those kinds of things exclusively. In short, what is the normative relationship between exclusive possession and use? That will be the subject matter of Chapter 7.

The second, considered in Chapter 8, is the justification of a natural right to exploit the material resources of the earth. Since the publication of the two works mentioned at the outset there has been a strong re-assertion of the Kantian theory of property rights. Two features of this account are pressing, at least for me. The first is that there can be no genuine property rights outside of a civil condition, that is, outside a legal regime imposed by the state. The second is that the very nature of any *right* to exploit the material resources of the earth (or indeed to acquire any rights as against others by entering into contracts) is necessarily a property right whose form is exclusionary. I disagree with both of these claims, and part of this chapter is devoted to saying why. Another claim I make in this chapter is that on any plausible conception of a natural right to exploit the external resources of the earth, the most that can be justified is a more or less extensive usufructory right, that is, a right to things which depends upon one's actually using them. It is only with the addition of other considerations that this natural right serves as part of the justification of the formally exclusionary property rights that we generally have under the law.

The third issue, dealt with in Chapter 9, is the ever-vexed issue of rights in land, in particular why land is or is not suitable as the kind of thing that should primarily be regulated by private property rights. Indeed, I shall suggest that the current regime, speckled though it is with many restrictions on landowners, gives insufficient weight to our common interest in the Earth. This, I hasten to say, will not be justified in relation to any idea that the Earth is 'owned in common' by the inhabitants of the planet. Common ownership is the wrong way to think about this common interest, in much the way that 'self-ownership' is the wrong way to think about the interest we have in our lives and our selves.

I am very conscious of the fact that this book only scratches the surface of many significant issues and controversies in property theory. It basically addresses a number of issues in the field that have come to preoccupy me, which doubtless reflect some lapses of attention and some failures of appreciation. Yet I hope to convince the reader of the importance of the ideas I do address, and in that sense this book can be regarded as something of a ground-clearing exercise for further reflection. I hope to be forgiven for clearing a smaller patch of ground than I might otherwise have done. This means that I have not addressed in detail the recent work of Larry Alexander, Alan Brudner, Eric Claeys, Hanoch Dagan, Larissa Katz, Chris Essert, Adam Mossoff, James Stern, Christopher Newman, Eduardo Penalver, and Carol Rose, all of whose work deserves devoted attention in its own right, and despite the fact that I have learned so much from them. My excuse, and my apology, is that I wanted this to be a book with a very focused few aims.

Finally, and most gratefully, this book has given me the opportunity to collect my thoughts about these issues, many of which I presented over the last twenty years in no systematic fashion. That thought provides a nice reason to turn to the help I have most bounteously received from others. I gratefully acknowledge my many debts to those who have spurred me to think again, and more deeply, about all of this. What this book presents, then, as my current thinking on the rather grand topic of property, was very much a collective endeavour in the best tradition of the academy.

I am grateful to Lisa Austin, Peter Benson, Michael Bridge, Alan Brudner, Rob Chambers, Eric Claeys, Rowan Cruft, Simon Douglas, Timothy Endicott, David Foster, David Frydrych, John Gardner, Josh Getzler, Aravind Ganesh, Shane Glackin, Leslie Green, Hanoch Dagan, Avihay Dorfman, Chris Essert, Andrew Halpin, the late Jim Harris, Norman Ho, Duncan Horne, Hu Ying, Larissa Katz, Dennis Klimchuk, Matt Kramer, David Lametti, David Lefkowitz, Jeremiah Lau, Tim Liau, Michael Littlewood, Mark McBride, Ben McFarlane, Tom Merrill, Charles Mitchell, Adam Mossoff, Steve Munzer, Chris Newman, John Oberdiek, Johan Olsthoorn, Mike Otsuka, David Owens, Dennis Patterson, Ronen Perry, Chris Pierson, Karluis Quek, Arthur Ripstein, Mathias Risse, Carol Rose, Luke Rostill, Nicole Roughan, Nick Sage, Irina Sakharova, Irit Samet, Seana Shiffrin, Andrew Simester, Henry Smith, Lionel Smith, Patrick Smith, Steve Smith, James Stern, Gopal Sreenivasan, Rob Stevens, James Stern, Zhong-Xing Tan, Peter Turner, Bill Swadling, Jeremy Waldron, Stephen Watterson, Ernie Weinrib, Leif Wenar, Fred Wilmot-Smith, Sam Williams, Sarah Worthington, and Katrina Wyman for comments, questions, and discussions over the years, and to many students in Singapore, Oxford, London, Toronto and elsewhere who were kind enough to let me share these ideas with them. I owe especial thanks for helpful comments and discussion as this project drew close to the finishing line to Chris Essert and Seana Shiffrin on Chapter 1, 1.4, to Mark McBride and Shane Glackin on Chapter 2, 2.3, to Michael Moore on Chapter 4, 5.4.4, to Chris Essert, Donal Nolan, and Arthur Ripstein on Chapter 7, 7.2, and to Peter Chau, Arivend Ganesh, Arie Rosen, Nicole Roughan, Steve Smith, Lionel Smith, and Rob Stevens on Chapter 8. Let me say to all of the above, I could not have written this book without you, and our conversations have inspired me to complete it, as well as making the whole project a great deal of fun. Huge thanks to you all.

I must also thank Jaya Appalasamy, Wendy Wee, and Kriz Zhao for helping me to find spare bits of time to plug away at this whilst I was Vice-Dean for Research at NUS from 2015 to 2018.

Finally, inexpressible gratitude to Duncan Horne, who read the entire manuscript and made the final result immeasurably better. And for so much else.

I am delighted to acknowledge the funding support of the National University of Singapore (Grant WBS Number: R-241-000-127-133).

Last, but never least, thanks to Jamie Berezin, the editors of this series, Timothy Endicott, John Gardner, and Les Green,—and—at Oxford University Press, who saw this through to the end.

Off we go.

Table of Contents

List of Abbreviations

BOR	The Bundle of Rights Picture of Property
BPrN	Basic Property Norm—The 'Property' Exclusionary Norm for Tangible Property
BUsN	Basic Usufructory Norm—The 'Usufructory' Exclusionary Norm for Tangible Property
FP	The Fluctuation Problem. As regards rights in rem, such as title to Blackacre, the actual aggregate of Hohfeldian multital jural relations is in constant flux as people are born or die.
GFPN	The Guidance Function Principle of Norms—That which is irrelevant to the application of a norm is not part of that norm
HMP	The Hohfeldian Multital Picture of Jural Relations—The 'picture' of our private law legal relations under which each individual is in an extensive web of one to one right–duty relations that links that person with every other person
SI	The Standing Issue, that is, the issue about who has right to bring a claim in respect of another's property, that is, about who has a recognized interest in the property of another
SPP	The Switched Places Problem, that is, the problem for claiming, in cases of the transfer of a right from A to B, that A's right is the same as B's, in view of the fact that the aggregate of jural relations B acquires has one jural relation that A didn't have—A's duty to B not to trespass upon Blackacre—and A had one jural relation B doesn't acquire—B's duty to A not to trespass upon Blackacre

PART I

The Complex Structure of Legal Title to Property

As I indicated in the preface, this book is a re-examination of the nature of property rights, which builds upon my prior work but reflects the development of my thought in the last twenty years or so. Our first task, undertaken in this part, is to look at what I have called the 'complex' nature of legal title to property. This complex nature is particularly evident in relation to property in land, where the law recognizes a number of different kinds of interests in land, such as easements and restrictive covenants. In the first chapter I hope to show how this complexity is best understood, taking as my foil the reigning convention when, many moons ago, I started writing about property: that property is best understood as a bundle of rights, a thesis I abbreviate to 'BOR'.

In the second chapter I look at two 'nominalisms'. The first, moral–political nominalism derives much of its force from BOR—indeed it might have been regarded as an entailment of BOR. Moral–political nominalism is the idea that property has a 'nominalist' ontology: roughly and briefly that we can apply the concept of property to particular rights or bundles of rights pretty much as we wish. In other words property, as a legal concept, has no central organizing features in consequence of which, if they were there, we cannot just treat any right or bundle of rights as property rights. This nominalism is 'moral–political' in so far as it holds that the only reasons for treating certain rights or bundles of rights as property rights are various moral and political reasons, moral and political reasons which are contested. As different contested moral and political viewpoints hold sway over time, our property rights will correspondingly vary. In so far as this thesis is correct, the legal concept of property is in ever-present danger of 'disintegration' as a working legal category because of that very ontology. The second, 'scientific reductionist' nominalism, is again a development of BOR, relying heavily upon Hohfeld's theory of jural relations. On this nominalism the reality of the legal relations which fall under the rubric of property are a battery or series or assemblage of Hohfeldian jural relations. Complexes of these jural relations, such as A's fee simple title to Blackacre, have no genuine or real normative force within the legal system. Legal normativity lies in, and only in, the normative force of the Hohfeldian jural relations themselves, taken one by one. If correct, and I hope to persuade you that it is not, this nominalism undermines the idea that there are, or can be, general norms, general legal rules, that structure the phenomenon of property rights.

One of the themes of these two chapters will be my disagreement with what might be called 'rights fundamentalism'. As I shall point out in a number of places, what seems to motivate both BOR and the two nominalisms is the idea that individual rights, understood as individual Hohfeldian jural relations, are the atomic, basic normative elements that structure our legal interpersonal relations. More general norms, such as rules of law that apply in many cases, are best conceived of as derivative of those jural relations. They are at best abbreviations or short-cut summaries of how our rights play out in practice. I take the opposite view. Call me a 'rules fundamentalist'. In the view I shall defend, the derivation goes the other way round. General norms, general legal rules, are basic, and whatever rights or Hohfeldian jural relations there are exist in virtue of the way those general rules apply in particular cases to particular individuals. At this point all of this is undoubtedly very abstract and schematic. I only flag the point here as a marker which I shall have to redeem as the argument proceeds. This theme will also resonate throughout Part 2 where I examine Hohfeldian jural relations in painstaking detail.

1

The 'Bundle of Rights' Picture of Property Revisited

In the near century since Hohfeld published the second of his two papers on fundamental legal conceptions,[1] his thought has been generally regarded as a bulwark of the 'bundle of rights' picture of property, BOR for short. It is the supposed contribution to that picture which begins the discussion in this chapter.

1.1 Hohfeldian Analysis and the Thesis That Property is a 'Bundle of Rights'

During the 2016 US presidential election it was said of Donald Trump's supporters that they took him seriously, but not literally, whereas the press took him literally, but not seriously.[2] Something similar can be said about the debate over BOR. Proponents of BOR take the BOR picture seriously, but not literally. They think, for example, that it generates a genuinely novel and informative perspective on, or theory of, property rights. So they take it seriously. But, as I will show, they do not really take it literally. There have been really no attempts to work out its details, and deal with its problematic aspects, which I am about to address.

[1] Hohfeld 1913–14; Hohfeld 1916–17.

[2] Selena Zito, 'Taking Trump Seriously, Not Literally' The Atlantic, 23 September 2016: https://www.theatlantic.com/politics/archive/2016/09/trump-makes-his-case-in-pittsburgh/501335/.

Property Rights. J. E. Penner, Oxford University Press (2020) © J. E. Penner.
DOI: 10.1093/oso/9780198830122.001.0001

By contrast, the opponents of BOR take it literally, but not seriously.[3] We don't think it generates any genuine insights and think that it leads to mistaken ideas about property. So we cannot take it seriously as a theory. But we do take it literally, which is why we think we can show that it cannot be taken seriously. Taken literally, that is, genuinely assessing what it *says*, shows it to be a failed theoretical programme in so far as it amounts to a theoretical programme at all (as opposed to being nothing more than a slogan).[4]

BOR, as a thesis about property, has two possible interpretations, sometimes taken together:[5]

(1) that the legal configuration understood as a property right, say a fee simple in Blackacre, is in fact an aggregate of norms, such as the liberty to enter Blackacre, the power to license others to enter, the liberty to build upon Blackacre, the power to grant an easement over Blackacre, and so on. However, there is no necessary and sufficient set of these constituting norms which make up the 'property right' to Blackacre. Different aggregates will occur in different circumstances, and so the legal labelling of some such aggregate as a 'property' right cannot properly be done on the basis of some central constituting norms, such as the right that others exclude themselves from Blackacre, or the right to deal with the title to Blackacre. Therefore determining whether, for example, rights in respect of excised human cells[6] count as property rights is largely a matter of policy considerations, not a matter of 'legal analysis'.[7] There is no 'internal'

[3] Besides myself, I would cite Tom Merrill and Henry Smith as prominent opponents: see Merrill and Smith 2001a, 2001b, 2007; Merrill 1998, 2011; Smith 2004b, 2011, 2012b. See also Ripstein 2009, 88; Ripstein 2013.

[4] Penner 1996a; Smith 2012b, 1694–5; cf. Halpin 2017.

[5] These were first distinguished clearly, as far as I know, by me in Penner 1996a.

[6] See, e.g., *Moore v Regents of the Univ. of Cal.*, 793 P.2d 479 (Cal. 1990), *Yearworth and others v North Bristol NHS Trust* [2009] EWCA Civ 37, [2010] QB 1.

[7] There is sometimes a claim that the bundle of rights theory, if true, makes us understand that only policy considerations are relevant in determining whether someone holding one or more sticks of the bundle should successfully be able to claim that it follows that some other stick in the bundle should be recognized as his. Thus, it would be false to argue from the fact that I have the right to immediate, exclusive possession of a chattel that I should also have the power to license another to use it. No sticks 'go together' legally on any genuinely normative account. I only point this out to say that I do not think that the anti-bundle theorist has any commitment in favour of or against policy arguments that would enlarge or restrict rights in property. (See also Merrill 1998, 753–4.) What the anti-bundle theorist argues is that one of the considerations relevant to determining the incidence of property rights, that is, whether a

organizing principle which makes sense of the fact that certain property norms, such as the right to immediate, exclusive possession of a tangible like Blackacre and the power to license others to do what would otherwise amount to a trespass, seem to go together.

(2) that the legal concept of property is a *concept* of a particular kind, whose application is not to be understood as applying a definition framed in terms of necessary and sufficient conditions as one would, say, in the case of 'chair' (a portable seat for one) or 'bachelor' (an eligible to be married yet unmarried male). The concept of property has a different mode of application; it might be a 'family resemblance concept', for example, applied in terms of paradigmatic instances with a broad similarity rider.

Whilst these two interpretations are related,[8] I shall not discuss the second here.[9]

Here I am concerned to address the intellectual foundations for the idea that a property right is a structural composite, in particular understood as an aggregate of Hohfeldian multital jural relations. I shall assume that property rights relate to tangible property in the first instance, land and chattels, though I will consider intangible property, choses in action and the like, where looking at them can be illuminating.

To foreshadow a theme of the book, if what I say here and in subsequent chapters is sound, then there is a larger payoff than just the result that a Hohfeldian BOR theorist cannot give an account of legal concepts such as the fee simple. It should also show that no system of private law can be exhaustively represented by interpersonal jural relations alone. It will also require the inclusion of norms that are not interpersonally relational in only this way, that is, general and impersonal *rules*.

proposed configuration of rights, duties, powers, and so on is a property right, is the internal structure of title; see 1.4.

[8] To the extent that a concept is applied on the basis of paradigms with some sort of similarity rider, applying the concept to a new instance might be framed as the examination of whether the instance shares some sufficient amount of features with one or other of the paradigmatic instances, that is, how many sticks found in a paradigmatic bundle it happens to have.

[9] For discussion see Penner 1996a. For a very different perspective on the conceptual structure of property, relating it to language in terms of communication of information, see Smith 2003.

(Those readers unacquainted with, or rusty on, the Hohfeldian scheme of fundamental jural relations, should pop over now to the beginning of Chapter 3, where the scheme is set out in detail.)

1.2 The Hohfeld–Honoré Synthesis and the Tripartite Structure of Title

The Hohfeld–Honoré synthesis[10] underpinning BOR rests upon a fairly serious mistake.[11] The property theory community has failed to notice two features of the synthesis. In the first place, whilst the Hohfeldian examination of jural norms is analytic if it is anything, Honoré's bundle of incidents going to make up the legal concept of ownership is anything but. For that reason, their concepts of property do not synthesize, unless Honoré's incidents are radically reconfigured. Secondly, and perhaps more importantly, when we do that reconfiguration, we see that many of the standard incidents have their origin in the law of obligations, not the law of property, properly understood. In consequence, the bundle of incidents which might be regarded as going with title to property is really nothing like the way BOR portrays it.

That Hohfeldian jural relations are analytic is evident. Hohfeld aimed to produce an exhaustive analysis of the fundamental relations out of which the legal position of any one person vis-à-vis any other can be comprehensively formulated. He had a limited success to this extent: in a large number of cases, any question that can be raised in litigation between two parties can be analysed as a question of which one of the four jural relations he identified obtains between the two with respect to a particular act (including speech acts or similar (e.g. signing or sealing a deed)) that one of them might have performed or might undertake to perform (i.e. the legal issue or question can be either backwards- or forwards-looking). In this sense, then, *any* legal issue arising between two parties can, indeed must, be framed as the

[10] See, for example, Munzer 1990, 17–27.

[11] Not adequately addressed, I now think, in Penner 1996a, 754–67; there I focused on the fact that Honoré's list of incidents depended upon the existence of a 'thing', some *res*, whereas Hohfeld's notion of rights in rem sought to displace things as an organizing feature of property rights; I still think that is right, but I proffer here a different difficulty, which I think has more traction in illuminating the tripartite structure of title. See also Penner 1997b.

question of which of the four jural relations obtains between the two with respect to the particular act. The success is limited because questions of jural relations arising by operation of law must supplement this picture, as must legal concepts, such as 'possession', which frame the law's characterization of certain acts. As we shall see, Hohfeld's understanding of the distinction between jural relations arising by the exercise of powers and jural relations arising by operation of law is flawed.[12] Moreover, it is not clear how a concept like 'possession', which concerns the relation of a person to a thing, not a person's relations to others, would figure in a scheme devoted entirely to interpersonal jural relations.

That Honoré's list of incidents[13] is *functional* is also plain. By 'functional' I mean that Honoré describes the situation of the owner, not principally in terms of his Hohfeldian powers, duties, and rights vis-à-vis others, but in terms of the social or economic advantages that an owner has by virtue of his position, and the terms and limitations of those advantages. Here's the list:

1. 'The right to possess, *viz.* to have exclusive physical control of a thing'[14]
2. 'The right to use ... use refers to the owner's personal enjoyment and use of the thing'[15]
3. 'The right to manage ... the right to decide how and by whom a thing shall be used. This right depends, legally, on a cluster of powers, chiefly powers of licensing acts which would otherwise be unlawful and powers of contracting'[16]
4. 'The right to the income'[17]
5. 'The right to capital ... the power to alienate the thing and the liberty to consume, waste, or destroy the whole or part of it'[18]
6. 'The right to security ... Legally, this is in effect an immunity from expropriation'[19]
7. 'The incident of transmissibility'[20]

12 Chapter 4, 4.1.
13 Honoré 1961.
14 ibid., 113.
15 ibid., 116.
16 ibid., 116.
17 ibid., 117.
18 ibid., 118.
19 ibid., 119.
20 ibid., 120.

8. 'The incident of absence of term'[21]
9. 'The prohibition of harmful use'[22]
10. 'Liability to execution'[23]
11. 'Residuary character'[24]

We can affirm Honoré's functional characterization of ownership by noting, first, that rather than framing the right to possess in terms of a right to the immediate, exclusive possession of a thing that correlates with a duty imposed upon all others not to interfere with that thing, Honoré speaks of the owner's 'exclusive physical control'. This is functional or empirical, concerning physical engagement and the possibilities that that affords. It is worth noting that in some respects the description is not even really apt. I am not sure what it means to be 'in physical control' of Blackacre, for instance. And my ownership of Black Beauty is not diminished in the least even if I am a terrible rider and cannot control him at all. Clearly the idea is something like the owner alone has the liberty to engage in various ways with the thing he owns. But even so, the notion of control is not easily framed in terms of jural relations, as Holmes long ago pointed out.[25] It is also worth noting that the issue of actual, factual possession or control principally arises in 'transition' cases, for example the first acquisition of a tangible, or when the question arises whether title has passed because the property in question was actually delivered, that is, whether a transfer of factual possession took place.[26] Once a right has been acquired, however, the owner is the beneficiary of the general property norm that one is not allowed to interfere with the tangible property of others. The owner need not continue to maintain any kind of actual, factual possession to remain a beneficiary of this duty, although she is said to remain in possession, however little physical control she may have over the thing in question, until someone actually displaces her possession by taking

[21] ibid., 121.
[22] ibid., 123.
[23] ibid., 123.
[24] ibid., 126.
[25] Holmes 1963, 174. 'The law does not enable me to use or abuse this book which lies before me. That is a physical power which I have without the aid of the law. What the law does is simply to prevent other men to a greater or less extent from interfering with my use or abuse.' This follows a passage, Holmes 1963, 173, in which Holmes states: 'Legal duties are logically antecedent to legal rights.'
[26] See Bridge, 2015, 33–4, 74–6; Holmes 1963, 186–7.

possession themselves. Holmes provides an example of the nature of the thinking at work here:[27]

> Suppose that a finder of a purse of gold has left it in his country-house, which is lonely and slightly barred, and he is a hundred miles away, in prison. The only person within twenty miles is a thoroughly equipped burglar at his front door, who has seen the purse through a window, and who intends forthwith to enter and take it. The finder's power to reproduce his former physical relation to the gold is rather limited, yet I believe that no one would say that his possession was at an end until the burglar, by an overt act, had manifested his power and intent to exclude others from the purse. The reason for this is the same which has been put with regard to the power to exclude at the moment of gaining possession. The law deals, for the most part, with overt acts and facts which can be known by the senses. So long as the burglar has not taken the purse, he has not manifested his intent; and until he breaks through the barrier which measures the present possessor's power of excluding him, he has not manifested his power. It may be observed further, that, according to the tests adopted in this Lecture, the owner of the house has a present possession in the strictest sense, because ... he has the present intent and power[28] to exclude others.

As to the second incident, the right to use, I think it is now fairly clear that there is, at common law, prima facie, no such thing.[29] I say 'prima facie' because whilst it is generally the case that one's property rights

[27] Holmes 1963, 187.

[28] It is not clear what power the imprisoned owner has, except in so far as the purse lies within his 'lightly barred house'. But the same continued possession would obtain in respect of his car even if it were parked on a public street. In any case it is quite clear that Holmes treats the continuance of possession as really a matter of the fact that by taking first possession or delivery from another a person becomes entitled to the benefit of the general duty not to interfere with goods not one's own. No less a figure than Kant recognized that the continuing right of the owner to his property has nothing to do with any factual or empirical control or possession. Rather his right is secured by the fact that others have a duty not to interfere with the property in question. See Kant 1996, [6:253], 43; Ripstein 2004, 27–8. Kant muddies his own thought by referring to this as 'intelligible' or 'noumenal' possession. The ongoing right of the owner does not turn on any notion of possession at all, noumenal or otherwise. Something's being my means requires it to be subject *to my choice*, not subject *to my possession*. See 8.3.1. (Whilst making some choices may require actual physical possession, e.g. eating an apple, this is not true in all cases. I can, for example, make the choice of transferring the title to the property by deed or by constructive delivery. See Bridge 2015, 75–8. More importantly, certain kinds of choices are by their nature non-possessory, e.g. choosing to treat a plot of land as a nature reserve.)

[29] See Penner 1997c, ch. 4; Ripstein 2013.

cannot be framed in terms of any list of legally defined particular use rights, nor is there a legally defined general, single, use right, it has been argued that the general duty not to interfere with the property of others is sometimes framed in terms of interference with use, in particular in the tort of nuisance to land. I shall look at nuisance in detail in 7.3. The general point is that the right to immediate, exclusive possession protects an owner's *interest* in using the things he owns, and thus this interest may justify the right;[30] indeed, one might say this exclusive liberty is the whole point of owning some things—clothing, bottles of wine, and so on. Nevertheless the idea of use does not prima facie inform any particular jural relations between the owner and others.

We can go on. I take it that the third, fourth, and fifth incidents speak for themselves as 'economic' incidents of ownership, not juridical ones. There is, in law, no right 'to manage', to 'income',[31] or to 'capital', per se,[32] and Honoré seems fully to appreciate this himself, when he says, '[The right to manage] depends, *legally*, on a cluster of powers, chiefly powers of licensing acts which would otherwise be unlawful and powers of contracting.'[33]

We could continue through the rest of the list,[34] but I take it the point is made. One cannot simply regard Honoré's incidents as substantial juridical norms which fill in or complete the battery of Hohfeldian rights (whether Hohfeldian claim rights, powers, liberties, or immunities) so as to generate a complete bundle of rights which an owner is supposed to have.[35]

Now I am not denying that a good Hohfeldian can reconfigure Honoré's incidents so that most of them can be represented as Hohfeldian jural relations. I say 'most of them' for three reasons.

[30] For a contrary view, see Ripstein 2013.

[31] Unless income is restricted to 'natural' income, like the apples on one's apple tree, or the calf born of one's cow.

[32] Of course, under a trust, separate income and capital interests are regularly created. But trusts are not merely proprietary devices, they are of course also a matter of the obligations that a trustee owes the beneficiaries.

[33] Honoré 1961, 116 (my italics).

[34] Some of the incidents, such as the absence of term, or 'residuary' character, could not really be counted as part of the BOR in any case, since they are meant to be important *defining features* of certain of the rights in the bundle.

[35] Munzer (2011) has recently stated (without elaborating the position in any real detail) that taking Bentham's analysis of legal powers provides a better basis than Hohfeld for BOR. To the extent that a Benthamite 'power of contrectation' or 'handling' might help assimilate Honoré's 'right to use' for example, there may be something in this. But see Hart 1972, 801–6, who seems to think this kind of 'power' is really just one sort of Hohfeldian liberty.

The first has to do with the nature of a function and its contrast with jural relations. A jural relation is not a function, at least in the sense Honoré is concerned with. Von Wright's distinction between results and consequences[36] is illuminating here. The exercise of a power bears an 'intrinsic' relation[37] to the *result* of its exercise, but not to whatever other *consequences* flow from its exercise. For example, when X exercises a power of sale over her laptop to sell it to Y, the result of that exercise is that title passes to Y. If Y does not acquire title, then there has been no sale. It may be the case, in consequence of this, that Y must pay sales tax. That is certainly a consequence of the sale, but not its result. The power of sale would be the same if sales taxes were abolished tomorrow. So it is a mistake to think that when X sells her laptop to Y she exercises a power to impose a sales tax on Y. So though it might, *might*, be a consequence of one's having various rights and powers in respect of one's property that one may manage it, this is a consequence of the exercise of those powers in a particular context, and depends on what one means by 'manage'. But such a functional 'power' to manage is not a jural relation of any kind with respect to anyone.[38] The second reason is that certain of the incidents, such as income and transmissibility, concern cases where title arises or passes by operation of law, for example on the birth of a calf or by inheritance, and Hohfeld never clearly analysed rights, duties, powers, and so on that arise or are transmitted by operation of law.[39] Finally, as we have already noticed,[40] certain legal concepts, such as 'possession' of tangible property, concern the relation of a person to a thing, not a person's relations to others. Hohfeld's scheme of interpersonal jural relations is not one in which such concepts find an obvious fit. One might say that X has, for example, a Hohfeldian power as against Y[41] to acquire title to a fox by taking possession of it by capture, so incorporating possession into the scheme by making it part of the definition of a Hohfeldian power. I think this would be the right, or perhaps only, move for the Hohfeldian to make, but as we shall see later when we look at Hohfeld's jural relations, in

[36] Von Wright 1963, 39–41.

[37] Raz 1990, 103; cf. Wellman 1985, 45.

[38] I am not casting doubt on the possibility that in other areas of legal doctrine, say that of company law, a legally defined office of manager can be part of the law, in the same way that the law of trusts creates the office of a trustee.

[39] We shall examine this in detail in 4.1.

[40] Text to note 13, 26, supra.

[41] Such a power is a Hohfeldian 'multital' power, discussed in detail in Chapters 4 and 5.

particular his ideas about legal powers, in more detail in Chapters 4, 5, and 6, this way of proceeding endangers the coherence of *general* legal concepts such as possession, which range over any number of specific Hohfeldian jural relations.

Putting these concerns to one side, however, one might be able to generate something plausibly like what I think most people think about when they think about BOR, that is, the various jural norms that might typify the position that an owner (or others) might occupy in relation to a particular thing, such as Blackacre. With regard to land, one immediately thinks of such interests as are found in the *numerus clausas*: possessory rights, powers of transfer, security interests, easements, restrictive covenants, and so on.[42] But if this line of thought makes sense, then it leads to the second proposition about BOR that I want to advance, which is that, as envisaged by the Hohfeld–Honoré synthesis, BOR essentially weds the idea of title to property to the power to undertake contractual (or similar) obligations. Let me explain.

Besides the right to immediate, exclusive possession, the power to license others to enter into or take possession whilst retaining title,[43] and the power to dispose of one's title, by grant of a lesser title or outright transfer, the other elements of the *numerus clausas* originated in contract.[44] A mortgage, a title-transfer security, was originally simply a conditional contractual transfer. The same was true of leases originally. And contract remains a basis for creating non-proprietary interests of similar kinds to the property interests one can create. Whilst, because of the interpretations of the Rent Acts,[45] English law now considers licences to enter and leases to be conceptually distinct in the sense that I cannot merely contractually license you to take exclusive possession of Blackacre for a defined term for a periodic payment, this is not the case on common law principles, and the same is clearly not true of other items in the *numerus clausas*. I can contractually license

[42] *Keppel v Bailey* (1834) 2 My & K 517; *Hill v Tupper* (1863) 2 H & C 121; Rudden 1987 is rightly credited for bringing the *numerus clausas* to the attention of this generation of property scholars. See also Claeys 2019.

[43] Under which I mean to include the power to put property in custody or 'representative possession' of the owner by another, and cases of bailment. See Bridge 2015, 39–40 and 59–68 respectively.

[44] See also Claeys 2018, 250–3; Claeys 2019, 65–8. By 'contractual' I mean to include binding obligations created by covenant and, in equity, trust obligations.

[45] *Street v Mountford* [1985] AC 809; and some difficulties remain: see the conflicting judgments of the Court of Appeal and House of Lords in *Bruton v London & Quadrant Housing Trust* [2000] 1 AC 406.

you to use a right of way over Blackacre for a period of ten years or for so long as I remain owner of the property, whichever is less. And I can contractually grant you a conditional power to take possession of Blackacre, and thereupon grant you a power to sell it, the condition for which is that I have defaulted upon repayment of a loan from you, which conditional power is to last as long as my debt to you remains outstanding, or for so long as I remain owner of Blackacre, whichever comes first. This may not be a particularly good form of security, but nothing in the law prohibits the creation of such a thing.

The point to grasp is that the powers of title to grant mortgages, leases, restrictive covenants, and so on arose because the law determined in its wisdom to allow certain *originally purely contractual* obligations of the owner to 'run with the land',[46] that is, to bind successors in title to the obligor and, in cases such as easements, to pass to successors in title of the obligee. The same is true of the trust, although the obligations were recognized in equity, not in the common law.

I am not in the least disputing that this was a good thing, but allowing this development of the law is quite clearly a matter of policy in the strict sense;[47] we don't extend all the same sorts of powers to owners of chattels, and civilians do not extend all of them to land and they don't (as a matter of applying civil law concepts, at least) recognize trusts at all.

If, therefore, we look carefully at these 'obligational' members of the *numerus clausas*, we can analytically reduce the 'closed number' to three: the possessory right, namely the right to immediate, exclusive possession, and the two powers that go with title, namely the power to license others to enter into or take possession whilst retaining title, and the power to dispose of one's title, by grant of a lesser title or outright transfer.[48] In certain cases, the exercise of these powers will give rise

[46] Or with property rights more generally, real and personal, in the case of trust assets.

[47] I distinguish policy in the strict sense from what might be called 'legal policy'. The former is a matter of deciding on a host of factors, social, moral, economic, and so on, whether a rule should be created, abolished, expanded, modified, reformed, and so on. By contrast, an example of a legal policy is something like a maxim of equity, for example, that equity will not perfect an imperfect gift. In the latter case, the policy exists so that the legal requirements of transfer, whether statutory or common law, are not undermined by a court of equity perfecting any transfer that fails for not meeting such requirements. Such a legal policy captures an element of the idea that the rules must work together as a whole with some degree, not only of consistency, but of coherence. Another obvious example would be the maxim 'Equity follows the law'.

[48] For an example which applies this sort of analysis to the trust, see Penner 2014b.

to obligations that will 'run' with the owner's title to her property,[49] or in others with both her and her counterparty's titles to the property.[50]

In these 'running with the land cases', these members of the list can then be understood to reflect various ways in which an owner may come under an obligation, for various purposes and with various conditions, now usually legally regulated and circumscribed, to exercise either or both of his two powers of title: (1) to grant possessory licences, for example, to license another to enter for a limited purpose (an easement or profit) or to take possession of the thing he owns whilst retaining title (e.g. a bailment, to give vacant possession to a mortgagee prior to the latter's exercise of a power of sale); and (2) his power to deal with his title, either by granting, where possible, a lesser title, such as a lease or a life estate, or by transferring his title outright. Both of these powers can sometimes be exercised by others (agents, pledgees, mortgagees, and so on).

Following this reduction to three, we do have a sort of 'bundle' of jural entities, one right and two powers, which characterize ownership. Ownership, or title to property, is 'complex' to that extent. Henceforth I shall call this the 'tripartite' structure of ownership, leaving aside the complexities of the *numerus clausas*, in particular as it relates to rights in land. Ownership, then, comprises an underlying right, the right to immediate, exclusive possession, plus powers to deal with that right. The case of intangible property, such as choses in action, is even simpler, since the underlying right confers no right to genuine *possession* of any tangible thing at all;[51] all we have is an underlying right, for example to be paid ten pounds, say, which is *inherently 'exclusive'* in the sense that nothing any third party does can extinguish this right in normal circumstances, and a power to deal with it, by assignment, etc.[52]

[49] For example in the case of a profit a prendre, which can be held 'in gross'.

[50] For example in the case of an easement, where there must be both a dominant and servient tenement.

[51] The case of documentary intangibles is a complication, not an exception. Certain intangible rights may be represented via the possession of certain tangibles, typically documents, whose exchange, for example, can result in the exchange of the intangible underlying rights.

[52] I therefore don't think one needs to show that the exchange value of intangible rights like choses in action is protected by exclusionary rules: see Merrill 1998, 751. No exclusionary rules are necessary when something is inherently intangible—there can be no crossing of a boundary where no boundary exists. That is, in the case of an intangible there is nothing to exclude anybody from. This leads to a mea culpa: if there is one part of Penner 1997c I would rewrite it would be pages 129–32, where I argued that legal choses in action partook 'indirectly' of the general duty not to interfere with tangible property, namely in the 'wherewithal' of the debtor. I should simply have stuck with what I said on the top of page 129, that as an abstract personal right a chose in action is inherently 'exclusive' in the sense that

Let it be clearly understood that this tripartite characterization of ownership is no concession to BOR *unless* no story can be told about how the three parts 'naturally' go together. The BOR theorist is, after all, committed to the idea that such juridical norms can be put together or pulled apart at will, such that any configuration is, more or less, a realization of our concept of property or ownership. But it is fairly easy to come up with a story about why the three elements of the tripartite structure do go together naturally. We shall turn to several such stories in the last part of this chapter.

But the immediate discussion also gives rise to a different point. The BOR theorist, by failing to realize the different *origin or source* of different property interests, fails to see the different *nature* of these interests.[53] These are not simply different configurations of Hohfeldian jural relations which any system of property might adopt. Rather, they reflect clear policy preferences having not just to do with the scope of property rights, but the power to voluntarily undertake obligations. In a sense BOR deracinates these interests, taking them all as being 'property interests' with a similar sort of standing, when they are clearly distinctive. For example, they typically[54] partake of a quite different 'in rem' nature.[55] A mortgagee's interest is 'in rem' in the sense that it binds successors in title to the mortgagor and, in that sense, could in principle bind anyone because anyone in principle might be a successor to the mortgagor. But it doesn't bind in rem in the same way that my right to immediate, exclusive possession of my wristwatch does. That right binds in rem in the sense that everyone, right now, is under a duty not to interfere with my watch. The creation of a mortgage does not impose any sort of in rem obligation on everyone, right now.[56] It is just

it cannot be interfered with in the way that tangible property can; all that I then needed to do, as I did in the following pages, was to show how the separability thesis (Penner 1997c, ch. 5) applies to choses in action.

[53] A point made in Penner 1996a, 727–8.

[54] The exception is the easement, which binds in both ways: the successor to the servient tenant owner is bound by the covenant creating the easement, and all third parties are liable in an action (in English law) for nuisance if they interfere with the easement-holder's right, for example, blocking the entrance to a right of way. This latter example is discussed further in 7.2.

[55] Penner 2006a; Penner 2019, [2.107]–[2.116].

[56] It is sometimes said that an easement, say A's right of way over Blackacre, which B owns, imposes a new, in rem, duty, because a person C who, for example, blocks access to the right of way will be liable to both A and B in nuisance. But C does not have a different duty than the one he had prior to the creation of the easement in A's favour. He is just *liable* for its breach to two persons, rather than one; See 5.4.3–4. The case is no different in structure from

this sort of important distinction, about as important a distinction as one could find in the law of property given the distinctive importance of rights in rem to the nature of property in tangibles, that BOR does not merely fail to accommodate and explain, but positively obscures.

The tripartite structure of title relates property both to the law of tort and to the law of voluntarily undertaken obligations or contract, broadly conceived to include the law of covenants and voluntary obligations undertaken in equity. Regarding the former, the right to immediate exclusive possession of tangible property is the counterpart formulation of the duty not to interfere with the property of others, whether by taking it or using it without permission or by causing damage to it. Those duties are expressed in the tort law rules governing trespass, conversion, negligent damage, nuisance, and so on. For purposes of abbreviation, I shall call this norm prohibiting these wrongs against property 'BPrN', for the Basic Property Norm—The 'Property' Exclusionary Norm for Tangible Property.[57] Regarding the property/contract interface, I have tried to show how much of the *numerus clausas* consists of hybrid property/contract legal relationships. Ignoring the contractual side is perhaps the worst facet of treating these relationships as just 'sticks' in a property bundle that can be handed out by an owner.[58]

Before leaving this discussion of BOR and the *numerus clausas* I must address a series of papers[59] by Merrill and Smith in which they seek to explain the *numerus clausas* from the perspective of information costs/transaction costs economic reasoning. The basic idea is that if one restricts property interests to a closed list of well-known interests, this is efficient in terms of information costs/transaction costs because property interests concern third parties: property interests are in rem in either of the two ways just described. If any sort of contractual

the case where B sells Blackacre to P and Q as tenants in common, that is, co-owners. If C trespasses he is liable to two persons, not one, but his duty not to trespass has not changed at all just because of the sale. From the Hohfeldian perspective no sense can be made of these examples because each liability is correlated with the breach of a distinct right-duty jural relation, and any jural relation must be between two and only two distinct individuals. (In principle, that is. This restriction falls apart completely when we consider Hohfeldian powers in Chapter 4.)

[57] In Chapter 10 I shall introduce a related but different exclusionary norm, 'BUsN', the Basic Usufructory Norm—The 'Usufructory' Exclusionary Norm for Tangible Property.

[58] Penner 1996a, 739–42; Penner 1997c, 74, 93–6; I thank Lisa Austin for making me emphasize these points.

[59] Merrill and Smith 2000; Smith 2009b.

obligation could be attached to title to a property, then this would impose costs not only upon the parties to the arrangement itself but on third parties; in particular, third parties seeking to deal with owners of the kind of asset in question would be required to investigate whether such an obligation 'ran' with the land, and the greater the range of such possible information, the greater the information costs that would fall on would-be transactors. This perspective is supplemented by Smith and Merrill's idea of a 'property' or 'exclusion' strategy which contrasts with a governance strategy in respect of the rules governing resources.[60] The moving idea here is that a system which instantiates use rights in resources can, under the 'property' or 'exclusion' strategy, 'delegate' to the owner the right to determine, amongst the range of uses to which a resource can be put, which uses will be made of that asset, by giving him the right to exclude all others from making use of it (or interfering with his uses of it). Alternatively, where the costs of achieving a particular social goal warrant it, a 'governance' strategy can be adopted. Under this strategy, either by allowing the owner to contract with others or by instituting public regulations, a more fine-grained 'rights to specific, enumerated uses' regime for the property can be realized. From this perspective, the story I have told about those members of the *numerus clausas* that originated in contract (or equitable obligations, in the case of trusts), and now 'run' with the property, are the product of a 'mixed' strategy, allowing a powerful but limited right to create particular property interests via a use-by-use governance strategy, the law of contract.

It is perhaps worthwhile to note here that the original English feudal system of tenures allowed the creation of a wide variety of positive obligations which 'ran' with the land; the inflexibilities and inefficiencies of the system became apparent almost immediately following the conquest, and they were all eventually commuted into money rents or abolished.[61] So I expect Merrill and Smith would have an easy time of

[60] Although Merrill and Smith are clear that these represent poles of a spectrum, and intermediate strategies will also be adopted where the information/transaction costs analysis warrants them. See, for example, Merrill and Smith 2000, 38; Merrill and Smith 2001a, 809–51; Merrill and Smith 2001b; Smith 2002, 2009b.

[61] Baker 2002, 223–9. Before leaving this section I should mention that Baron 2014 offers a qualified defence of BOR, largely directed at Smith 2009a, 2012a, 2012b. The gist of her thesis (see Baron 2014, 61) is that the BOR metaphor encourages us to specify the actual jural relations between the parties, clarifying the normative or policy choices we make when we construct property-like jural relations. This will be particularly important when we look at new 'assets' in the 'netherworld between property, privacy, and intellectual property'.

tracking this steady move away from an excessive governance strategy to a simpler exclusion strategy.

1.3 Actuality and Potentiality

One recurring theme of BOR is the idea that property can be conceived of as a 'bundle of rights' in the sense that every owner of property has a bundle of sticks, represented by all the jural relations in which she stands to others, and furthermore that the grant of a property interest, such as an easement, is to be likened to the transfer of one of the sticks in her bundle to the person to whom she grants an easement.[62] The burden of this part is simply to establish, once and for all I hope, that this bundle of sticks variant of BOR is basically nonsense.

In his second 'Fundamental Legal Conceptions' article [63] Hohfeld describes multital rights as follows:

> A multital right, or claim, (right *in rem*) is always *one* of a large *class* of *fundamentally similar* yet separate rights, **actual and potential**, residing in a *single* person ... but availing *respectively* against persons constituting a very large and indefinite class of people.

We shall discuss Hohfeld's 'multital' rights idea in detail in Chapter 5, but for now we only need to notice that Hohfeld introduced the concept of a multital right to explain rights in rem, rights 'good against the world', as a set or class of individual rights. Thus the owner of Blackacre is in a right-duty jural relation with everyone else in the legal jurisdiction who has a duty to stay off Blackacre, for example in such a relation with A, in such a relation with B, with C, D, E, and so

Given what I have already said about the policy choices which gave rise to the 'obligational' members of the *numerus clausas*, I do not think this critique has any weight against my anti-BOR claims. Anti-BOR theorists need not maintain any brief in favour of treating any particular new right as a property right. The anti-BOR theorist's very point is that the BOR 'metaphor' provides no workable distinction between property and other rights, and nothing Baron says makes the opposing case on this point. The anti-BOR theorist pursues intellectual clarity, not property imperialism. If anything, it is the BOR theorist who seeks to expand 'property' by including within the category jural relations which can include any configuration with any sticks which 'looks' to the BOR theorist as being 'property-like'.

62 This section borrows from, but also substantially extends, Penner 2011.

63 Hohfeld 1916–17, 718 (italics original, my bold).

on. So the owner of Blackacre stands as in the hub of a wheel with right-duty jural relations radiating outward like spokes to all the other individuals in the legal jurisdiction.

In a footnote (fn 19) to the words in bold, Hohfeld writes:

The reasons for including the words, 'actual and potential' must be discussed at a later time, after a general consideration of the distinction between 'actual' and 'potential' jural relations.

As is well known, Hohfeld never completed his project, and he never returned to specify how he understood this distinction. I shall argue that the idea of a 'potential' jural relation represents a problem for the popular 'bundle of sticks' version of BOR. The mistake is similar to the one, exploded by Wittgenstein,[64] in which a rule is somehow conceived of as encapsulating its infinite applications within itself.

BOR is generally intended to contrast with the 'layman's picture of property,' that is, that property is a 'right to a thing'. I contend that the layman is essentially right. By thinking of property as a right to a thing, the layman does not think that a right to property is a right 'against' a thing, as if he could take Blackacre to court if it resisted him in his intended uses of it; that is obviously a fatuous construal of anything any layman might possibly think. Rather, the layman quite properly thinks that the nature of his right vis-a-vis others is *mediated* by a thing. His rights and others' duties are understood to be in respect of the things he owns. The layman understands that he is wronged in his property rights when someone interferes not with him, with his person, but with his property—trespasses on Blackacre, for instance. The layman understands that he benefits from the practice of self-exclusion, which the law institutes to make the right to property the norm that it is. The layman understands that everyone, himself included, has a duty not to interfere with property that is not his own and that everyone benefits from the observation of this duty, that is, to comply with BPrN.[65]

But the supposed contrast of BOR with the layman's view is not simply a limping contrast with the layman's view to the extent that

[64] Wittgenstein 1958, [143]–[242]; Baker and Hacker 1984.

[65] Even the currently property-less benefit from it, since when someone addresses their need and hands them the money or the bowl of soup, they are only legally secured in their receipt of it by the self-same duty upon all others not to snatch it immediately away from them again.

it gets the layman's view wrong—in its explanation of the grant of property interests, and in its conception of transfer, it is conceptually misguided. It purports to provide an alternative *analysis* of the rights, liberties, powers, and so on that go with the ownership of property. On this view, when an owner grants a lease to Blackacre, the correct analysis of this transaction is not that he exercised a power to create an interest in Blackacre that did not exist before—that again would be the layman's (correct) understanding—but rather that he transferred some pre-existing lease-stick in his bundle to the lessee. The popularity of stick theory—amongst some theorists at least[66]–requires that we address it in some detail.

One point before proceeding. The 'bundle of sticks' version of BOR is clearly anti-Hohfeldian in one respect—I leave it to stick theorists to determine how much they care about this—namely that Hohfeld explicitly stated that rights (or rather jural relations) cannot be transferred. He places scare quotes around the word 'transfer' whenever he employs the term,[67] and in the two passages in which he specifically considers the alienation of rights in rem he says the following:

> A has the legal power to alienate his interest to another, i.e. to extinguish his complex aggregate of jural relations and create a new and similar aggregate in the other person ... [68]
>
> The power of an ordinary agent (while his factual authorisation continues) to divest the rights in rem, etc, of his principal and create new and corresponding rights, etc., in the transferee; ... [69]

Thus, for Hohfeld, what lawyers call a 'transfer' of a right is not really a transfer at all: the alienor's right is understood to be extinguished, and the alienee's right understood to be one newly created.[70] So if one

[66] Munzer 2011; Epstein 2011.

[67] Hohfeld 1913–14, 24; Hohfeld 1916–17, 757 ('"shifting" of title'), at 762 fn 208.

[68] Hohfeld 1916–17, 746.

[69] ibid., 757.

[70] Ernie Weinrib has urged me to read these passages more sympathetically, as follows: A has the legal power to alienate, that is, transfer, his interest to another, *by* extinguishing his complex aggregate of jural relations and creating a similar aggregate in the other person. He urges me to do so because it would be unfair to attribute to Hohfeld, on the basis of these passages, the view that there can be no genuine transfer of a property right. But I do think we should take Hohfeld at his exact words. In the first place, re-reading passages in this way does not change the fact that Hohfeld himself places quotation marks around 'transfer' when he uses it. Secondly, given his multital rights thesis about rights in rem (as we shall see in

of the supposed advantages of stick theory is that it allows us to treat the creation of a new property interest as the division of the owner's previous rights or sticks by transfer of one or some of them to others, they must break faith with Hohfeld, at least on this point.[71] (See what fun you can have if you treat BOR *literally*?)

If we really wanted to conceive the grant of licences, leases, easements, mortgages, and so on, as transfers of previously existing rights which the owner himself already had, then we would have to hold that the owner has an infinite number of rights. After all, an owner has the legal power to grant anyone any right in the *numerus clausas* to do anything that can be done with his property. The 'bundle of sticks' view holds that an owner has one stick corresponding to each right in his bundle, which together form a bundle of sticks comprising rights to do every possible thing with his property, each of which on the Hohfeldian multital model of rights in rem is multiplied so as to be pre-assigned to every other individual.

Besides the implausibility of the idea that an owner has an infinite number of rights to transfer away his property, on Wittgensteinian grounds this idea seems both unmotivated and unsound. To exercise a power is to follow a procedure so as to produce a result. It is akin to following a rule to obtain a result, like following the rule of addition to add 23 to 68 to get 91. But in the same way that a rule doesn't 'contain' all possible applications of it, as if the competent possessor of the rule for addition somehow had within him all possible sums, a power-holder does not 'have', prior to the exercise of his power, all the possible exercises of it that he might make, or rather, all the possible results of all the possible exercises of it that he might make. Where, and how, could he possibly 'have' them? The bundle of sticks metaphor seems wedded to a mythology of normative human behaviour exposed and disposed of long ago by Wittgenstein.[72]

Furthermore, since the 'sticks' that we are talking about are themselves *norms*—a legal power is a power to create or alter the norms that apply to oneself or others—we must remember what a norm is: it is a standard which guides the behaviour of one subject to it. If A has all the norms that he could possibly generate by the use of a power he

Chapters 6 and 7), it would seem that that thesis more or less commits him to the view that the right X 'receives' from Y cannot be the right Y himself had.

[71] See Penner 2011.

[72] Wittgenstein 1958, [143]–[242]; Baker and Hacker 1984.

has, do they all *guide* him or impose a standard on him in some way? Clearly not. It would be impossible for them to do so—there are far too many and they conflict. Thus, the whole idea of 'having' a bundle of norms which do not act as norms, that is, do not guide behaviour, is misconceived.

There is a further conceptual problem with the 'bundle of sticks' view for Hohfeldians, which turns on the fact that Hohfeld did not conceive of rights as free-standing 'things' or 'sticks' that any individual might *have*, but as jural *relations* that obtain between him and others. The bundle of sticks treatment of the easement reveals the problem. A grants B an easement over Blackacre, say a right of way, for five years. The relevant feature of the easement is that, following the grant, A owes B a duty not to use his land in any way that interferes with B's right of way. Now let us account for this stick in A's bundle *before* he transferred it to B. Not only did A have the right of immediate, exclusive possession of Blackacre in virtue of his fee simple but surprisingly he also had the duty to exclude himself from interfering with B's right of way; that, after all, was one of the sticks in his bundle. On the 'bundle of sticks' picture, if we take it seriously as an analysis of what A's jural relations with B are, A's bundle of rights (sticks) includes both a right to the immediate, exclusive possession of Blackacre, and the duty to exclude himself from B's right of way over it because he has that particular 'easement-stick' in his bundle as well; though he hasn't transferred it to B yet, on the bundle of sticks view it is still there in the bundle, and if a right (or duty) actually exists it means it guides the behaviour of those subject to it. But of course it doesn't actually exist, and A does not have any pre-existing duty to exclude himself from B's right of way. In short, then, many of the exercises of powers which create rights in the Bs of this world must, by definition, create duties in A. If these rights are somehow *already* in A's bundle, then so are the duties. This is incoherent. Duties which A 'has' but need not comply with are, *at most, potential* duties, not actual duties which as yet have simply not been transferred. This shows that the bundle of sticks idea fails *in limine*.

Another way of seeing this Hohfeldian problem is this: for Hohfeld, the idea that analysis requires attention to jural *relations*, not just one end of any jural relation, is bedrock. That is to say, a new legal position is not to be conceived of as the *movement* of 'one end' of a jural relation from one person to another—transferring a *right* or a divisible part of a *right*—but a *change* of one jural relation for another jural relation. A jural relation is what it is, a relation between A and B where the identities of A and B at each end of the relation are essential to the identity of the jural relation. When A 'transfers' Blackacre to B it cannot be the case that the prior jural relation is simply moved to B, because on the Hohfeldian account no one *possesses* a jural relation. Moving the right–duty relation from A *to* B under which A is the owner and B has a duty to keep off from A to B simply makes no sense. What has to happen is that their positions under the jural relation are reversed, in the sense that B is now the right-holder and A the duty-ower. Another way of noticing the point is to see that if the idea is that every new interest in property arises because a right is 'transferred', then so, on a Hohfeldian rendering of BOR, must the correlative duty be 'transferred', for all legal norms are conceived of as jural relations. Indeed, this aspect of Hohfeld's theory seems to be overlooked on the bundle of sticks idea of granting new interests in a thing. If the right-sticks are in the owner's bundle already, then so must be the corresponding correlative duty-sticks in the putative grantees' bundles. But then the best metaphor for a grant from A to B would be something like 'activation', making A's and B's new jural relation actual, not merely potential. Indeed, it is not clear whether a coherent notion of *transfer* would even apply here. If, as Hohfeld himself suggests in the quoted passage above, there are actual and potential jural relations, then the potential ones are there at the outset. No idea of transfer is either needed or, indeed, possible.

The picture of course gets worse if we also apply the Hohfeldian multitality thesis about rights *in rem*, for then A must have a five-year lease-stick in his bundle for every other individual. And notice, these sticks could never genuinely co-exist as actual rights in A's bundle: the actual existence of any of these multital lease-sticks would *exclude* the actual existence of all the others: they are, as an economist would put it, *rivalrous*. So, again, these rights can only really be conceived as potential, not actual, rights which A might create by the exercise of his powers. So they do not exist before A creates them, so they are not there for him in his bundle of sticks, and so he cannot transfer them, for there is nothing to transfer. Any normative system whose purpose is actually to guide people's behaviour, including how they should think about what they are doing, must founder on the kind of profound confusion of potentiality with actuality that the 'bundle of sticks' version of the 'bundle of rights' picture so misguidedly counsels.

To diagnose why the bundle of sticks transfer picture has any attraction at all is fairly straightforward. The view holds, as we have seen, that the power to grant interests is the power to transfer one's own interest. So the power to grant a different, 'lesser' interest must be a power to 'divide' one's interest, handing a piece to X. And, I suppose, the idea is that my original interest must be infinitely divisible.[73] Here is how the story would go with something like the power to grant a lease. A transfers five years' time in Blackacre, which he would otherwise have kept for himself, in granting a five-year lease to B. Thus he transfers the right to five years' immediate, exclusive possession of Blackacre to B. Since A already had the right to the next five years' worth of possession, that right already existed, and so it can be the subject of a transfer. This analysis, of course, is perfectly correct in the case where A does actually transfer the actual interest he has, say his fee simple, to B. But in the case of a right like a lease the analogy to the transfer of a fee simple is a cheat.

Whilst a legal system could provide a 'divisible' fee simple, such that (e.g.) one's fee simple ownership was conceived of as a battery of rights to time in the land, say one right for each day, and so the grant of a lease for a year would amount to the transfer of 365 such rights, that is not the way a lease is actually conceived of in the law. In the case of a lease, just as with the easement, its creation is conceived of as the grant of a particular right to the lessee which does not just take a part of, but *burdens*, the fee simple of the lessor. It is for this reason that there necessarily exists a relationship of privity of estate between the lessee and lessor, which, for example, supports the web of covenants typical of leases. The fact that the lessee acquires rights in rem does not mean that they are the *same* rights in rem that the lessor held. Indeed, we know that the lessor retains some rights in rem, as, for example, against those who would injure the property reducing the value of the lessor's reversion. Another example where the principle of division doesn't work are the cases of non-exclusive licences and co-ownership. When I grant a licence to X to come onto my land, I do not lose any of my possessory rights. Such a licence doesn't carve out a portion of the land for the licensee. Of course, I cannot literally stand in the same place as my licensee, but that is a practical matter, not a juridical one. My licensee's ability to 'use the land', to wander here and there for instance, is

[73] Smith 2011, 286–7 accuses the BOR theorist of committing the 'fallacy of division'; to be clear, I am not claiming that here.

not a 'reduction' or a 'transfer' of my right to do the same. The same is true when title is conveyed from a sole owner to co-owners. Similarly, a grantor of an easement of right of way does not lose his own rights to cross his property. A grantor of a restrictive covenant does lose something in terms of his liberty to use, but the grantee does not gain anything in terms of the benefit of the burdened property; instead she gets an indirect right that benefits her own property, but not by expanding any legally defined use or choice she can make in respect of it. None of this works on the division paradigm.

All of the right/duty relationships of this kind are special and in personam; they have specific right-holders and duty-owers essentially (although by transfer or other forms of transmission the specific lessor and lessee may change over time). They are *conferred*, not *transferred*.

A final point on stick theory. Glackin analogizes the Hohfeldian sticks in any particular bundle of rights to the relation of subatomic particles vis-à-vis any properties and relations that may arise:

> anything true we can say about the world ultimately reduces to statements about the distribution of perfectly natural properties and relations; there are no necessary connections between the individual perfectly natural properties and relations; and those perfectly natural properties and relations are the intrinsic properties of subatomic particles and the spatiotemporal relations between them.[74]

But on the actuality/potentiality point, the analogy would seem to undermine, not support, stick theory. Given the properties of subatomic particles, they can combine in various ways to form, for example, different chemical elements, according to the physical/chemical laws that govern their interactions. Their properties give them this *potential*. But no physicist would say that for any subatomic particle (or any number of them), they already contain in some *actual* way the various bondings with other particles so as to compose the chemical elements of which they might form a part. Whatever bondings they actually form are a matter of their intrinsic properties, in particular their potentiality to bond with others, *plus* the facts of natural history, that is, what happened in terms of the forces that actually acted upon them so as to cause them to enter into whichever bonds are

[74] Glackin 2014, 5.

actually formed. *Mutatis mutandis* with jural norms, the 'natural history' here being the facts of individual power-holders having exercised their powers (and, again, the operations of law) to generate whatever jural norms actually obtain.

1.4 The Internal Coherence of the Tripartite Structure of the Right to Property

The anti-BOR theorist is committed to the idea that the tripartite structure of title is not simply some bundling together of disparate jural norms on the basis of fluctuating, historical, policy considerations (as we have acknowledged to be true of those other 'running with the land' interests falling within the *numerus clausas*), but rather that they go together because of their very nature.

One fairly easy way of showing that the right to exclude plus the two powers of title which make up the tripartite structure go together is to envisage cases in which they are pulled apart. Obvious problems leading to a diminishing realization of the usefulness of having property rights would immediately arise. So, for example, assume that A has the right to exclude, but B has the power to license what would otherwise be a trespass, and C the power to transfer. Clearly, some uses that A would wish to make could be thwarted by B, but B's exercise of this power, except in so far as he licenses himself singly or with others, would be of no benefit to B per se. The same could be said of C's power to transfer. But notice also that we are assuming one clearly important aspect of all of this which, up until now, I have not drawn express attention to. The right to exclude is a right of immediate exclusive *possession*, protected by BPrN, which entails via that possession the liberty to use the property as one wishes. Of course for a Hohfeldian there cannot be a right to use or possess—rights to *do something* can only be liberties or powers. So a Hohfeldian must pull the liberty to use and the right to exclude apart. The former liberty correlates with a no-right, the latter with a duty.[75] We shall return to the intimate connection between the liberty to use and the right to exclude in Chapter 7, but for now I wish merely to point out that a right to exclude uncoupled from a liberty to use is not what we

[75] Hohfeld 1913–14, 30, 32–3.

would normally conceive of as a right of ownership. A security guard may have the legal powers to exclude, or even to be a gatekeeper, but that alone does not make him an owner of what he is guarding.[76] Similarly, a trustee has the title to the trust property and has the right of immediate exclusive possession of the trust assets, and so he is the one who has the protection of BPrN, but he holds that title and that right for the benefit of others, the beneficiaries—he has no liberty to use the property for his own benefit, which is why he is not the beneficial owner of the trust assets.[77] He owns, one might say, in form but not in substance.

Different authors have proposed different explanations of the internal coherence of the tripartite structure. Let me begin by offering a reprise, with some amendments and modifications, of what I said about this in the past.[78]

Like the commentators I shall shortly discuss, the prime focus here is on human agency. In order to realize any number of interests, individuals must be able to exercise their agency in dealing with the external resources of the world. In Chapter 8 I shall consider the justifications that have been offered to provide moral grounding for the right to do so, but here I am concerned to spell out the structure of such a right, in particular the tripartite structure of title that I have identified. When I wrote about this twenty years ago, it seemed obvious to me that the different elements of the tripartite title to property demanded paying attention to different facets of our agency, which is to say, the different interests we realize when we use things in one way rather than another. So though I noted that the purpose of the law of property was not to make people into hermits, at the same time I suggested that an *individual's* right to benefit from BPrN was the foundation of the right to property. I then went on to explain the right to share (to permit what would otherwise be a trespass) and the right to transfer as aspects of our agency as regards acting with others. I still think this form of explanation is correct.

[76] Penner 1997c, 70.

[77] See, generally, Penner 2014b.

[78] Penner 1997c, 68–97, 207–8; Penner 1996a, 754–67, 799–67; Mossoff 2003, 375, groups me with those who he thinks 'pick a single stick—the right to exclude—and attempt to reduce property to this single right'. This is fair in so far as I used the terminology of 'derivation' in relating the powers of title to the right to exclude. But I think that a look at the literature just cited belies this characterization; I have always endorsed and elaborated a theory of title to property which make essential reference not only to the right to exclude simpliciter but also to the powers of title.

Some idea of the personal independence of individuals strikes me as the obvious starting point in this story. The basic point has to do with personal autonomy and the unique relationship each of us has to our individual lives, our enacted agency grounding the 'authorship of our life story' function Raz aims to describe in his well-known theory of autonomy.[79] I am not saying here that we are not social creatures, nor that anyone with any sense makes whatever choices they make about their person or their property without at the same time understanding the way those choices will shape and be shaped by the interests of others. But there is a difference in making a choice in the context of the interests of others, and making a choice for or with the intention of implicating the interests of others. It is neither a discounting of, nor a failure to appreciate, the interests of others when I choose in the circumstances that the interests of others are not, or not at least principally, featured in the reasons for which I make such a choice. Even though consensual interactions with others may be empirically inevitable, they must be seen to be *normatively not inevitable* if they are to be regarded as *indeed consensual*. So the two powers that go with title, it seems to me, need to be regarded as related, but distinct, aspects of title, with related, but distinct, justifications. This is particularly so with the power to transfer, and in fact I have argued that we must distinguish the justifications of gift transfers from those transfers that fulfil contractual obligations and those that fulfil non-contractual obligations (such as the obligation to give money to the poor or transfer money to fulfil a tax demand). Other sorts of alienation, such as the right to leave property by will or the descent of property by inheritance, all need their own substantive justifications.[80]

With this in mind we can turn to two accounts which seek to unify the tripartite structure in different ways.

Christopher Essert,[81] taking a cue from Shiffrin,[82] argues that there is a 'transcendental' or 'metaphysical' argument to show that the tripartite structure of ownership I have described is in fact unitary, such that there is really only one jural norm in evidence here. In other words, the tripartite structure I have described is not actually tripartite at all.

[79] Raz 1986, chs 14, 15.
[80] Penner 1997c, 84–100.
[81] Personal communication with the author.
[82] Shiffrin 2008, and further personal communication with the author.

Rather, there is just one jural norm, but given its outworking in different contexts of application, this can result in the misleading appearance of three jural norms. This seems to be the claim that Shiffrin makes concerning our right that others do not interfere with our person; that is, such a right also entails that we have the power to license others to touch us, that is, to do what would otherwise be a trespass to the person.

Whilst the paper in which Shiffrin discusses this body norm is ultimately concerned to establish a non-conventional basis for the power to promise, Shiffrin first uses the right to our body to show the shape of her 'transcendental' argument.[83] Here is the relevant passage:[84]

When an agent gives consent to another—to a doctor to perform an examination or to a worker to enter the agent's apartment—she transforms, in the way intended, the moral situation between the parties simply through the transmission of her will to do so. Prior to conferring consent, the agent's right to control her body, and her property, forbade touching or entering as forms of assault and trespass. Simply by expressing her will, the consenting agent morally transforms the situation as intended, thereby generating a permission for another....

One *could* imagine a conception of autonomy without consent in which an agent exercised complete sovereignty over her body and other personal spaces, such as the home, but had no ability to share or transfer these powers to others. That is, the agent could not grant consent to others to exercise these powers in lieu of or alongside herself. Such a structure is imaginable but so impoverished as to be utterly implausible. As Joseph Raz has argued, the development and realization of our central autonomous capacities requires a diverse and rich set of meaningful options. Rights of autonomous control that were inalienable to this degree would render (morally) impossible real forms of meaningful human relationships and the full definition and recognition of the self (not to mention making medical and dental care cumbersome, dangerous, and awfully painful). To forge meaningful relationships, embodied human beings must have the ability to interact within the same

[83] Shiffrin 2008, 498: 'My strategy is indirect. It offers a reductio of the distinctive elements of conventionalism and a transcendental argument for concluding we have the power to promise.'

[84] Shiffrin 2008, 500–2 (italics original, citations omitted). For discussion of Shiffrin's reference to Raz's account of autonomy, see Penner 2014a.

physical space, to share the use of property, and to touch one another. They must therefore be able to empower particular people. A plausible account of autonomy would have to reject the isolation the constricted model of self-sovereignty would enforce as inconsistent with affording opportunities to lead a decent life and realize one's central capacities. It would have to include the power of consent to share at least some of the powers associated with self-sovereignty.

I agree entirely with what Shiffrin says in the final passage and have quoted it with approval more than once.[85] Yet, at first glance, this doesn't seem to look much like a *transcendental* argument, at least in the conventional Kantian sense of that term.[86] The basic form of such an argument is that if one cannot conceive of *x* without its having a certain feature or property *y*—for example, if one cannot conceive the external world except in terms of its being extended in space—then that is a sufficient reason for believing that *x* does have the property or feature *y*.[87] Yet in this passage 'One *could* imagine ...' suggests that a world in which people do not have the power to license others to touch them is perfectly *conceivable*, and moreover that Shiffrin's argument for such a power is straightforwardly *moral*, making reference as it does to the value of autonomy.

Perhaps, however, the transcendental flavour of the argument can be framed in this way: the moral normativity of the right not to be touched not only underpins that independence from the interference of others but also transfers seamlessly to the power to license others to touch one. The idea, though I may be expressing it badly, is that one's right to one's body is not primarily as an excluder, but as a gatekeeper. This is an idea that others, Merrill for one,[88] seems to think comes 'naturally' in the context of property rights. This thought leads to framing the necessity/conceivability point in this sort of way: whilst it is conceivable that I have the right without the power, it is also not conceivable that I do not conceive the right and the power going together, that is, it is not conceivable that I do not conceive of the possibility of the gatekeeper idea of the right.

[85] Penner 2013, 264; Penner 2014a, 122.

[86] For an illuminating discussion, see Harrison 1982.

[87] Although as Harrison 1982 points out, that does not entail that necessarily x has the feature y.

[88] Merrill 1998, 740–52.

Put more formally:

(1) There is a normative requirement, here having the moral power to allow others to commit what would otherwise be a trespass to the person or to property.
(2) We are capable of meeting it. For the purposes of the argument we can take this as an assumption or premise but if challenged it would seem fairly straightforward to provide an argument, on the basis of our rational nature.[89]
(3) The normative requirement has a metaphysical presupposition, namely necessarily creatures who are capable of complying with the norm by which one must not interfere with the bodies or properties of others are capable also of complying with the norm which empowers people to permit what would otherwise be a trespass.
(4) From (1) to (3) the moral power to permit what would otherwise be a trespass necessarily obtains whenever the moral norm by which we must not interfere with the bodies or properties of others obtains.

I am not sure how much turns on the difference between Essert and Shiffrin, on one side, and me on the other, so I shall simply welcome their company as anti-BOR theorists—if the tripartite structure is metaphysically unitary, then BOR is metaphysically ruled out. That which metaphysics binds together, no policy argument can put asunder.

Arthur Ripstein offers another alternative. Ripstein argues that only Kant's perspective in the Doctrine of Right can refute BOR, on the ground that Kant shows how the incidents of the right to property form an integrated whole.[90] As Ripstein points out, the structure of our right to tangible property is very similar in structure to the rights we have over our own bodies.[91] Although I cannot alienate myself except in cases where voluntary entry into actual chattel slavery is recognized,[92] I have the first other two norms in the tripartite structure, the right of

[89] Either on some Kantian account or, which I would prefer, a Razian/Gardnerian account: see 8.4.1.

[90] Ripstein 2009, 88; Ripstein 2013. Weinrib 2018, 132, disputes BOR by framing all aspects of the right to property, both the right to immediate exclusive possession and the two powers we have been discussing, as all forms of 'usability', a broad notion of use which is essentially reflective of the owner's exclusive right. In this respect it seems to me to be on all fours with Ripstein's relational account, without the same reference to 'authority'.

[91] Ripstein 2004, 11–14; Ripstein 2013, 175.

[92] For reasons explored in Penner 1997c, 122–5, I don't really think this amounts to a transfer of my rights in my body for the simple reason that my agency with respect to my body is

immediate exclusive possession, protected by BPrN, and the power to license others to do what would otherwise be an unlawful interference. The structure of the property right, like the right we have in the exclusive possession of our own bodies, is relational. I get to decide what to do with my own body and my own property because others don't. And this right to decide has the structure of an authority relation over others. They must defer to my authority in the sense that I get to decide what to do with my body and my property. Since it is clearly possible that I might decide that what I want to do with my body or property involves others, respect for my ability to choose would seem to encompass the two powers of title, the power to license what would otherwise be a trespass, and the power to transfer; these powers are just aspects of my authority over others with respect to my property; they are just outworkings of the deference relationship in which they stand to me.

I demur from this view because it seems to me to suggest a misleading equation of ownership with a kind of authority, which Ripstein first put in this way:

> Property has an authority structure; the right to exclude is generally exercised by the owner, in relation to all non-owners; ownership both empowers the owner with respect to the thing and restricts others. Non-owners must defer to the owner's authority, even if the owner is not present to exercise it, and even if the owner is incapable of exercising it; how the thing is used is up to the owner *as against all others.*[93]

I think this notion of authority darkens, rather than illuminates, our understanding of ownership, as I shall go on to explain momentarily. Much of what I say reflects Ripstein's own current thinking,[94] and he has reframed his characterization of ownership as a kind of authority more recently as follows:[95]

> Your rights to your body and your property can be characterized as a kind of authority relation, but [their] negative [and relational] character makes them narrower than other familiar examples of authority.

unique, and cannot be endowed upon a separate, other, agent. But we could always concoct some science fiction 'external control of my bodily actions, feeling, etc device' if we wanted to pursue this line of thought, which I hope is very much peripheral to the discussion at hand.

[93] Ripstein 2013, 169 (italics original).

[94] Personal conversations with Ripstein.

[95] Ripstein 2016, 33.

As I shall now hope to persuade you, it is not clear that any concept of authority, however narrow, is a useful way of explaining how an owner stands in relation to others.

In the first place, BPrN does not owe its existence to the directive of any particular owner, or all of them; rather it is a rule of law that makes ownership what it is; BPrN is what constitutes (in part) the title of the owner. Just because you own something does not make you any kind of authority over me just in virtue of the fact that I therefore have no right to it. BPrN is not, then, as Ripstein (and other authority theorists of title[96]) seem to suggest in the first passage, an authoritative directive emanating from owners. It is an authoritative directive emanating from the law, or by reason of morality if it is assumed that there is a natural or human right to property apart from the law.

Moving on to the powers of title, the powers to license and transfer, could one not say that these *powers* have an authority structure, empowering the owner to selectively relax BPrN, thereby making the owner a 'part-owner' of BPrN, or a joint directive-maker as regards BPrN, along with the law itself? No, one could not, or not in the relevant sense. An authoritative directive is either duty-imposing or power-conferring.[97] In the case of licences, the 'directive' is power-conferring, not duty-imposing. When the owner of Blackacre proposes to license me to come over for dinner, that 'directive' empowers *me* to decide whether to do so, that is, take up the licence. It is, I suggest, only a very strained sense of authority that would make the owner an authority over me on this basis. Your being in charge *of an object* is only very tenuously understood as your being in charge *of me*. As owner you might, by refusing to grant me a licence, thwart my desires, but thwarting my desire to something I have no right to is not an interference with my rights. To the extent that I do not have any actual desires with regard to Blackacre (and there are loads of things owned by others that I have no interest in whatsoever), the owner of

[96] Dorfman 2012, 2014, for example, seems to extend this thought to an exorbitant extent, saying that the owner *establishes* the content of what would otherwise be BPrN individually with each non-owner. For discussion see Penner 2013, 260–1.

[97] For the purposes of this discussion, only these two sorts of directive are relevant. There are also permission-granting directives, but although we sometimes say that by granting a licence to enter Blackacre we 'grant permission' to enter, this is the exercise of a legal power, not simply the grant of a permission, the structural features of which are different. See Raz 1990, ch. 3.

Blackacre does not even have a 'power' to do that.[98] The same point applies, *mutatis mutandis*, to the power to enter into legally binding agreements; the law is not telling me what to do, but only telling me that *if* I want to enter into such agreements I can. That is how power-conferring directives work.

I am not denying that the owner can be conceived of as an authority in this power-conferring sense, but the owner is, unlike the legal system, capable of being *only* a power-conferring authority, not a duty-imposing one, which makes the claim that ownership is a kind of authority anomalous vis-à-vis the more typical cases of authority as Ripstein makes clear in his more recent formulation.[99]

Furthermore, the owner-as-authority idea leads to the misleading language found in the passage first cited:

> ownership both empowers the owner ... and *restricts* others. Non-owners must *defer* to the owner's authority, *how the thing is used is up to the owner as against all others.*[100]

As commonly understood, each of the italicized phrases is relevantly false. What *restricts* others in the sense of imposing duties upon them is BPrN, not any directive of the owner. By observing BPrN, I am not *deferring* to any particular owner's authority, nor indeed to any owner. And it is not true that how a thing is used is up to the owner as against all others in so far as how that thing is used *involves others*.

[98] The situation with respect to your ownership of your land is even less authority-like if we consider the state's sovereignty over its own territory. The state of France has no authority over me if I stay in England, but if I go to France (or rather French officials allow me to enter France, under the counterpart of an owner's licensing me to enter their property) I am under the sway of its authority; so in this negative respect the owner and France are in a similar, power-conferring position only; so long as I don't care to enter your land or France, neither of you has any authority over me whatsoever. But if I do get into France, the French state may impose duties upon me as it likes. But you as owner cannot do so if I enter your land. You cannot just impose duties upon me at will. You can terminate my licence, of course, but that is not the same thing at all.

[99] The notion of authority Ripstein sets out in Ripstein 2004 pretty clearly links authority with the right to coerce, for example, to issue duty-imposing norms. Dorfman 2012, 595–6 seems to regard a mere power-conferring authority, as in contract, as not the right sort of authority to constitute the ownership of property. I do not see how he can regard licensing or transfer, which depends on a power-conferring authority, to be an aspect of ownership, whose authority, he says, has an 'unconditional character'.

[100] Ripstein 2013, 169 (my italics).

An owner cannot just recruit me to do things with his property. The rules are entirely facilitative, power-conferring on both sides, not duty-imposing. We might as well say that I, the non-owner, have authority over the owner when it comes to entering Blackacre under a licence, because whether I do so or not is as much up to me as it is to him.[101] Consider also, for example, the plight of the owner who wants to sell but can find no one to buy.[102]

Another way of seeing this point, which reveals a flaw in the 'gatekeeper' theory of ownership, is to contrast the notion of license with the notion of waiver.[103] Licensing someone to come onto one's property is not some selective diminution of BPrN conceived along the lines of swinging open a gate or tearing down part of a wall. Licences are always given on terms which establish a new legal relationship of licensor and licensee, terms which reflect the purposes of the licence, the particular use, if you will, to which the property will be put. When I invite you to come over for dinner I do not thereby abrogate my rights under BPrN. You are not thereby entitled to pick flowers from my garden or spend the night in my bedroom. What licenses allow an owner and another to do is to jointly benefit from BPrN, so that they may engage their individual agencies in a co-operative fashion as regards any particular thing.[104] Viewed in this way, the licensee becomes a kind of 'part owner', on terms of course, with the actual owner. In saying this I am not denying that as a matter of legal doctrine a mere licensee acquires no interest in the land or chattel of his licensor[105]—the point is simply that the

[101] For a discussion of the way that Locke's spoilation proviso and the theory of justice in contracting interact in the case of land-owners bargaining with the landless for the latter's services, see Penner 2018.

[102] I should point out that for Kantian reasons Ripstein 2009, 90, 96–106; 165, and Weinrib 2018, 133–5, hold that first appropriation does count as the exercise of an authority over others, and so is illegitimate without legislative sanction. I disagree with this, and say why at 8.3.1. But the point is irrelevant to the present discussion, since it turns on the nature of a legal owner's present powers however he may have come into possession, by first acquisition or by transfer.

[103] The same thought applies to transfer, which will come to the fore when I discuss the 'directional abandonment' conception of transfer at 6.5.

[104] In the same way, when you and I decide to have sex, I hope our understanding of what follows is richer than thinking we are merely mutually consenting to what would otherwise be a trespass to the person.

[105] As against the owner—at common law a licensee in exclusive possession does acquire a title in virtue of his possession against third parties under the doctrine of relativity of title.

licensor–licensee relationship is itself situated within BPrN, and is not principally a deviation from it.[106]

1.5 Conclusion

This has been a long opening chapter. It has largely consisted of analytic criticism of a host of ideas that have sustained, for many, the plausibility of BOR, the bundle of rights picture of property. But what I really hoped to have achieved is to convince the reader that BOR is both unilluminating and 'unmotivated', philosophically speaking. When we have a firm grasp on the tripartite nature of title, and the way in which the powers of title and the power to contract interact to explain the *numerus clausas*, we have all we need to make sense of property rights.

[106] See further Penner 2006b. Parenthetically, it should be noted that Kant's actual views on property and contract may mirror my own better than Ripstein and Weinrib as regards the tripartite structure of title. As we shall see in Chapter 8, 8.2.1 Kant clearly distinguishes between three kinds of acquired rights: property rights, contract rights, and status rights. To the extent licences and leases are obligational relationships, the power to create them would seem to fall into the contract or status categories of acquired rights (for the purposes of this point, it doesn't matter which); they are, then, acquired rights with a hybrid property/contract or status structure, which is exactly my view. Unfortunately Kant doesn't discuss such hybrid rights.

2

Two Nominalisms

Moral–Political Nominalism and Scientific Reductionist Nominalism

One of the defining features of BOR is its nominalist thrust. The idea is that there is no core, or essential, structure to ownership or property rights, such as the tripartite structure of title to tangible property I identified and defended in the last chapter. Rather, one can assemble any of the different rights, duties, powers, and so on into one or more bundles, each of which one can 'call' property (hence the 'nominalist' tag),[1] the only constraints being human ingenuity and policy considerations.[2] It is to two versions of this BOR-related nominalism that we now turn.

2.1 Moral–Political Nominalism and Conceptualism

Joseph Singer has persuasively claimed that one of Hohfeld's intended contributions to the understanding of legal doctrine was to show that 'high level' abstract legal concepts, like 'property' or 'title', do not

[1] Contrary to received wisdom, Halpin 2017, 1, claims that Hohfeld intended his analytic scheme to apply equally to 'aggregate' legal positions, such as the fee simple. So it is possible that in later work Hohfeld would have made clear that he was no BOR advocate.

[2] Mossoff 2003, 372–4, summarizes the idea nicely. See also Merrill 1998, 737–9; Smith 2015, 2059.

Property Rights. J. E. Penner, Oxford University Press (2020) © J. E. Penner.
DOI: 10.1093/oso/9780198830122.001.0001

do the organizing work that classical jurists, 'conceptualists' under this terminology, believed they did. Singer explains the distinction this way:

Conceptualism is the belief that concepts at a high level of generality and abstractness are operative, in the sense that they correspond to elements of the real world and are the basis of numerous and concrete subrules that can be deduced from them. Austin and Mill were conceptualists in this sense. Nominalism is the belief that concepts at only a very low level of generality and abstractness are operative. Thus general concepts, such as 'law' or 'property' or 'rights,' are seen merely as convenient categorizations of experience. We put into those categories the rules and meaning we choose to put into them. They do not of themselves determine their scope or consequences. This perspective is characteristic of Bentham and Hohfeld.

Nominalists as well as conceptualists claim that at some level, words and concepts correspond to objects or experience in the real world. The difference is the level of generality at which concepts are thought to be 'real.' Whether one is a nominalist or conceptualist depends on a comparative judgment of the level of generality of operativeness of concepts.[3]

The flavour of this kind of nominalism with regard to property rights is suggested in the following passage:

It is important to remember that policy arguments had always been involved in rationalizations of the legal system, even at the height of the conceptualist school. Hohfeld demonstrated that the policy that underlay the theory of self-regarding acts was incapable of justifying either uncorroborated liberties or damnum absque injuria. As such, Hohfeld's insight was crucial to legal realism. Precedential reasoning became far more problematic. Previously, a case holding that someone had a legal liberty would be good precedent for the proposition that other people had duties not to interfere with the acts permitted by the liberty. Similarly, a case establishing a property right would be good authority for all the liberties, rights, powers and immunities that make up the general right of property. After Hohfeld, a precedent establishing a legal liberty would not be relevant to a case in which the legal issue

[3] Singer 1982, 1016–17.

was whether to impose duties against interference. Thus, any old cases that relied on such faulty reasoning were wrong since they were decided on the basis of a logical error. Further, every case now had a much more limited range of application so many more cases would have to be decided on their merits as cases of first impression rather than by mechanically applying rules established in earlier cases.[4]

A similar claim is made by Thomas Grey in his influential 'The Disintegration of Property':

[D]iscourse about property [amongst property 'specialists', i.e lawyers or economists] has fragmented into a set of discontinuous usages. The more fruitful and useful of these usages are stipulated by theorists; but these depart drastically from each other and common speech. Conversely, meanings of 'property' in law that cling to their origin in thing-ownership are integrated least successfully into the general doctrinal framework of law, legal theory, and economics. It seems fair to conclude from a glance at the range of current usages that the specialists who design and manipulate the legal structures of the advanced capitalist economies could easily do without the term 'property' at all.[5]

It seems to me that a good case might be made that 'nominalism' about property has had a significant impact in American jurisprudence.[6] Our concern here, however, is whether it is a helpful stance to take as a theorist of property. I shall argue it is not. I shall contend that there are indeed 'high' level abstractions about property which we cannot plausibly do without if we are to understand property rights and property law doctrine, and furthermore, that Hohfeldian analysis does not assist us in making sense of these abstractions; indeed, it seems quite clear on examination that the Hohfeldian analysis of fundamental jural relations positively obscures our understanding of these high level abstractions.[7]

[4] Singer 1982, 1054.

[5] Grey 1980, 69.

[6] See, e.g., the majority decisions in *Moore v Regents of the Univ. of California*, 793 P.2d 479 (Cal. 1990), *United States v Craft*, 535 US 274 (2002), and *State v Shack* 277 A.2d 369, 372–5 (N.J. 1971); see also Smith 2015, 2074–83.

[7] For a different criticism of Hohfeld's nominalism than the one mounted here, focusing on corporate entities, see Kramer 1998, 51–7.

2.2 The Conceptualist's High Level Abstract Concepts of Property Law

So what are these high level abstractions of property law that one, donning the mantle of 'conceptualism', can claim to be operative, operative in the sense of being foci of legal norms and generally structuring our understanding of property law? As I argued in Chapter 1, the answer is that property law in respect of tangible property, that is, land and chattels, is structured by one fundamental right and two fundamental powers: the possessory right: the right to immediate, exclusive possession; and the two powers that go with title, namely the power to license others to enter into or take possession whilst retaining title, and the power to dispose of one's title, by grant of a lesser title or outright transfer. The only other idea that is required to make sense of the other property interests that compose the *numerus clausas*[8] is the idea of a contractual[9] right's 'running with the property'.

But even with only the three basic norms of tangible property I have identified in mind, it seems fair to cite a couple of passages where Singer himself seems to accept that the right to immediate, exclusive possession and the powers to deal with title are treated as more or less essential or characteristic features of tangible property.

Singer writes:

> But is individual ownership an apt model to use in thinking about business property? I believe it is not. If individual ownership is seen as the basic model, we are led to assume that owners generally have a right to do what they will with their property. They have the right to exclude all others, and a right to determine the terms upon which they will allow others access to their property.[10]

I am happy to share Singer's concern about applying the model of individual ownership to business property, but his characterization of individual ownership, which is the paradigm of common sense notions

[8] See, for example, Rudden 1987; Merrill and Smith 2000.

[9] 'Contractual' construed broadly to include the power to undertake binding obligations by way of covenant and, in equity, the power to impose/undertake trust obligations.

[10] Singer 1991, 48–9.

of property, is an admirably succinct expression of it in terms of the possessory right and the powers of title set out above.

In another article, Singer says:

> The core of possessive individualism is based on a particular model of private property and freedom of contract. This model contains several features. First, ... the presumption is that the legal rules identify a single owner of all valued resources and that *that owner has the legal power to control those resources to the exclusion of others*. Second, there is a general presumption in favor of free use of property. Owners are generally allowed to do what they like with their property—including destroy it if they wish—even if their use interferes with the interests of others. Limits to freedom of action are narrowly defined and exceptional. This presumption promotes a policy of autonomy and self-reliance. Third, the free market model 'promotes individual *freedom of disposition* as the basic mechanism for allocation.' *Property owners are generally free to decide when and to whom to convey their property*. This means that property owners *have the legal power to transfer or share their property on terms chosen by them* and that they are immune from having their property interests transferred to others against their will.[11]

Again, I am happy to agree with Singer that the concept of property thus described is a model that is deeply implicated in a possessive individualist perspective on interpersonal moral and political relations. But it is more or less *the* model of property that the law seems to work with, and again, he accurately characterizes it in terms of the right to exclusive possession and powers to deal with title so as to transfer or share it (i.e. license others to use it).

These passages suggest that Singer's 'nominalist' anti-conceptualism was more a matter of rhetoric than substance. That is, when actually addressing cases, he seems to rely just on the higher level concepts he seeks to undermine. His nominalism seems to be little more than, well, nominal.

Singer has recently retreated from a pure or purist nominalism.[12] In view of the work of Merrill and Smith, he is willing to acknowledge standard packages which make up the property interests the law recognizes. He now joins a particular tradition of legal scholarship, in which I very loosely group figures like Gregory Alexander,

[11] Singer 1988, 634–5 (footnotes omitted, my italics).
[12] Singer 2009, 1021–2, 1023–5.

Eric Claeys, Eduardo Penalver, Hanoch Dagan, and Avihay Dorfman, which aims to understand these various packages in terms of a richer moral-political perspective in which different political values such as autonomy, liberty, solidarity, and community ground the contours and features of the various interests in the *numerus clausas*, in particular to try to show what justifiable limitations upon the basic right of exclusion and two powers of title can exist.

In any case, moral–political nominalism fails. The high level or abstract concepts I have identified in the tripartite structure of title *do* structure our understanding of property rights and property law doctrine, and do so splendidly. They organize our ideas about property rights from 'first principles', so to speak, and illuminate (with the help of the law of obligations) the *numerus clausas*. This seems apparent from the latter two passages of Singer's that I have quoted. But besides what I have myself claimed on this point, we have seen from the last chapter that the work of Merrill and Smith, Ripstein and Shiffrin/Essert, in various ways shows the internal connections between the three norms of title I have identified.

But the point can be pressed further. Higher-order or abstract-legal concepts, which from the nominalist/BOR perspective are merely provisional legal 'complexes' like the fee simple, or the trust, or the contract, regularly feature in laws which are followed all the time. To just consider legislation, consider s. 1 of the Law of Property Act 1925, the Trustee Act 2000, and the Contracts (Rights of Third Parties) Act 1999, which frame genuine legal rules in which feature the concepts of the fee simple absolute in possession, the trust, and the contract, respectively. The examples can, of course, easily be multiplied. The concept of damages for breach of contract, with variants such as expectation damages and reliance damages, are very general and abstract, but they do essential work nonetheless. So also does the concept of trespass, which applies to many different sorts of particular fact situations. These sorts of considerations prompt a point which shall be developed throughout this book. Hohfeld's analysis was in terms of fundamental jural relations each of which explicated a different notion of 'right'. Moreover, the idea was that a complete legal picture of the way that each individual stood, as a matter of law, vis-à-vis all others could be framed in terms only of these jural relations, seeing the individual in a web of jural relations, as it were. Assuming that this analysis is to be understood as a comprehensive analysis of existing law and how it applies to individuals, then it seems to suggest that the notion of a legal rule qua high-level abstraction (of which a legal definition is a kind), is somehow not part of legal reality. But this seems patently absurd so long as we remember that the *source* of the individual jural relations in which one person stands to others is the application of legal rules, both duty-imposing rules and power-conferring rules. Doing away with these 'abstractions' and treating only the resultant configuration of jural relations as legally real would seem to give rise to a loss of legal understanding—we would be blinded from understanding why any particular jural relation arose in the first place. Framing the law in terms of rights (of whatever Hohfeldian kind) can be illuminating, as can be framing the law in terms of rules. The point here is simply that to the extent Hohfeldian analysis makes the former the exclusive analysis, as nominalism seems to suggest, it deprives us of the latter way of making sense of the law, via its rules, which I shall throughout this book claim is essential.

2.3 Scientific–Reductionist Nominalism

A different argument has recently been advanced by Shane Glackin.[13] He claims that a non-nominalist account of ownership or property, such as the one I advanced in Chapter 1, which he calls 'essentialist',[14] is irredeemably flawed, and he draws upon the philosophical concept of 'supervenience' to show why. I think his claim is misguided in several respects, but since, as far as I know, it is the only truly original defence of BOR that someone has proposed in the course of my professional lifetime, it deserves a careful hearing.

Glackin does not himself use the term 'nominalism', but his 'anti-essentialism' about property is, in my view, more or less identical to

[13] Glackin 2014. One point at the outset: To the extent that Hohfeld concentrated on legal disputes, and judicial reasoning to resolve those disputes, rather than on how the law operated outside the context of disputes and courts, Glackin seems to bring a similar focus. See Glackin 2014, 5: 'relevant to the legal dispute'; 6: 'relevance to ... judicial decision-making'; 9: 'judicial determinations'; 17–18: discussing the judicial opinions in *International News Service v Associated Press* (1918) 248 US 215 and *Moore v Regents of the Univ. of California*, 793 P.2d 479 (Cal. 1990); 17: 'judges will make a decision'; 24: 'actual processes of judicial reasoning'. I do not detect in his paper any reference to the way that law guides behaviour outside the process of adjudication. Hohfeld's focus on adjudication will be discussed in Chapter 3, 3.1.

[14] Glackin undertakes several other criticisms of my support for the anti-BOR view, which are not relevant here.

Singer's 'nominalism' about higher-order legal norms. So, for example, Glackin says:[15]

The bundle theory regards these individual and separable rights, or 'sticks', *as having no substantive, essential connection to each other.* To the extent that any two or more of them tend to accompany each other, *their conjunction is contingent rather than intrinsic; from a logical point of view, we might as easily have tied any other combination of the possible interests in the chattel or property together in the bundle.* In our ordinary commercial transactions, we can and do take these bundles apart, redistributing the sticks among others' bundles, and replacing them with new ones.

Who, then, is 'the owner' of some particular piece of property? The question, for a bundle theorist, involves something like what Gilbert Ryle would have termed a 'category error'. *Since the number and kind of such interests in the property, all vested in different individuals, may be almost unlimited depending on the legal jurisdiction, it makes little intuitive sense to pick out any one interest bearer as 'the' owner. No particular interest or right, and moreover no particular combination of those interests and rights, is either necessary or sufficient to establish ownership.*

As to the 'scientific' aspect of his nominalism, Glackin grounds his position by applying the concept of 'supervenience'. He sets out the basic thought as follows:[16]

[A]nything true we can say about the world ultimately reduces to statements about the distribution of perfectly natural properties and relations; there are no necessary connections between the individual perfectly natural properties and relations; and those perfectly natural properties and relations are the intrinsic properties of subatomic particles and the spatiotemporal relations between them.

'Supervenience' more generally is a philosophers' term of art for a relation between sets of properties; A-properties supervene on B-properties if and only if all differences in A-properties must be accompanied by differences in B-properties. Thus, for instance, the brittleness of objects is said to supervene on their physical microstructure; if one windowpane is more shatter-resistant than another, then the atoms composing the two must be differently arranged. Conversely, a different arrangement of atoms does not

[15] Glackin 2014, 4 (footnotes omitted, my italics).
[16] Glackin 2014, 5–6 (footnotes omitted).

entail a different level of brittleness, and my coffee mug may be just as prone to shattering as a windshield while clearly being differently constituted.

The last sentence adverts to the phenomenon often referred to in the literature as 'multiple realisability':[17] the same higher-order property, here brittleness, can supervene on different physical microstructures.

The anti-essentialist argument for BOR then proceeds by analogy:[18]

> For the subatomic particles ... we may substitute individual 'sticks' in the bundle of property rights. The bundle theory holds, then, that anything we wish to say about what are commonly termed 'property' and 'ownership' can be said *by reference exclusively* to the properties of the sticks in question, that none of those sticks or their properties are necessarily connected with or related to any of the others, and that nothing above and beyond these sticks and their properties and relations is of relevance to 'true'—that is, legally valid—judicial decision-making. Statements about 'property' and 'ownership' in every case are therefore *either redundant—being reducible in full to their constituent claim-rights—or simply false, invoking mysterious entities of which we have neither evidence nor a coherent understanding.*
>
> In metaphysical terms, the bundle theory is therefore ... a naturalist and an antiessentialist, position. It is naturalist insofar as it *denies the existence of any further relation of 'property' or 'ownership' over and above the specific claim-rights*; once these have been inventoried, *there is nothing more the law needs to know.* It is likewise antiessentialist, because it denies that there is any particular 'core' claim-right or set of such rights that determines how the concepts of 'property' and 'ownership' are to be applied.

As to the 'reductionist' aspect of Glackin's views:[19] roughly and briefly, in philosophical scientific discourse 'reductionism'[20] has different but related meanings, but the basic idea is that the scientific findings of one science, say behavioural psychology, can be 'reduced' to, that is, explained by, laws or properties of a more basic science, say neurophysiology. In principle, the reduction could go 'all the way down', via

[17] See, for example, Fodor 1997.

[18] Glackin 2014, 6 (footnotes omitted, my italics).

[19] In email correspondence with the author Glackin reminds me that it is wrong to characterize supervenience as in any way straightforwardly a 'reductionist' position. I think that is quite right, as I shall go on to discuss. The question is whether Glackin's paper suggests a leaning towards a reductionist position, and I think there is ample evidence that it does.

[20] See generally Fodor 1974.

biology, to chemistry, to the basic laws of physics. In principle, reduction in this way would lead to a kind of 'eliminativism'; that is, if all psychological properties and laws could be reduced to neurophysical properties and laws, then we could do without dealing with the less basic properties of psychology. Although Glackin does use the terminology of 'reduce' and 'reduction' in a couple of places,[21] he does not come out and explicitly say that we should eliminate talk of higher level concepts like 'ownership' and 'property' in favour of speaking only about the more basic Hohfeldian jural relations, the 'atoms' which form the 'microstructure' of complex legal bundles. Taking together the passages italicized in the preceding two quotations with two further things Glackin says, [22] we get:

- 'Statements about "property" and "ownership" in every case are therefore either redundant—being reducible in full to their constituent claim-rights—or simply false, invoking mysterious entities of which we have neither evidence nor a coherent understanding'
- BOR 'denies the existence of any further relation of "property" or "ownership" over and above the specific claim-rights; once these have been inventoried, there is nothing more the law needs to know'
- 'Any *unitary* notion of "ownership", then, denoting a single canonical relation between person and property, seems to drop out of the legal picture altogether, surviving as a mere "folk-legal" concept in the discourse of laymen'
- 'while everyday talk ascribes an essence or "core" content to the concepts of property and ownership, no such entity in fact exists. For the bundle theorist, then, the terms represent a sort of primitive hangover from outdated theories that legal science has now dispelled'

That all sounds rather reductionist, if not outright eliminativist, about 'property' and 'ownership' to me. Be that as it may,[23] my response will be twofold. First, I shall suggest that the current state of play in the philosophy of science regarding supervenience and reductionism does not deny the efficacy of the discourse in which higher-order concepts figure. So even if 'property' and 'ownership' did supervene on various

[21] Glackin 2014, 'reduce(d)' at 8, 13, 21, 22 'reduction' at 11, 21, 'reducible' at 6, 16.
[22] Glackin 2014, 5.
[23] Glackin 2014, 20–1 seems to take a less eliminativist stance, as least for laymen.

configurations of Hohfeldian jural relations, that would not show anything about their analytic usefulness. Secondly, I shall suggest that the supervenience relationship that applies to properties like brittleness and something's physical microstructure does not apply by analogy to legal norms, or norms in general for that matter.

First, as to the 'reductionist' programme in science.[24] Taking it the way Glackin seems to do, it suggests that nothing can usefully be said, 'scientifically speaking', about higher-order properties, higher-order properties such as brittleness that supervene upon an open disjunction of basic level arrangements of atomic particles. But this is clearly false. Physics may be the most basic science, but there are lots of 'special sciences', that is, those which study higher-order (higher than physics) organizations of matter, like biology or psychology, sciences that can and do discover robust empirical generalizations framed in terms of properties that do not figure in the basic laws of physics. To take one example, Bergmann's rule is a principle of population biology that states, roughly, that in the case of warm-blooded animals of the same genus or species that are widely distributed across latitudes, those animals at higher latitudes (or more accurately, in colder environments) will be of larger size.[25]

Now there is a serious philosophical debate[26] about the status of laws in the 'special sciences', in particular whether the properties which figure in the empirical generalizations they discover and describe are natural kinds in the way that it is understood that the properties which figure in the laws governing elementary particles are. For example, the laws in which sub-atomic particles figure are thought to be exceptionless,[27] whereas the laws in the special sciences are generally not—they are generally taken to have implicit or explicit *ceteris paribus* clauses. Bergmann's rule is not exceptionless, despite its framing a very robust causal generalization. So one might think that the properties that figure in exceptionless laws must be of a different kind than those which figure in laws that are not. This interesting thought need not detain us.

[24] For a prior consideration of this issue in the context of contesting a similar thought underlying Dworkin's model of the judge Hercules, see Penner 2005.

[25] The normal explanation for the rule is that evolutionary processes have been shaped by the fact that, having a lower surface area to body volume ratio, larger animals radiate relatively less heat and therefore stay warmer (or rather, have to expend less energy in keeping warm per unit of mass) than smaller animals do.

[26] See Fodor 1974, 1997; Kim 1992; Block 1997.

[27] This is so whether the laws are fully deterministic or are, in part or in whole, probabilistic.

The point is, whatever the right answer to this might be, no one denies that the special sciences do discover genuine robust empirical generalizations, even though they are framed in terms of kinds or properties which do not figure in the laws of physics. Moreover, framing laws and speaking in terms of these kinds or properties is not 'optional', that is, is definitely not just a matter of 'convenience'; whatever the status of the reductionist thesis in the philosophy of science, there simply are no relevant reductions available in the vast majority of cases, and the special sciences do perfectly fine without them.

Applying this thought to the law by way of analogy, Glackin's anti-essentialist nominalism would seem to be wholly unreflective of our knowledge of and understanding of the law. It is abundantly clear that all kinds of working legal norms, by which people, including lawyers and judges, reason and guide their actual behaviour, that is, genuine *norms* in the law, have no available reductions to the elementary particles of Hohfeldian analysis, nor are such reductions regularly sought (or, in my view, obtainable[28]). Rather, legal 'complexes' like the fee simple, or the trust, or the contract, regularly feature in laws which are followed all the time. Consider again the legislation cited above: s. 1 of the Law of Property Act 1925, the Trustee Act 2000, and the Contracts (Rights of Third Parties) Act 1999.

Considering 'ownership' and 'property' specifically as examples of such higher-order legal concepts, it is perhaps worth remarking that 'property' and 'ownership' are tricky examples. There is, for example, a long-running debate as to whether English law even has a genuine concept of ownership.[29] But, for example, the concept 'personal property', as opposed to just 'property', though obviously multiply realized, without doubt *does* figure in legal norms.

To take another example, consider the concept of 'passing of title', which is obviously important throughout the law of property: whether title has actually passed from A to B is a question of extreme importance, in matters of succession, insolvency, security, and much else. But title is obviously multiply realized—one can have title to land, to shares, to goods, to equitable interests, and so on, each of which will have a different Hohfeldian configuration. To take a couple of examples which make this point explicit: title to goods inevitably involves in rem (or for the Hohfeldian, multital) incidents, whereas title to shares does not.

[28] See paragraph following n. 40, below.
[29] Harris 1986.

A share is a kind of alienable, exclusive right, but the exclusivity of the right lies not in its being the subject matter of a duty upon all not to interfere with it. No one could if they tried. A share is a kind of chose in action, not a chose in possession, in the same way as a debt is a chose in action, not a chose in possession.[30] But whilst the rules about passing of title to each of these may vary to some extent (e.g. with regard to formality requirements), the concept operating here, the concept of title, is not sensitive to the particularities in the underlying realizations in terms of fundamental or 'atomic' legal relations.

The basic idea here is that the reductionist programme goes awry if it is imagined that because a reduction is possible in principle,[31] robust causal generalizations which define brittleness as a meaningful scientific concept are robust causal generalizations *of the more basic science*.[32] This is false. Brittleness is at best a concept of applied physics or engineering. There are no laws of basic physics in which the concept of brittleness figures. The same goes for the BOR reductionist. The robust legal norms in which concepts of title figure, real and genuinely normative as they are, do not figure in the array of 'basic' jural relations which a BOR reductionist alone regards as real.

It seems to me that what Glackin suggests is at best a programme for reform, not an analysis of the law of property or any other area of law with which I am familiar. And as a programme of reform, I think it no more likely to be successful than any reductionist programme in science has been (if indeed there is one).[33] The special sciences flourish, new ones popping up all the time all with their own proprietary concepts which figure in the robust empirical generalizations which they produce. And the analogy with law is exact. New areas of law emerge all the time, again generating their own proprietary legal concepts, that is, multiply realized 'complexes' of more basic jural relations. Furthermore, as far as I am aware no one has ever produced the long-awaited reduction of a property law concept such as the fee simple absolute in possession or any other legal concept, like the contract of sale or the trust or the agency relationship, to some perspicuous

[30] Of course some tangibles, 'documentary intangibles', are embodied in paper, so those chattels are protected in the same way other choses in possession are.

[31] Via a typically unknown, 'openly disjunctive' series of 'bridge statements'; see Fodor 1974, 107–11.

[32] I do not claim that Glackin makes this mistake himself; I set this out just to frame the relevant issues.

[33] Fodor 1974.

Hohfeldian–Honoréan analysis.[34] There has really been nothing but hand-waving here. As I've previously remarked,[35] BOR looks more like a slogan or picture than it does an actual *reduction* of property to anything, much less anything that is analytically fruitful in terms of the doctrinal norms that actually shape the law of property. To put this point another way, if an 'analysis' is meant to import the idea of illumination, it cannot simply amount to pulling apart and setting out particular parts of the phenomenon under examination. Dissecting and setting out the parts of the human circulatory system, heart, lungs, veins, arteries, and so on, is not on its own helpful, unless that is followed by an explanation of how they work together to make the circulatory system what it is.

One notable disanalogy with scientific reductionism is that one of the attractions of scientific reductionism lies in the fact, as previously noticed, that the laws of physics are understood to be exceptionless, whereas the laws of the special sciences are not—they are typically taken to be defeasible,[36] or to put it another way, subject to *ceteris paribus* clauses. But Hohfeldian jural relations, even taken one by one, are clearly not exceptionless. Take the multital jural relation that A has a right that B not trespass on Blackacre. That is not exceptionless; cases of necessity may arise. And like any other legal norm, these cases are not predictable, that is, are not themselves law-like, just as in the case of any law of the special sciences. So it is not clear, in terms of understanding, what resort to the 'basic level' of Hohfeldian 'atomic relations' (in analogy with physics) is supposed to give us as a matter of understanding of legal doctrine, much less in the efficacy or efficiency of judicial decision-making. This is particularly so since, as far as I can tell, the exceptions that B will be able to claim as a defence to what otherwise would be a trespass draw upon *general* considerations, such as necessity, in the same way that excepting someone from complying with a contractual obligation might turn on considerations like duress,

[34] One 'a priori' reason for doubting the possibility is in virtue of the fact, first clearly noticed by Wittgenstein, that it is not that *no rule* could be constructed from any finite set of acts but that there are indefinitely many rules that could be constructed to account for them. By parity of reasoning, an indefinite number of rules of private law could be constructed from a collection of contracts analysed in terms of the atomic Hohfeldian multital norms they individually instantiate.

[35] Penner, 1996a, 714.

[36] H. L. A. Hart was the first modern theorist to examine the defeasible character of legal rules: Hart 1994, ch. VII.

or undue influence, or frustration, and so on. None of these considerations are specific to any individual jural relation.

None of this should be particularly surprising since, unlike atomic particles, legal norms are human artefacts, and they can be framed at different levels of generality. Hohfeld sought to show that in the case of any dispute, the dispute could be framed in terms of one of his fundamental jural relations.[37] Seeking such 'lowest common denominators', Hohfeld provided an analysis which, if it was complete, could do without more general norms. For reasons that will occupy us in the next part, I don't think the analysis is complete in this way. The law only works on the basis of norms more general than Hohfeldian jural relations. If this is right then the reductionist/supervenience relations between higher-order properties and the properties of physics is an unsustainable model for the relations between more general and more specific laws. In particular, if the general rules are doing most of the work in determining the existence of the more specific Hohfeldian jural relations, which I claim they do, then the 'supervenience' relationship goes the wrong way round. The higher-order property determines the more 'basic' one. That is, there is no change in any of the jural relations in which X stands to others unless some application of a rule occurs based on acts or events, or someone exercises a power, a power conferred and itself determined by some power-conferring rule.

But, and this is my second objection, 'supervenience' is not a relationship that applies, even by way of analogy, to the relation between more concrete and more general norms. As regards natural phenomena, supervenience is the idea that the properties that figure in the laws of a special science, for example, brittleness, exist 'in virtue of' properties that figure in the laws of a more basic science, for example, physical microstructures, where 'in virtue of' reflects some kind of nomological necessity.[38] That is, the supervenience relationship is determined by the laws of nature that apply. But the relationship between more and less general norms is not like that.

As Glackin emphasizes, concepts like property are 'multiply-realized' only in the sense that different aggregates of Hohfeldian jural relations[39]

[37] This aspect of Hohfeld's thinking will be set out in detail in Chapter 3, 3.1.

[38] A least nomological necessity; I mean not to foreclose the possibility that some supervenience relationships, or indeed all of them, are metaphysically necessary.

[39] At Glackin 2014, 5, Glackin says that the Hohfeldian jural relations making up the 'sticks' in BOR are 'observable', whereas 'property' and 'ownership' are not. I am not sure what this means, given that norms are abstract entities which are not present to the senses.

can satisfy the correct application of the concept 'fee simple'. But this is not because of any kind of relationship of nomological necessity, but one of concept application. Having the concept of fee simple allows one to apply that concept to all of its proper instantiations, which of course doesn't rule out that the concept is vague or does not determinately apply to every possible candidate instance. More generally, the relationship between more general and less general norms is essentially one of norm application or specification. The principle of justice, 'gives others their due' is very general and abstract, and needs to be specified in order to apply it to particular instances. There will doubtless be more or less general, more or less abstract specifications, along the way, from 'keep your agreements', to 'deliver the promised goods under a contract of sale', to 'transfer title to 7 tons of barley to Fred', the last of which we can frame as a Hohfeldian right–duty jural relation. Thus Hohfeldian jural relations, unlike physical microstructures, cannot be described independently of whatever other higher-order 'properties' might or might not 'supervene' on them. They are the products of applying 'higher-order', that is, more abstract, norms. Without having applied the power to enter into a contract, given under a power-conferring rule, the final concrete Hohfeldian jural right–duty relation would not exist. Similarly, we do not 'induce' higher level norms from more concrete ones. We come to understand that more specific norms are proper instances of more general principles that justify or organize the more specific norms in some illuminating way, that, for example, property rights whether in land or chattels or choses in action relate individuals to each other in a different way than contracts do. In short, the relation between more general or abstract norms and more concrete norms, and I take it that for Glackin individual Hohfeldian jural relations are the stopping point of concreteness in so far as they are basic, is one dependent upon the 'ontology' of rules and rule applications, not upon the ontology of natural laws or supervenience.

Showing this will be the burden of the next part, but is it useful here to engage in a wee thought experiment, in which we attempt a genuine Hohfeldian analysis. Consider A, a subject of English law. Now present yourself with the panoply of Hohfeldian jural relations in which he stands. All of them, in some sort of list. Given this, and only this, what sense do you make of his legal situation? I don't mean make sense of his legal situation when for one reason or another one of these jural relations is made salient, perhaps because of a legal dispute, but his legal situation in general as one subject to the English legal system. From this list could you discern the Law of Property Act 1925 and all of its particular provisions? How on earth? Consider this analogy—you are to determine the rules of a game by being given a list of all the possible moves a player may make, vis-à-vis all the other actual and potential players, in all possible circumstances. Rather than trying to figure out what the game is like from that list, wouldn't you just rather have the rule-book for the game? The claim here is that if actually ever carried out, a Hohfeldian analysis would generate a *loss* of understanding of the actual law.[40]

It is well to notice two other features of such an analysis which makes the picture even more problematic. The first, which I shall also discuss in some detail in Chapters 5 and 6, is what might be called the fluctuation problem arising from Hohfeld's multitality thesis. Because all jural relations obtain between identified individuals, each time a person is born or dies in the jurisdiction in which A finds himself, his list of Hohfeldian jural relations changes from moment to moment. His legal life is one of constant, and more importantly for A, *unnoticed and unnoticeable* flux. Given this, it is difficult to see how such a list could be normative for A, that is, could serve to guide his actual behaviour. He could never, on this analysis, know where he really legally stands.

The second pertinent feature here is that certain things which we would normally regard as aspects or elements of a norm, in particular its source, are barred by the analysis. Hohfeld is clear, for example, that a contractual duty owed by B to A to stay off the property of C is no different, 'intrinsically considered', than the duty B owes to C himself to stay off C's property. So the Hohfeldian analysis again seems to require a loss of understanding if the source of a right is an important aspect of its legal nature, which it clearly is. If B does interfere with C's property, he is liable for damages for breach of contract to A, but to C for damages for trespass. This sort of example is easily multiplied. Is A's duty to pay B £10 intrinsically considered the same as C's duty to pay B £10, given that A's duty to do so is a contractual debt and C's duty arises from a tax demand? Who knows? As far as I know no one has made any clear sense of what Hohfeld actually thought 'intrinsically the same' means, and it is doubtful he had any very clear idea himself.[41] Obviously, however, a Hohfeldian would have to work out what jural

[40] cf. Katz 2018, who claims that Hohfeldian analysis makes it impossible to recognize what she calls legal 'forms', such as ownership or trusteeship.

[41] See Chapter 5, 5.3.

relations are intrinsically considered identical to each other to make the scheme comprehensible.

All of these points lead us to discuss the normativity of rules, jural relations, or any other kind of norm.

2.4 The 'Guidance Function Principle of Norms' or GFPN

My identification of the tripartite structure of title or ownership reflects the guiding idea of this book, which is that norms, including of course Hohfeld's jural relations, set standards on the behaviour of persons. The norms of English grammar are standards for producing grammatical English sentences, or judging the grammaticality of English sentences. The norms of arithmetic provide standards for adding, subtracting, multiplying, and dividing integers. Moral norms set standards on our behaviour in a different way. But besides this truism, there is a feature of the guiding function of norms which I shall emphasize in certain places and which has, I think, been underappreciated in the discussion of legal and moral norms, which is this: *that which is inessential, extraneous, or irrelevant to the guidance function of a norm is not part of that norm.* This is the Guidance Function Principle of Norms, or GFPN.

The basic idea can be explained with an example. Numbers may be odd or even, but that is irrelevant to following the rule of addition. This is so even if we have learned that the sum of two even numbers must be even (that the sum of two odd numbers must be even, etc), and use this as one way of checking that our sums are correct. So whether a number is odd or even is irrelevant to applying the rule of addition, that is, following its guidance, even if I have the concept of odd or even numbers and can make use of this concept to check my sums. Any number of other features of the world are more obviously irrelevant to following the rule of addition; whether it is Tuesday today, whether I am calculating numbers written in green ink, whether I am hungry or not, and so on indefinitely.

Applied to legal or moral norms, duties guide one's behaviour by telling one what one must or must not do. If X understands the duty not to trespass on the property of others, X knows that she cannot walk uninvited into Y's house, but that merely gazing at Y's house from the public highway is fine. It is irrelevant to X's duty that Y's house is painted purple. More significantly, it is irrelevant to X's duty that it is *Y's* house. Legal or moral *powers* guide in a different way; they do not require you to exercise them, but they tell you what you must do *to* exercise them. X can exercise a power to transfer title to a chattel to Y by delivery to Y with the intention that Y becomes the owner, or by executing a deed of gift of the chattel to Y and delivering that to Y with the same intention. It is irrelevant to the validity of X's exercise of the power that Y has false teeth. More significantly, it is irrelevant to the exercise of the power that the class of persons to whom X *might* have given the chattel is of one size or another, that is, whether X is in a city of millions or is on a desert island with only Y for company.[42]

As we shall see in Part 2, the Hohfeldian analysis of property appears to violate this principle on several occasions. But before leaving this chapter, we can use one more example to undermine the efficacy of Hohfeldian analysis.

There are different ways in which one can, via the use of different norm formulations, achieve the same results. To consider the case of addition, one could either apply the rule of addition, or memorize a series of conditionals. Thus by memorizing the following conditionals, one could achieve the same results as applying the rule of addition to all combinations of the integers 1 to 3:

If 1,1→2
If 1,2→3
If 1,3→4
If 2,1→3
If 2,2→4
If 2,3→5
If 3,1→4
If 3,2→5
If 3,3→6

Consider this a Hohfeldian analysis of the rule of arithmetic for the first 3 natural numbers. I take it that everyone would agree that memorizing this set of conditionals is not learning the rule of addition, even for the integers 1 to 3. To think so would be a confusion, identifying

[42] Nothing in GFPN forecloses inquiries into what sort of guidance particular norms of private law provide; for an ongoing dispute of this kind regarding strict liability in tort law, see Smith 2014; Gardner 2014; Ripstein 2016, 130–5. Thanks to Nick Sage for prompting me to make this clear.

different norms that attain the same results as the same norm.[43] My claim here is that the Hohfeldian analysis reveals just such a confusion. It purports to explain or analyse a norm of general applicability as a series of special individual jural relations. The thought here is that even if we could spell out exhaustively all the jural relations in which A stands, we would have no understanding of the laws that govern A.

All of this grants the Hohfeldian the assumption that, in principle, at any time one could provide a complete snapshot of A's legal position, *expressed* as a series of Hohfeldian jural relations between identified individuals. The point of this example and the ones above in 2.3 is to show that this does not amount to an *analysis*. It provides no insight into the norms that make up the law and, indeed, it tends to obscure them because, purporting to be fundamental, it suggests that nothing further needs to be said.

2.5 Conclusion to Part 1

There is, I think, a large theoretical payoff that follows from revisiting BOR and looking at the two nominalisms in this chapter, which can initially be put in this way: it seems, upon examination, that pursuing a jural relations-level Hohfeldian analysis is guaranteed to generate a loss of understanding about whatever area of law we are looking at. As we shall see in Part 2, there are particularly important cases of such a loss of understanding when we assess the application of Hohfeld's scheme to various property rights and rules.

[43] This is not to say that a radical interpreter could not (mistakenly in this case) infer that X was following the rule of addition when observing X apply the conditionals; nor, if one accepts a 'naturalist' ontology for the succession relation, that could X himself not 'induce' the rule of addition when applying the conditionals in some sufficient number of cases.

PART 2

Hohfeldian Analysis and Legal Property Rights

In the last two chapters we saw the ways in which Hohfeld's theory of jural relations was seen to give support to the Bundle of Rights picture of property (BOR). In this part our task is to examine Hohfeld's theory of jural relations *simpliciter* as it were, disentangled from any BOR thinking. I shall be examining different features of that theory to determine whether it illuminates or obscures our understanding of legal property rights.

Although some of my criticisms have been foreshadowed by others, as far as I know much of the work here is genuinely original. In particular, when we get to Chapters 4, 5, and 6, I hope to show that the property scholarship community in particular, and the Hohfeld scholarship community in general, has failed to drill down into what Hohfeld actually said, particularly in relation to the way he conceived his analysis of jural relations in so far as they are taken, or assumed, to help us understand property rights.

3

Hohfeldian Liberties

In this chapter we begin to assess whatever illumination of the nature of property rights and property law is generated by Hohfeldian analysis. Before we undertake a specific examination of Hohfeld's characterization of liberties, we must examine the bilaterality, or bilateral structure, of Hohfeldian jural relations, and Hohfeld's 'disambiguation project', that is, his project to ensure that the ambiguous term 'right' can be revealed to show that it covers four different sorts of 'right', and how this disambiguation of the term assists in legal, particularly judicial, reasoning.

3.1 Jural Conceptions and Jural Relations

Hohfeld identified eight fundamental jural conceptions, and four fundamental jural relations, the latter being identified and individuated by relating one pair of the eight jural conceptions; the jural relations are as follows:

right[1]–duty
liberty–no right
power–liability
immunity–disability

[1] Aka 'claim right': Hohfeld 1913–14, 31, 33.

Property Rights. J. E. Penner, Oxford University Press (2020) © J. E. Penner.
DOI: 10.1093/oso/9780198830122.001.0001

There being a right then, according to this more or less orthodox reading of Hohfeld,[2] is both necessary and sufficient for there being a duty, and vice versa.

It follows that although we speak of X having a right, or a liberty, or a power, or a duty, and so on, strictly speaking such a locution is a solecism on Hohfeld's scheme. To say that X has a right to be paid $10 by Y is to say that X stands in a right–duty jural relation with Y, the subject matter of which is Y's paying X $10. This jural relation is not something either X or Y can 'possess'. Of course, there is a sense in which we say that X 'owns' his right to be paid $10 by Y, and this has a certain practical validity because in the case of this right X can alienate this debt by assigning it to Z, for instance. But for Hohfeld, this possibility of assignment is expressed by saying that X is in a power-liability relationship with Y such that X can extinguish the right–duty jural relation that obtains between X and Y and create a new such relation between Y and Z—thus this 'ownership qua alienability' of the right does not follow from the right–duty relationship itself, but from the distinct jural power–liability relations X has in respect of Y and Z.[3]

This tenet of Hohfeld's 'correlativity thesis'[4] can be stated as follows:

1. Rights and duties and any of the other six fundamental legal conceptions are not to be conceived of as free-standing norms themselves, but are only representations of opposite poles of a jural relation; only jural relations (or moral relations where the Hohfeldian scheme is applied to analyse moral norms) correctly characterize norms.[5]

Two other tenets of the correlativity thesis are also recognized as orthodox:[6]

2. Each jural relation obtains between two, and only two, persons. Another way of putting this is that the identities of the parties related by the jural relation are essential features of the relation.

[2] See, for example, Finnis 1972; Kramer 1998, 7–51; Radin 1938; Halpin 1985, 438–40; Wilson 1980, 195–6; Rainbolt 2006, 2.

[3] As we shall see in Chapter 4, 4.2, this formulation of X's power or powers in this case is very problematic, but it seems as if this is the way Hohfeld himself would have put the point.

[4] Kramer calls this Hohfeld's 'Correlativity Axiom': Kramer 1998, 24.

[5] Raz 1984a, 1984b, 1986, ch. 7, and MacCormick 1977 famously reject this tenet of the correlativity thesis; I think their rejection is mistaken. See Penner 1997c, 306–14.

[6] Halpin, 1985, 439; Finnis 1972, 379–82; Kramer 1998, 7–14; Radin 1938, 1147–8.

3. Each jural relation concerns an act or omission of only one person in the jural relation.

Restricting our attention to right–duty jural relations and liberty–no right jural relations, 3. applies as follows: in the right–duty jural relation, X's right concerns an act or omission of Y's, who has the correlative duty either to φ or not to φ. So a Hohfeldian right always concerns only the acts or omissions of the duty-ower. As regards liberty–no right jural relations, the position of the act or omission is reversed: in this relation, it is an act or omission of the liberty-bearer, X, which is in question, and the correlative position of the no-right-bearer, Y, is that Y has 'no right' that X φ or forbear to φ. In other words, X has a liberty to φ where X has no duty not to φ.

Distinguishing right-duty and liberty–no right jural relations in this way was the most significant move in Hohfeld's 'disambiguation project'. He was concerned that the word 'right' was used ambiguously, being capable of referring to any one of his four relations: sometimes it referred to rights (the right–duty jural relation), sometimes to liberties, sometimes to powers, sometimes to immunities. In particular, Hohfeld applied his scheme so as to show that having a liberty to φ, in so far as that turns on claiming that one is under no duty not to φ, neither entails nor even implies that another person has any duties with respect to one's φing, whether not to interfere with one's φing or in any other respect (assisting one, empowering one, and so on). Whenever a litigant (or a court) claims that the latter can be inferred from the former, this is mistaken; such an inference is clearly illicit.[7] It is also perfectly right to observe that where this sort of mistake is made, it normally occurs with the backdrop of an unexamined premise, that is, that a substantive justification for a court's finding, say, a duty on one who interferes with a liberty is hidden by the false claim that such a liberty entails a duty upon others not to interfere with the acts the liberty refers to.[8]

Now it has been argued that in the context of the law, a claim to have a liberty to φ always involves a second claim to a right–duty relation, along the lines that when X claims a right, say, to build a house on his land, he is not merely claiming that a stranger, Y, has 'no right' that he doesn't, but that Y is under some duty or set of duties that would

[7] For discussion, see Thomson 1990, 46–55. For an elaboration of this point with regard to Hohfeld's discussion of *Quinn v Leatham* [1901] AC 495, see Simmonds 1998, 169–73; Perry 1977; 1980; cf. Hudson and Husak 1980.

[8] See, for example, Simmonds 1998, 187–95; Singer 1982, 987–994.

prevent Y from interfering with X's building his house. Hart referred to this as a 'perimeter' of protection.[9] But even if it is true that where X claims a liberty to φ 'in a legal context'[10] he is claiming that Y is under some sort of duty which would protect to some extent or in some ways his φing, this is beside the point. The correct, Hohfeldian, point is that, as a matter of the logic of duties, we can conceive of the absence of a duty to φ or not to φ apart from any other duties which others might or might not have.[11] Moreover, if we observe GFPN, we see that although Y has a duty to X not to φ (to trespass on Blackacre) which *in fact* provides some protection to X when he ζ's (builds a house), that does not mean that Y has a duty not to interfere with X's ζing, along two dimensions.

First, so long as Y does not commit a trespass, he may interfere with X's building his house in other ways. So, for example, at common law neighbouring landowners owe each other a duty of support—they are not entitled to excavate on their land so as to cause a landslip or a subsidence of their neighbours' land. But this duty only extends to the land (the soil) itself. A landowner is not required to keep his land (soil) in such a state that his neighbour can build any structure, however heavy, upon it. Thus in this case Y is free to excavate his land so as not to cause a landslip or subsidence of X's land (soil) itself, but in a way which would prevent X from building the (massive, heavy) house that he wants because now, because of Y's excavations, X's land will not support it (or will not support it without an expensive foundation structure). Second, neither Y's duty not to trespass nor Y's duty of support is framed in terms of X's house-building activity. To discharge his duty to X, Y must not cross the boundary of X's land and must not cause a landslip or subsidence. In the case of the latter duty, it is more properly framed as saying that Y must act so as not to be the *sole* cause of a slip or subsidence on X's land, to cause this independently of X's use of his land. So Y's right here does make reference to X's use of the land, but not so as to 'protect' it in so far as it relates to any particular project for her land that X entertains.

So far so good. We can now proceed to another idea which is associated with the Hohfeldian analysis, but which is not mandated by any

[9] Hart 1982, 171.
[10] For discussion see Halpin 1985, 445–52.
[11] Rainbolt 2006, 6–7.

explicit endorsement by Hohfeld himself. The point was most sharply put by Radin in an early essay on Hohfeld's scheme:

> We are concerned with an algebra that will enable us to describe some precise and repeated situations, the actual judgments of courts, in such a way that any judgment can fall into the scheme.[12]

This is not correct, for it fails to address cases in which what is at issue is the operation of law.[13] The distinction between events that constitute changes in jural relations arising by operation of law and events that do so because a person has exercised a power is something we shall have to examine in Chapter 4, but the point is obvious. For example, under X's contract of house insurance with Y, X can claim that the lightning strike that destroyed his house gave rise to a right to be indemnified by insurance company Y. Hohfeld clearly understood that certain events gave rise to changes in jural relations by operation of law, and it does no harm to his scheme to add this possible court judgment. So amended, it is clear that for any plaintiff and defendant engaged in private law litigation (to which we shall restrict our attention[14]), the answer to any question about the legal relationship between X and Y can be framed in terms of Hohfeld's scheme, giving one and only one of the following answers:

1. With regard to X's φing, X is in a liberty–no right relation with Y.
2. With regard to X's φing, X is in a right–duty relation to Y (such that if this is so, X is under a duty either to φ or not to φ).
3. With regard to X's φing, X is in a power–liability relation with Y, such that by φing X changes the legal position of Y.
4. With regard to X's φing, X is in an immunity–disability relation with Y, such that by φing X does not change the legal position of Y.
5. With regard to some event, upon its happening X's and/or Y's legal position(s) will change.[15]

[12] Radin 1938, 1147. See also Wellman 1985, 9, 12, 15, 18.

[13] Wellman 1985, 15, seems to miss this point.

[14] As this book is concerned with private property rights, this restriction is sensible. For the issue whether the Hohfeldian scheme is applicable to other areas of the law or to morality generally, see, for example, Kramer 1998, 27–60.

[15] For the view that answers 1 and 2, and answers 3 and 4 are not independent of each other, 1 and 2 concerning the existence or not of a duty, 3 and 4 concerning the existence or not of a power, see Halpin 1985, 440–5, 452–6.

Notice that the answer will not resolve the dispute in cases 2, 3, and 5.[16] In each of these cases the court must look at further facts[17] to see whether, in 2, X discharged or breached his duty to Y, in 3, whether X in fact φed, in fact exercised the power, and in 5, whether the event occurred. By contrast, in the case of 1 and 4, any further facts about what actually happened are irrelevant to the resolution of the dispute.

3.2 The Non-Regulation of Liberty–No Right Relations

On its own terms, the claim that the Hohfeldian scheme may be employed to provide a comprehensive battery of answers to the questions any litigant may put to the court, a court which is bound to provide a resolution of the dispute, is successful. The question to be addressed now is how we are to understand the significance of this with respect to a court's giving 'answer 1' from the list above. There are two views: the first, which I shall endorse here, is that when the court delivers 'answer 1', the court holds that X's φing and/or not φing is *unregulated* by law. The alternative view, endorsed by Hohfeld, is that X's φing is *'negatively' regulated* by law—roughly, the thought is that what the law does not prohibit it permits, where 'permits' carries the connotation of approval or endorsement. Hohfeld puts the point this way:

It is difficult to see ... why, as between X and Y, the 'privilege + no right' situation is not just as real a jural relation as the precisely opposite 'duty + right' relation between any two parties.... A rule of law that *permits* is just as real as a rule of law that *forbids*; and, similarly, saying that the law *permits* a given act to X as between himself and Y predicates just as genuine a legal relation as saying that the law *forbids* a certain act to X as between himself and Y. That this is so seems, in some measure, to be confirmed by the fact that the first sort of act would ordinarily be pronounced 'lawful', and the second 'unlawful'.[18]

[16] Unless the litigants merely seek a declaration of their legal relation, for example that a contractual term is valid under the law.

[17] That is, facts beyond those which go to establishing the existence of the duty or power, or the event's happening giving rise to a change in X and Y's legal position.

[18] Hohfeld 1913–14, 42 n. 59 (italics original).

It is of course true that the law does regulate certain liberties: where X, a landowner, exercises her power to grant a licence to Y to enter Blackacre, X and Y now stand in a liberty–no right relation with respect to Y's entering. The same is true of the case where Y is relieved of his duty not to enter Blackacre by operation of law in the case of necessity. The dispute between the two views just set out concerns the status of liberty–no right answers, 'answer 1' above, where the liberty in question *is not an exception to a general duty-imposing rule*, such as the rule against trespass.

The reason why the first view is right and Hohfeld's view is wrong is that only the first reflects GFPN. It helps to show this by first considering moral norms and then turning to legal norms.

Moral reasons, or reasons of morality, do not engage many sorts of act. Outside of special contexts, there are no moral reasons to choose vanilla ice cream over chocolate. This is so even if there are recognized norms of other kinds—for example a norm which says you should vary your ice cream choices in order to broaden the range of your palate—which do apply to the act in question. Outside of special contexts (e.g. I am under contract to you as your accountant) it is not a moral error to fail to comply with the rules of arithmetic. Nor, outside of special contexts (e.g. I am drafting a complex contract for you), is it a moral wrong to speak or write ungrammatically. Nor is it a moral error to make an aesthetic misjudgement. It may be a fashion outrage to wear a striped shirt with tartan[19] trousers, but outside a special context (e.g. I am going to a job interview at *Vogue* and I need the money to support my family) it is not a moral wrong to do so. The reason is simple. In such cases, there are no moral reasons which apply to make one way of acting preferable to the other. Since morality gives no reasons either way, it provides no guidance, that is, no standards by which the act can be judged. Therefore there are no moral norms that apply. The act in question is simply not regulated by morality.

So too with any number of kinds of acts and the guidance of the law. It is a mistake to think that what is not prohibited is permitted, in the sense that the law provides reasons for, and sets standards upon, all such 'permitted' acts. This is reflected in the way courts typically express 1-type answers when they give them. Where Y claims that X is under a duty to Y in respect of X's φing, and Y's claim fails, the action

[19] In North American English, 'plaid'.

does not normally proceed to trial. X will successfully have the action struck out at the preliminary stage for 'disclosing no cause of action'.[20] In other words, the facts, even if proven, would not be facts about any action of X's that the law regulates.[21] Hohfeld would frame this answer in terms of the court's finding a 'real' liberty–no right jural relation, but the actual formulation used by the courts is clearly preferable because it more accurately reflects the nature of the court's decision.

The second, wrong-headed, view seems to trade on two ideas: (1), which seems to have been the view of Bentham,[22] that because in theory the law *could* prohibit any action, where the law doesn't forbid an action it in some sense endorses it, and (2), to which we see Hohfeld was partial, that the liberty–no right relation is just as 'real' as the duty–no right relation. Neither withstands scrutiny.

As to the first, to adapt a thought of Ripstein's,[23] one might try to extend the sense of 'regulate', adapting Sartre's view that to fail to decide is to decide against deciding, so that failing to regulate is a kind of regulation, but this extension drains the concept of legal regulation of any content. Moreover, it clearly misdescribes the nature of legislation (including, in this context, judicial law-making). Legislators legislate by exercising a power to do so, and exercising a power is an act. Where a legislature has not exercised a power to legislate with regard to some matter, it has not legislated. In addition to this, it is clear that some legislatures have no power to legislate on certain matters. 'Congress shall make no law ... abridging the freedom of speech' is conventionally, and rightly, interpreted to mean that (exceptions aside, e.g. libel, obscenity) Congress has no power to legislate so as to regulate the content of speech, and that any Act purporting to do so would be invalid. And this is so even though, or indeed because, this reflects the First Amendment-makers' positive attitude towards speech—so in this sense the law's determination not to regulate this area is an endorsement of the liberty–no right relation with regard to actions constituting speech, but that endorsement is given effect to by a constitutional

[20] The court must give an answer whether the plaintiff has any ground for a claim or not. After all, as Lord Esher put it: 'Anybody can bring an action though he has no right at all.' (*Attorney General v Sudeley* (1896) 1 QB 354 at 359), cited by Hohfeld, 1913–14, 54, fn 88.

[21] My use of the word 'regulate' must be distinguished from that of Raz 1983, 181–13. For Raz, an 'unregulated' dispute occurs when there is a 'gap' in the law in the sense that the law is indeterminate on the point in question.

[22] Halpin 1996, 136.

[23] Ripstein 2013, 160.

act, the enactment of a *prohibition on regulation*. That prohibition does not itself regulate citizens' speech: it regulates the legislature.

As to the second, it is false that failing to provide a reason not to φ is giving a reason to φ. In indefinitely many cases where we are at liberty to φ, there just are no reasons (or no good or valid reasons) to φ (which is, after all, *why we don't φ*), and the law doesn't give us any. An absence of a reason either to φ or not to φ is just that, the absence of reasons. As Raz puts the point, permissions of this kind, 'weak permissions' as he calls them, 'contribute nothing to practical reasoning'.[24]

This, I should stress, is not a matter of labels; it is the distinction that is important. For all anyone should care one could call the case where the law does impose standards of behaviour, as when it imposes a duty or tells people how to exercise a power validly, as Regulation Type A, and call the case where it provides no standards at all as Regulation Type B.

The point is not whether law-makers, legislatures, or judges, have decided consciously or not to regulate an area, but whether they have in fact done so. Of course where a legislator or a constitution-maker or a court decides that some type of conduct is not to be regulated, that becomes part of the law. The court will, for example, have to determine what counts as 'speech' when determining the scope of the area in which 'speech' is unregulated. And when a court holds that X has no claim against Y because of the content of Y's speech, this ruling adds to the law. So it is perfectly correct to say that the law regulates, really regulates, the liberty–no right jural relations of its subjects in these senses. But that does not undermine the significance of the distinction, nor its usefulness.

So, for example, as to its usefulness: on one variant of BOR, a property right is a bundle of use-rights, that is, a bundle of liberty rights to use one's property. If correct, the point taken here demolishes the very notion; a bundle of 'non-norms', that is, a situation where no legal norms govern anything, cannot properly characterize the genuine legal relations that actually obtain between persons.[25] As I pointed out in 1.2,[26] the uses the owner makes of this (tangible) property are

[24] Raz 1990, 90. See also Thomson 1990, 46–55, discussing the weakness of such privilege in contrast to what she calls 'liberties'; at 49 she points out that the mere absence of a duty would endow 'non-human entities of all sorts – including your left shoe' with privileges (cf. Rainbolt 2006, 8–9), and Kocourek 1920–21, 21, 34–35, 35 fn 28; Kocourek 1921; Kocourek calls unregulated liberties and immunities (re: immunities, see Chapter 5, 5.4) 'anomic'.

[25] See also Penner 1997b, 168–70.

[26] See also Ripstein 2013, 158–9, 160–1.

generally unregulated. Moreover, considered as Hohfeldian 'multital' jural relations, which we shall examine in detail in Chapter 5, the reality of multital *liberty–no right* jural relations is problematic in a further way. All sets of multital rights are of course indefinite, as the group of duty-owers fluctuates as people are born and people die, but multital liberty–no right jural relations are indefinite in a different way: there is no way, even in principle, of setting out a list or compendium of such rights. That is, there is no way in principle of individuating any reasons which are supposed to guide our actions. Hohfeld himself grasped this,[27] but did not consider how this undermined the 'reality' of such relations.

It is worth noting in passing a recent Hohfeldian manoeuvre by McFarlane and Douglas to show that X's property right in tangible property, land, or chattels, can only be explained as a Hohfeldian right, that is, in terms of X's multital *right–duty* jural relations with others, not in terms of any multital liberty right that X has to use her property.[28] Consider X's liberty to drive her car. True, X is in a liberty–no right jural relation with Y regarding this use of her car. But so is everyone else: Y has no right that W not drive X's car, no right that Z not drive X's car, ad infinitum. Similarly, W, any third party, is at the liberty-holder end of an infinite number of liberty–no right jural relations, wherein Y, Z, Q, and so on have no right that W not drive X's car. What distinguishes X from W, Z, Q and everyone else, what allows us, that is, to identify *her* as the owner of the car rather than anyone else, is not the existence of a multitude of liberty–no right relations with respect to the particular car, but the fact that as between herself and each of the others, she *does not* have *no right* that *they do not drive the car*—rather, she *has* a series of multital *rights* that *they do not drive the car*, that is, they are under a duty not to commit a trespass or conversion of her car, that is, they must exclude themselves from it.[29] For the purpose of making their point, McFarlane and Douglas are happy to assume that these myriad liberty–no right relations between non-owners are genuine legal norms,[30] but the correct way of seeing the point is just

[27] 'A [a fee-simple owner] has an *indefinite number* of legal privileges of entering the land, using the land, harming the land, etc' (my italics). Hohfeld, 1913–14, 746.

[28] Douglas and McFarlane 2013, 220–1.

[29] In Chapter 8 I shall explain why the right to exclude in the absence of a right to use does not serve to identify an owner. But the right to use in question is not happily framed as a Hohfeldian liberty.

[30] Douglas and McFarlane 2013, 220.

to understand that the law simply has no concern to regulate the relations between individual non-owners of X's car with respect to their individual dealings with it. They simply have no duties between themselves in this respect, for a completely obvious reason: it is not their car. How anyone, including X, deals with X's property[31] is simply no concern of Y's, W's, or anyone else's.

3.3 Conclusion

The preceding points can be summarized as follows: unless an act constitutes one or more of the discharge or the breach of a legal duty, or the exercise of a legal power, or an act giving rise to a change in legal relations by operation of law, the act has no legal *significance*.

For this reason, genuinely legally or morally regulated liberties are better called 'licences' or 'permissions'. Note, we are not concerned here with the idea that often when someone says they have a legal liberty, or a legal right, to do something themselves, like scratch their head, it is perfectly possible to translate this statement into the Hohfeldian schema by saying that the claim is one to a right–duty jural relation in which some other or others have some one or more duties which are framed in terms of protecting X's doing something; X may be claiming that he has the right to scratch his head because Y is under a duty not to physically interfere with him in doing so.[32] Here, rather, we are concerned with legal relations of the Hohfeldian liberty–no right kind; these attract genuine legal attention because they form exceptions to the background normative position, that is, to the position prior to the exercise of a power so as to permit or license what would otherwise be a breach of duty, as when X licenses Y to come onto her property, or by operation of law, as in the proverbial example where Y by virtue of necessity is permitted to break into X's mountain cabin in a severe snowstorm.[33] Therefore, except in fruitless litigation of the kind in which the claim is struck out for disclosing no cause of action,

[31] Assuming, of course, the dealing in question is not itself unlawful.

[32] See text to n. 22 above.

[33] Exactly the same lesson applies *mutatis mutandis* to the immunity–disability relationship. These are not generally regulated by law or morality at all. They only arise against a backdrop where a person would normally have a liability to the exercise of a power by another, being an exception to the general normative situation. See further, chapter 4, 4.4.

the liberty–no right question always concerns the existence of powers and their proper exercise, or the operations of law which would allow in certain circumstances a person to commit what would otherwise be a breach of duty.

A final point: despite Hohfeld's apparent support for treating liberty–no right jural relations as 'real', in the sense that the law regulates the behaviour of the parties in such cases, Singer has correctly emphasized the fact that Hohfeld's bringing the liberty–no right relation to our attention was profoundly significant for theorists because it showed those large areas of human conduct in which the law did not regulate people's behaviour, with the result that X can injure Y without Y having any legal redress, that is cases of *damnum absque injuria*.[34] Vividly put, this was where the law decides that a 'state of nature' prevails. And, for what it's worth, this important observation can be given a Kantian framing.

Arthur Ripstein[35] and Nicholas Sage[36] elaborate the Kantian distinction between those cases in which X alters Y's genuine normative relations with X or others, and those cases in which X merely 'changes the context in which Y operates'. When X buys the last pint of milk from the shopkeeper C, Y has not suffered any genuine change in his legal relations with either. Although X's purchase may be detrimental to Y in various ways (Y may have a contract with D to bake a cake and his failure to purchase the milk may cause him to breach that contract), in the eyes of the law no wrong is done to Y for Y has no legal interest in the pint of milk so long as it is C's. A second example is that of market competition, which Singer emphasizes in his discussion of X's opening up a shop next to Y's which may lure away Y's customers, but X's doing so does not interfere with any legally recognized interest of Y's, though clearly it changes the context in which Y operates. In Hohfeldian terms, X and Y are in a liberty–no right relations in these cases, which is to say that X's acts are not regulated by law, and Y is not regarded as being in any genuine jural relation with X in respect of these acts of X.

[34] Singer 1982, 994, 1013–14, 1055–7.
[35] Ripstein 2009, 40–50.
[36] Sage 2012.

4

The Problems with Powers

4.1 The Nature of Legal and Moral Powers

Before tackling the question of how powers fit, or fail to fit, into the Hohfeldian scheme of jural relations, it is essential to address a controversy over the nature of legal and moral powers. Hohfeld explains powers in the following way:

> A change in a given legal relation may result (1) from some superadded fact or group of facts not under the volitional control of a human being (or human beings); or (2) from some superadded fact or group of facts which are under the volitional control of one or more human beings. As regards the second class of cases, the person (or persons) whose volitional control is paramount may be said to have the (legal) power to effect the particular change of legal relations that is involved in the problem.[1]

It is orthodox to refer to changes in legal relations falling in class (1) as changes arising by operation of law; for example, X's right to make an insurance claim against Y, her insurance company, arises by operation of law when her house is destroyed by lightning. The problem with Hohfeld's characterization of powers, that is, events falling into class (2), is that it seems overbroad, as was pointed out by Raz.[2] There are many things that one does which may effect a change in legal relations that do not seem to be properly described as the exercise of a power. Raz gives the example of moving house, with the consequence that

[1] Hohfeld 1913–14, 44.
[2] Raz 1990, 102–4.

Property Rights. J. E. Penner, Oxford University Press (2020) © J. E. Penner.
DOI: 10.1093/oso/9780198830122.001.0001

one's tax liabilities change. We would not normally describe someone as having the legal power to change their tax liability by moving house. To take a different sort of example, consider Halpin's 'legal maverick'[3] who commits a petty crime in order to be gaoled, so as to have a warm bed and food for the winter. Again, it seems awry to say that individuals have a power to acquire the right to accommodation and board by committing a crime. Fortunately, class (2) can be narrowed to accord with these intuitions.

Two considerations counsel against equating the exercise of a power with any act over which the actor has 'volitional control' that has legal consequences. The first, which is reflected in this way of framing the issue, is the distinction between results and consequences. As we said with the sale of a laptop example in Chapter 1, 1.2, the exercise of a power bears an 'intrinsic' relation[4] to the *result* of its exercise, but not to whatever other *consequences* flow from its exercise. Similarly with the example of moving house: the *result* is that I now reside elsewhere. It may be a *consequence* of this that my tax liability changes, but this is not an intrinsic aspect of moving house. With regard to the legal maverick, it is a result of the maverick's petty crime that he has breached a duty of the criminal law. The consequence of this, or to put it another way, the law's response to this, is that he is liable to punishment. Thus the law may respond to the exercise of powers in any number of different ways, but any such consequential changes in legal relations arise by operation of law, and thus fall into class (1).

The second consideration has to do with the normative guidance of morality or the law. One has a moral power to consent to being touched, that is, give permission for what would otherwise be a trespass to the person, because it allows one to act co-operatively with others in valuable ways.[5] One has no moral (or legal) consent to murder because murder is not a worthwhile co-operative project for people to engage in.[6] Similar considerations underlie the moral and legal power to enter into binding agreements. True, X can act so as to make it the case that he will owe an enforceable debt to Y in different ways, but not all of them amount to the exercise of a legal power. X can do so by entering into a valid contract in which this debt is one of the

[3] Halpin 1996, 141–7.

[4] Raz 1990, 103; cf. Wellman 1985, 45.

[5] See Chapter 1, 1.4.

[6] See, for example, Ripstein 1998, 201–8.

terms, and X can do so by battering Y so that Y will have a valid cause of action against X which will conclude with the court's ordering X to pay Y a certain sum in damages. But only the first, of course, is the exercise of a power by X. The law does not empower X to become Y's debtor by committing battery.

The distinction between the exercise of powers and the operations of law is, therefore, a conceptual one. This does not entail that the distinction is always easy to apply. To take one historical example, consider the following:

> Once upon a time, one might have said that all uses [the equitable forerunner of trusts] arose by operation of law. By undertaking the moral (not Equitable, in the sense of being governed by a rule of the Court of Equity) obligation to hold his powers of title for the benefit of the feoffor, the feoffee to uses was not conceived to be answerable in Equity because Equity regarded the feoffor as having the power to create a use; rather, the use was imposed upon the feoffee by Equity to prevent his unconscionable exploitation of his title. But as time went on, and Equity's intervention became not only predictable but certain, landowners could intentionally take advantage of this so as effectively to create uses. At some stage, but certainly well before the Statute of Uses, this reliance upon the predictable reaction of Equity came to be understood by all concerned as a new power accompanying title, that is a power to create a use.[7]

This story is exactly as one would expect: in so far as Equity came to regard the use or its successor, the trust, as a valuable legal device, it came to recognize the acts creating one as the exercise of a power to do so.

The distinction between powers and the operations of law can be complicated in another way too. Consider the concept of possession in English law. The law empowers an individual to acquire title to a tangible thing simply by taking possession of it. This is true even of property that is already owned, but for ease of explication let us assumed the thing in question is unowned. It seems right to say that acquiring title to possession is the exercise of a legal power. It facilitates the creation of a title, and in general, the law is neutral or positive on doing such a thing. But there is an important difference between

[7] Slightly modified from Penner 2014b, 493–4.

this power and, for example, some powers to license or to transfer, which can often be accomplished by mere words, 'come on in', or by a procedure, such as registration. These acts effect a legal change via conformity with a form that could obviously be otherwise. Signing a document and affixing a red wafer to it bears no necessary conceptual connection to the act of transferring property. Such an act has no particular normative significance except in virtue of the fact that the law treats complying with it as an exercise of a power, an act which most people are trivially capable of performing. Things are different in the case of acquiring title by possession. Possession reflects pre-legal notions about acts which are not merely a matter of more or less arbitrary form. To say this is not to deny that the legal concept of possession is a matter of law, or that its contours have not been shaped by any number of legal considerations. The thought is rather that unlike speaking some formula, a requirement that a person take possession, in so far as it draws upon pre-legal notions of 'control' or 'capture', imposes substantive constraints on the exercise of this sort of power. In other words, the 'operations of law' come into play in the exercise of the power to acquire title by taking possession in the sense that success in this area has a substantial factual element, success which is determined by the law and not merely by the actor's choice to exercise the power.[8]

One further thing to note about this, though I am not sure how much we should care, is that the law of possession is not really a matter of 'jural relations' between individuals, but about what physical steps are necessary for the law to conclude that an act of possession has taken place. What is involved is a relation between a person and a tangible thing, not his relations with others. Of course this relation is only legally relevant in so far as it is relevant to his legal relations with others; successful taking of possession by A is relevant because it establishes his title in the thing and thereby brings himself, regarding that thing, under the protection of BPrN, or as Hohfeld would have it, establishes all the multital rights that others not interfere with it. How we relate the rules about taking possession to various other rules, in particular to Hohfeldian jural relations, is basically a question about the individuation of laws.[9] All I am noticing here is that not all rules of law are

[8] The same substantial inquiry will attend cases of transfer where effective transfer turns on 'delivery', for example.

[9] For discussion, see Penner 1997c, ch. 3.

illuminatingly framed in terms of jural relations, at least in terms of the substantive work they do.

Pointing all this out is not, of course, to say that we couldn't have a purely legal idea of connection of a person to a thing that had nothing to do with any empirical relation such as possession between a person's body and a tangible thing like land or an object. As we have seen,[10] BPrN does not require for its operation any such connection.[11] We could abolish the power to acquire title by taking possession—perhaps a person wanting something unowned could apply to some central registry. That might be very inconvenient but it is not inconceivable.

4.2 Powers and Correlative Liabilities

The problem here can be straightforwardly identified. A power to change a jural relation will always involve at least two individuals at the liability pole of the power–liability jural relation. To take a simple case, a judge has the power to create a judgment debt between X and Y by ordering Y to pay X a certain sum. The judge has the power to do this, and necessarily, given that the power is a power to impose a right–duty jural relation, both X and Y are simultaneously and necessarily subject to this judge's power. Thus they both fill the place at the liability pole end of the power–liability jural relation. Therefore the power–liability jural relation violates tenet 2 of the orthodox reading of Hohfeld's correlativity thesis set out in Chapter 3, 3.1, namely:

2. Each jural relation obtains between two, and only two, persons.

According to this tenet, any fundamental jural relation obtains between two and only two distinct individuals, and the four distinct jural relations are individuated as distinct types by the way in which the disambiguated 'right' pole of a jural relation between X and Y correlates with a different one of the four non-right poles. Indeed, the main thrust of Hohfeld's first paper was to show that the word 'right' can only be disambiguated by showing how it represents a pole of each of

[10] Chapter 1, text to n. 25.

[11] Of course, BPrN does necessarily involve a substantive factual element in terms of determining what counts as interference with tangible property, for example what counts as a trespass. But this issue is orthogonal to the one in the text, which concerns the exercise of a power to acquire title to a tangible thing, not what counts as an infringement of such a title.

the four distinct jural relations, that is, just in so far as it correlates with a differently characterized pole at the other end. In the case of powers, the correlativity thesis is supposed to work as follows: one specified individual, X, has a power in relation to another specified individual, Y, who has the correlative liability. That is to say that under the power–liability relation, X is in a relation of power–liability with Y, X being at the power pole of this bilateral relation, Y being at the liability pole.

It is worth pointing out that Hohfeld was very unclear, in both of his 'Fundamental Conceptions' papers, about how he conceived of a power and its relation to the correlative liability. Certainly, he seemed to accept in a number of places power–liability jural relations which violate tenet 1.

Tenet 1 is set out in Chapter 3, 3.1 as follows:

1. Rights and duties and any of the other six fundamental legal conceptions are not to be conceived of as free-standing norms themselves, but are only representations of opposite poles of a jural relation; only jural relations (or moral relations where the Hohfeldian scheme is applied to analyse moral norms) correctly characterize norms.

That is, he seemed to indicate in a number of passages that X's exercise of her power (singular) effected a multitude of legal relations involving more than one other individual. But Hohfeld nowhere relates this acceptance to his apparent commitment to tenet 2.

To take but one example of the violation of tenet 2 which Hohfeld clearly accepts: the same individual can be at both poles of the power–liability jural relation. Indeed, his first example of a power he provides is a power of X to abandon property, thus changing X's own normative situation;[12] in such a case X's power correlates with a liability that X herself has. So if it is a tenet of Hohfeld's notion of correlativity that distinct individuals occupy the poles of any Hohfeldian jural relation, then this tenet is violated by any number of legal powers.

The intuition underlying the thought that a power–liability relation can have only one person at the liability pole can, perhaps, be shown by way of analogy to physical relations, along the lines of X's having some ability to affect the physical location of Y. Owing to her physical 'power' or strength, X can push Y from one place to another, changing

[12] Hohfeld 1913–14, 54, n. 90.

Y's location. One might say, therefore, that X and Y stand in a physical relation such that X, by the exercise of her own power, can change Y's physical location. In this way of reading the situation, Y's physical location is not characterized or identified on the basis of how she stands physically in relation to others. We determine Y's location, say, by latitude, longitude, and altitude.

Now consider an alternative account of such a power to change Y's location. We could also frame a physical relation of power, of X's power to alter Y's location, in terms of X's power to alter Y's location in relation to others, say in relation to W and Z. In such a case, however, X would have a power over Y's location which would not necessarily involve X's coming into physical contact with Y; she could alter Y's relative location by pushing W or Z or both in various directions. Indeed, if it were the case that Y was rooted to the spot, X could only alter Y's location by so dealing with Z or W or both. On this reading, the power to change Y's location necessarily implicates Z and W, for that is how 'position' is understood.

It seems clear that for anyone who accepts tenet 1 of the correlativity thesis, the latter 'relative' notion of position is the correct analogy. Our legal position is always to be conceived in terms of the array of jural relations in which we stand to others.

Could things be different in the moral realm? Consider the following example. It seems conceptually possible that there are moral duties without correlative rights. Assume X has a moral duty, not correlating to any other person's rights, to repent for her malicious behaviour, say by secluding herself and devoting herself to meditating upon her deed for a period of time. Assume also that her spiritual advisor, Y, has a power to relieve her of this duty, or limit it to some extent, if X has shown genuine remorse. This power–liability relation seems to comply with tenet 2: Y has a power to alter X's normative situation and only X's. But even this example doesn't really work, because by exercising the power to relieve X of her duty of repentance, Y has 'spent' the power (at least in the case of this occasion of X's repentance), such that Y no longer has that power over X's duty. Thus Y is also liable to the exercise of Y's power because afterwards Y no longer has the power, thus the exercise changes Y's normative situation as well.

It seems clear, then, that those individuals who might stand at the liability end of the power–liability jural relation cannot do so singly. Can we repair this by taking the view that powers are complex in the sense of always being 'paired'?[13] Can we say that the judge, in ordering Y to pay X $100 in damages, really has two powers, a power to impose a duty on Y and separate power to confer a right upon X? No, because there is no such thing as a 'half-power', by which one could impose a Hohfeldian duty on Y without conferring a correlative Hohfeldian claim right on X, and vice versa.[14] Unless one is willing to abandon the most defining tenet of the correlativity thesis, tenet 1, the 'half-powers solution' to the problem posed by tenet 2 is unavailable.

However problematic it might be for the Hohfeldian scheme, it seems preferable to abandon tenet 2 in the case of power–liability jural relations, and not only with respect to the idea that two and only two persons are involved, or the idea that the same person cannot appear at each pole of the relation (to accommodate powers whose exercise affects the power-holder's own jural relations). *What needs to be abandoned is the idea that powers are powers over persons taken singly, rather than powers over jural relations that obtain between persons.*

These considerations would seem to require the invocation of a new tenet, 2★:

2★. In the case of powers, the relation is between a specified individual[15] who fills the power pole of the jural relation and one or more jural relations obtaining between specified individuals that fill the liability pole of the jural relation; such a specified individual can be the power-holder herself.

The 'one *or more* jural relations' is significant. According to Hohfeld, when X transfers title to Blackacre to Y by exercising his power of transfer, X extinguishes the (multital) right–duty relations obtaining between X and a multitude of others who have the duty not to trespass on Blackacre and creates a new set of such relations where Y is at the right pole of these relations. As I shall explain in Chapter 7, this is a mistaken view of what a transfer is, but insofar as we retain tenet 2. for right–duty relations, as Hohfeld would insist we do, then this definitional move is necessary.

[13] At the very least paired. We would need to do further joining or bundling if the exercise of the power altered the jural relations of more than two people which, as we shall see in the next part, many do.

[14] Rainbolt 2006, 20 seems to attempt a 'half-powers' solution to the problem, but I cannot see how this squares with his acceptance of the correlativity axiom: he is explicit (at 2): 'Claims and duties are, to use a well-worn phrase, two sides of the same coin.'

[15] Or specified individuals in the case of a power that must be exercised jointly.

I should point out that Wellman, Kramer, and Rainbolt have all noticed the fact that Hohfeldian powers create or extinguish jural relations, and so a power cannot relate to only one individual; they also noticed that the power-holder himself could be subject to the exercise of the power.[16] But they seemed content to continue to treat individuals as the occupants of the liability end of the power–liability jural relation. For his part Wellman defines a Hohfeldian power in this way: [17]

X has a legal *power* **over Y** with respect to some legal relation if and only if X is able to perform some action that changes this legal relation of Y in some way.

He repeats this way of putting powers later when he says:[18]

In addition to fundamental legal powers of X over Y, there are legal powers of X over X, of X over X and Y, and of X over Y and Z.

It seems to me that holding onto the locution of powers 'over' individuals just obscures the truth that powers are in relation to jural relations. If Wellman had just stuck with his original thought this sort of spelling out the individuals in this sentence would be unnecessary. Finally, it is clearly incomplete. A law-maker, including a judge in a private law dispute, has the power to introduce legal rules that bind everyone, thus changing everyone's rights or duties or powers and so on.

4.3 The Interdependence of Some Powers

We must now notice another feature of power–liability relations. Power–liability relations can be interdependent in a way that Hohfeldian right–duty and liberty–no right relations are not. As Hohfeld himself insisted,[19] Y's duty to X not to trespass on Blackacre is independent of W's duty to X not to trespass on Blackacre; Y's breaching his duty neither depends upon nor entails anything about W's breaching hers. In similar fashion, X's liberty to Φ as against Y is independent of X's

[16] Wellman 1985, 24, 42; Kramer 1988, 20–2; Rainbolt 2006, 3, 19–22.
[17] Wellman 1985, 8 (italics original, my bold).
[18] Wellman 1985, 44.
[19] Hohfeld 1916–17, 742.

liberty to Φ as against W. The same obtains between different contractual duties owed to X, and the same independence can be seen in the case of X's power to license entry onto Blackacre. According to Hohfeld, X has a multital power to license Y to enter Blackacre, another multital power to license W to enter Blackacre, and so on. The same independence relation applies here to X's exercise of one of these multital powers. Exercising the power to license Y to enter Blackacre neither depends upon nor entails anything in regard to X's power to license W to enter Blackacre, or with regard to any other of the multital power–liability relations X is in with P, Q, R, and so on. The independence relation holds true as well of X's (multital) power to enter into contractual relations with Y, of his power to enter into contractual relations with W, and so on.[20]

But this independence relation does not hold when we consider X's power to transfer title to Y. When X exercises this power, he at the same time *extinguishes* all of the other multital power–liability relations he has with everyone else to exercise the power to transfer title to them. The same is true, for example, of a trustee's multital powers to appoint property amongst a class of objects, and of the court's multital powers to appoint a person or persons as administrator(s) of a deceased's estate.

It is not at all clear how we might adapt Hohfeld's scheme to accommodate this feature of some multital powers. That is, there do not seem to be any resources the scheme can draw upon which make sense of the analytical dependence between these sorts of power–liability relations. Another way of putting this is to say that this sort of complexity is one which the scheme does not seem suited to illuminate.

Consider, for example, what might seem to be an obvious way out. Why could you not conceive X's power to transfer Blackacre as correlating with a *class of persons*, all of those out there, Y, W, Z ad infinitum, and explain the power as a power to transfer title to one or some of them? Upon exercise, X's power would be 'spent', and so therefore it would no longer exist for X to make another transfer to anyone else. This is a defensible move, but it is not clear Hohfeld can make it if he wants to hold onto his thesis about multital jural relations; as we shall

[20] This is true even if by entering into one contract X exposes herself to an unavoidable liability for breach of contract. For example, if X contracts with Y to sell Blackacre to Y, and then the next day contracts to do the same with W, X must breach at least one of the contracts. Yet both are still valid contracts.

see when we examine the multitality thesis in detail in Chapter 5, a jural relation in which X is at one pole, a class (in this case an indefinite class) of persons at the other, is just the sort of relation the reality of which Hohfeld's claims about multitality are specifically intended to deny. According to the multitality thesis, X stands in *independent*, one-to-one jural relations with each member of the class.

4.4 Powers, Inalienable Rights, and the 'Unprovided-for' Nature of Immunities

Hillel Steiner has argued that if we take Hohfeld's analytic scheme seriously, he can show that there are no inalienable rights.[21] The argument has several steps. We saw in the last chapter[22] that Hohfeld believed that the liberty–no right jural relation was just as legally 'real' as the right–duty jural relation. I gave reasons for thinking this was wrong, arguing that liberties in so far as they correlate, as Hohfeld insists, with 'no rights', are not legal relations, but merely show that liberties so defined are legally unregulated. I shall conclude something similar or relevantly equivalent here: that immunities are not legally real either, but in the sense that they are not legally *provided for* as opposed to being not legally *regulated*.[23] But Steiner contends the opposite, and would apply the same idea of the 'normative reality'[24] of liberty rights to immunity–disability jural relations.[25]

As far as I understand him, Steiner would treat each 'right' pole of the four fundamental Hohfeldian positions as waivable in principle. That is, each claim right, liberty, power, or immunity is in principle accompanied with a power to 'waive' the right, liberty, power, or immunity. By waiver one essentially turns the jural relation into its Hohfeldian 'opposite'; thus for X to waive his right–duty relation to Y that Y Φ is for X to exercise the power to change this relation to one in which Y is under no duty to Φ or not to Φ; following the

[21] Steiner 2013.

[22] Chapter 3, 3.2.

[23] In doing so I am grateful to draw upon Biasetti 2015, though I would not hold him to the arguments I am about to proffer. In particular, I am sure I have missed some technical refinements in the way he presents his objections to Steiner.

[24] Moral or legal normative reality as the case may be.

[25] Steiner 2013, 237.

exercise of this power Y is in a liberty–no right relation with X such that Y has the liberty to Φ or not Φ.[26] Similarly, for X to waive his power–liability relation to Y with regard to some jural relation in which Y figures, call it α, is for X to exercise the power to change this power–liability relation to one in which Y is no longer liable to the exercise of that power with respect to α; thus Y is now in an immunity–disability relation with X such that Y is immune vis-à-vis X from changes, extinctions, or creations, of α.

I am afraid I must now introduce some notation to keep these Hohfeldian moves legible for, as we shall see, things get complicated quickly.

Consider what might be regarded as an unwaivable right, or strictly speaking, an unwaivable right–duty relation. X is in a right–duty relation with Y such that Y not Φ where Φ might be, as it were, 'murder X'. I shall render this relation in this way:

(1) X RD (for right–duty jural relation) Y: Y not Φ; leaving out the expansion in parentheses we get: X RD Y: Y not Φ

Similarly LibNR for 'liberty–no right jural relation', PL for 'power–liability jural relation', and ID, for 'immunity–disability jural relation'.

Thus X's power to change a jural relation in which Y figures, say a power of a judge to order Y to pay Z $10, is framed thus, where → indicates the change of jural relation upon the exercise of the power:

(2) X PL Y and Z[27]: Y LibNR Z: Y pay Z $10 → Z RD Y: Y pay Z $10

Where X is in a disability–immunity relation with Y as regards a jural relation in which Y figures, such that X has no power to order Y to pay Z $10, we get:

(2*) Y (and Z) ID X: Y LibNR Z: Y pay Z $10 → Z RD Y: Y pay Z $10

Where a right–duty relationship is waivable, this means that one party to the relationship has a power to negate it. Since we are concerned with those at the right end of jural relations, we will think of the person at that end having the power, though there is nothing in Hohfeld's scheme to rule out the duty-holder having the power to 'waive', that

[26] As I read Steiner the power of waiver of a right to Φ is the power to create a pair of Hohfeldian liberties, that is, the liberty to Φ and the liberty to not Φ.

[27] As I explained in 4.2, powers are always over a jural relation, in this case a jural relation between Y and Z that the judge can create. But for the sake of ease of exposition, I am expressing the power as one over both Y *and* Z in this case, with the tacit understanding that this does not mean X has two separate powers, one over each of them.

is, extinguish the relationship, if in principle all jural relations can be subject to a power of 'waiver' or extinction.

Thus, if the right–duty relation of (1) is waivable by the right-holder, it is accompanied by the following power:

(3) X PL X and Y: X RD Y: Y not Φ →Y LibNR X: Y Φ or not Φ

If the right-duty relationship is not waivable, we have:

(4) X and Y ID X: X RD Y: Y not Φ →Y LibNR X: Y Φ or not Φ

X and Y are the beneficiaries of an immunity right as regards X: X is disabled from changing Y's duty not to murder X into a liberty to murder X or not as Y chooses.

The important move in Steiner's argument now follows, which is the move my argument below shall block. Steiner asks what prevents X from *waiving his immunity* (4). If an immunity is a right, in principle it can be waived; but if X can waive his immunity, we get:

(5) X PL X and Y: (X and Y ID X: RD Y: Y not Φ →Y LibNR X: Y Φ or not Φ) → X PL X and Y: X PL X and Y: RD Y: Y not Φ →Y LibNR X: Y Φ or not Φ.

By substitution of (3) and (4):

(6) X PL X and Y: (4) → (3)

Thus, by exercising this power to waive the immunity in (6), X can make the unwaivable right waivable again, by empowering himself, that is, X, by waiving the immunity X has against himself. The power in (6) is X's, but one could grant the power of waiver to Q, a third party. The point is that so long as an immunity can be extinguished, the immunity right does not prevent the underlying right from being extinguished after all. The reason I have been granting X the immunity right is that in cases of what we call waiver, we normally think of the individual with the underlying RD right to be the person who 'waives' the right. This allocation is not necessary under the Hohfeldian schema; in principle anyone could have powers in relation to any other jural relation whether she figured in it or not. And notice, allocating this power of waiver to X, where X is at both ends of the power–liability relation, must, as we saw above, be permissible under the Hohfeldian scheme under revised tenet 2*.

Now we see how the prospect of an infinite regress looms. We can ask, can X waive the power in (6)? Given that all rights are in principle waivable, the answer must be 'yes'. This would yield:

(7) (4) → (3) ID X

But can X waive his immunity right given by (7)? Yes, and on we go. Thus Steiner concludes that if we were to try to insulate any jural relation from waivability we could only do so by way of an infinite regress. Steiner thus concludes that if the Hohfeldian analysis is correct, then all rights, liberties, powers, and immunities are waivable; unwaivable rights are in principle ruled out. Another way of putting this point is that the mere *possibility* of waiver under the Hohfeldian scheme means that no right can ever be unwaivable because of the way that the nesting of powers and disabilities works—any denial of a power of waiver at one stage can be undone at a subsequent one.

This conclusion can be blocked. As commentators have pointed out,[28] Hohfeld's notion of jural 'opposites' is really one of negation. A liberty, the 'opposite' of a duty, is just a 'no duty'. By parity of reasoning, an immunity is just a 'no liability', and a disability is just a 'no power'. As a matter of logic, the absence of X entails everything and nothing about the state of the world. For our purpose here, it does not entail the existence of any actual jural relation. Therefore, if an immunity is just the correlative of a 'no power' in Hohfeld's system, which it is, it has no more jural reality than a liberty does, which is just the correlative of a 'no duty'. So there is nothing to be waived in (4), for the immunity right is not a genuine jural relation. That is the general case, which sorts out Steiner's problem. Of course, just like what I have called genuine 'permissions', some immunity rights could be real under the Hohfeldian system, where they provide specific exceptions to more general powers, such as a police officer's immunity from prosecution for carrying a concealed weapon. In this case the law genuinely provides for the general power, here to prosecute for carrying a concealed weapon, and provides a genuine exception to that power. But just as in the case of unregulated liberties, unprovided-for powers and any possible exceptions to them in the form of immunities, have no normative reality.

If Steiner has got Hohfeld right, then Steiner's error is Hohfeld's too, though of course there is no evidence that Hohfeld followed Steiner to Steiner's conclusion, or that he would have done had the argument been put to him. I only address this matter here because the structure of private law seems to turn on a number of unwaivable rights and powers. One is not able to waive one's right to life in the general case.

[28] Kocourek, 1921; Halpin 1985, 441–5.

But more importantly, one is not able to waive one's power to enter into contracts, or one's power to license, transfer, or acquire property.[29] If Steiner were right we would be in big trouble. As I shall explore in Chapter 8, the law's conferral of powers reflects important facets of our 'natural' rights as agents in the world. That we might waive our powers as agents would permit a kind of waiver of our humanity, and I am glad that Steiner fails to prove that we must be able to do so.

4.5 Conclusion

Summing up, we see that powers put a significant strain on the general applicability of the Hohfeldian scheme of jural relations. We have had to add tenet 2* to accommodate powers at all, and this added complexity alone indicates that any simplifying function of the scheme appears to be overstated; tenets 1 and 2 of the correlativity thesis only really apply to the right–duty and liberty–no right relations. Moreover, the scheme cannot account for and arguably obscures the nature of power–liability relations which are not independent of each other. As we shall see in Chapter 6, this will cause serious headaches for the Hohfeldian in trying to account for the transferability of title to property, and the concept of an interest in property itself. Finally, we have met Steiner's claim that Hohfeld's analysis requires us to deny the possibility of unwaivable rights.

[29] One can of course enter into contractual or trust obligations not to exercise a power, but that is not the same thing as waiving the power itself.

5

Multital Jural Relations

5.1 The Multital 'Picture' of Jural Relations

I have found this chapter the hardest in the book to write. The reason for this is that the idea of multital jural relations, against which I shall be speaking, is intuitively attractive. It is a kind of 'picture' of our private law legal relations. It depicts an extensive web of one-to-one right–duty[1] relations that links us with every other person. I nevertheless think it misrepresents our legal relations in a serious way. Pompously, perhaps, I would say that the task I have to undertake in this chapter is akin to the task Wittgenstein set himself when he sought to undermine the 'Augustinian picture' of language.[2] The modus operandi of discharging this sort of task is to nibble away at the picture from different angles, in this case to show in what particular ways the picture allows us to, or makes us, misunderstand our actual jural relations one to another.

I couldn't say whether the multital idea was Hohfeld's invention, but I am happy to thank him for making the kind of moral and legal world view it expresses more or less explicit. Let us call this the Hohfeldian Multital Picture of jural relations, or HMP.

[1] And liberty–no right, power–liability, immunity–disability jural relations, of course; see Chapter 3, 3.1. I am assuming here that Hohfeldian liberty–no right and immunity–disability jural relations are genuine normative relations, but I have denied this in Chapter 3, 3.2 and Chapter 4, 4.4 respectively.

[2] Wittgenstein 1958, [1]–[3].

Property Rights. J. E. Penner, Oxford University Press (2020) © J. E. Penner.
DOI: 10.1093/oso/9780198830122.001.0001

One facet of this picture recasts an ancient distinction between rights in rem and rights in personam. Traditionally, a right in rem was regarded as a right 'good against all the world', that is, good against everyone. My right to bodily security or my right to my property are the standard examples. By contrast, a right in personam was a right good only against a specific individual (or a few specific individuals). The typical example is a contractual right Y might have against X to be paid £10. As we shall look at in detail below, Hohfeld's move to reconfigure this distinction gives rise to a number of complications, but the idea is simple and, for many, intuitively appealing: a right in rem is not *one* right good 'against the world'. Rather it is a *battery of one-to-one rights in personam*; X has a right that Y not batter him, a right that W not batter him, a right that Z not batter him, and so on so as to include everyone alive, or at least everyone alive in the relevant legal jurisdiction if we are speaking of legal rights. It seems to explain why, when X batters Y, X breaches a duty X specifically owes to Y, and Y's right is violated by X's act. It is why Y can say X violated *her* right.[3] What could be clearer and simpler than that? Unfortunately, as I shall go on to show, this clarity and simplicity is deceptive.

To help frame our discussion of multital jural relations, it is useful to set the scene by recalling the norm of property law which is at issue, BPrN, which I introduced in Chapter 1, 1.2. To remind the reader, this is one of the basic norms of property law in respect of tangible property, that is, land and chattels, which is the general duty not to trespass on property that is not one's own. (As we saw in Chapter 1, 1.2, the other basic norms are the power to license what would otherwise be trespasses and the power to transfer title.) Two things about BPrN should be borne in mind as we proceed. Both concern the information that the duty-ower needs to apply it, following GFPN. First, there is the information about what property the duty-ower himself owns. Arthur Ripstein, relying upon Henry Smith's insight, puts the point this way: [4]

[3] Essert 2013, 426 (footnote omitted), expresses this intuition well. Of an owner who suffers a trespass he says:

> Her claim is grounded in her special status as owner and is not a claim that rests on a general duty not to trespass; in fact, the owner does not and need not care how much trespass in general happens. All that she cares about is that her own property not be trespassed upon.

[4] Ripstein 2013, 159.

Henry Smith has noted this is an epistemically undemanding rule, which requires almost no information to apply; such information as it does require is autobiographical, and so typically available to each person.

The other sort of information required is a general familiarity, which is relative to the particular culture and legal system in which the duty-ower finds himself, with the sort of things that are privately owned and those which, in contrast, are not, such as public highways and wild animals. This familiarity is also typically easily acquired, so on this score as well BPrN is epistemically undemanding.

The grounding outlook of HMP is that BPrN, so conceived *as a rule imposing a general duty*, is misconceived or misleading. For Hohfeld, there is no such general relation between duty-owers and title-holders which characterizes their normative relation(s). Rather, X, as title-holder of Blackacre, is in a set of multital right–duty jural relations with Y, W, Z and so on, such that X has a right that Y not trespass on Blackacre, has a right that W not do so, and so on ad infinitum.

The distinction between rights in rem and rights in personam relate to a right's scope, that is, to the number of duty-bearers there are whose duties correlate to the right. This distinction must be contrasted with another, the distinction between *general* rights and *specific* rights. This distinction concerns not a right's scope, but rather its incidence—how the right comes into being. These distinctions can be confused, but confusing one distinction with the other was not Hohfeld's confusion, although, as I shall show presently, observing the two distinctions helps us to see where his confusion lay. Briefly, his confusion was twofold. Hohfeld failed to see that the rights in rem/rights in personam distinction is not one of empirical numerosity, but of normative guidance; secondly, his characterization of multital rights turns on an unexplained notion of the 'intrinsic similarity/identity' of norm acts. I shall first set out these distinctions, and then show the way that Hohfeld's idea of 'multital jural relations' leads us astray. Very briefly, Hohfeld's programme is both otiose and misleading—it doesn't do anything to explain the *incidence* of rights, and it misleadingly suggests a weird notion of normativity, that is, that norms only guide as between specific individuals. I shall then go on to explain the correlativity of property rights to the general duty not to trespass via the mediation of a rule, in this case BPrN.

5.2 Multitality and Generality

Hohfeld defines multital rights as follows:

A multital right, or claim, (right *in rem*) is always *one* of a large *class* of *fundamentally similar* yet separate rights, actual and potential, residing in a single person (or single group of persons) but availing *respectively* against persons constituting a very large and indefinite class of people.[5]

Proponents of the Hohfeldian scheme generally accept that the size of the class is irrelevant to the nature of multital rights,[6] and rightly so, for the size of the class does not distinguish between rights in rem and rights in personam, and this is easily illustrated. Assume that because of some cataclysm X, Y, W, and Z find themselves the only ones alive, and washed up on a desert island. X would still have rights in rem against each of Y, W, and Z that they not, for example, batter him or take his property. By contrast, consider this sort of case: Singapore Telecommunications Ltd ('Singtel') has contractual duties to provide mobile phone services on a standard basis to more than a million customers, under which contracts each subscriber has to pay Singtel $50 each month. This is certainly a large class of fundamentally similar (not identical[7]) yet separate right–duty jural relations and yet this does not make Singtel's rights rights in rem. As Kramer puts the point:

[T]he crucial feature of a right held 'against the world' is not the *numerousness* of the parallel rights, but the *indefiniteness* of their number.[8]

'Indefiniteness of their number' needs to be elaborated. It cannot mean that at any one time it is impossible to set out exactly the number of rights in rem that X has, as our desert island example shows. X has precisely three such rights, obtaining against Y, W, and Z respectively. The only thing that 'indefiniteness of number' can mean here is that,

[5] Hohfeld 1916–17, 718 (italics original).

[6] See, for example, Kramer 1998, 10 fn 2; cf. Merrill and Smith 2001a, 783–6, who argue that numerosity does have a role to play with regard to what they call 'intermediate' cases of property rights.

[7] W's duty to pay Singtel $50 each month is a duty that *W* pay this money each month, Z's duty that *Z* pay this money each month and so on; the same applies to the duty of each of them has to X not to enter Blackacre.

[8] Kramer 1998, 10 fn 2 (italics original).

whether empirically possible or not (X, Y, W, and Z could all be men, so that at least no other persons will be *added* to the class), the class can fluctuate, either diminishing or expanding in size. Yet even on this 'fluctuation' reading of 'indefiniteness of number', the multital jural relations so defined fail to capture the underlying idea of rights in rem, or to put it another way, rights held 'against the world'.

Consider again the Singtel example. The class of duty-owers, that is, the subscribers, could fluctuate, contract, and expand for a host of reasons. The class would shrink when subscribers die or exit the contract, and enlarge when new subscribers sign up. Note that it is not to the point here to object to this example by saying these departures and additions all happen within the law of contract. From the standpoint of a Hohfeldian analysis where numerosity is replaced by indefiniteness of number, *why* the class in question is capable of fluctuating is irrelevant. Of course one could say that Hohfeld implicitly assumed that the only changes in the size and composition of the duty-owing class countenanced by the multital analysis should occur by operation of law, though that is neither explicitly suggested nor even hinted at. But regardless of what Hohfeld himself thought, it does not do the trick of identifying rights in rem. We can replicate the same situation by referring only to the operations of law. Assume Assurance plc insures a number of policy-holders for $1m with regard to the risk of their houses being destroyed. The class of those with an enforceable claim right to be paid $1m dollars will enlarge each time one of their houses is destroyed, and will diminish on each occasion when, through effluxion of time, claims that are not yet enforced are barred by a statute of limitations.

The result is that on the basis neither of numerosity nor indefiniteness of number are multital rights, as defined, equivalent to rights in rem, and this is so irrespective of whether the fluctuations in the class arise by the exercise of contractual powers or the operations of law.

The only thing that generates the concept of a right in rem is the concept of a general, as opposed to a special, *duty*.[9]

General *rights* are those which everyone has by virtue of their humanity or citizenship within a jurisdiction, for example the right not to be killed or the right to vote. General rights need not be exceptionless: in jurisdictions with a death penalty, a person may lose their

[9] The following passage on the general/special rights distinction is modified from Penner and Melissaris 2012, para. 7.2.4.1

right not to be killed, and children are not allowed to vote. Special rights, in contrast, are those which arise for other reasons, such as rights under a contract, rights which therefore only specific individuals have. This is the sense in which the general/special rights distinction concerns the *incidence* of rights, that is, when they arise.

The in rem/in personam distinction concerns the scope of a right, that is, the class of people who owe a correlative duty to the right-holder. Rights in rem correlate with a general duty. A general duty is a duty that everyone has simply in virtue of their being alive or within a jurisdiction. Everyone has a duty not to interfere with the person or property of others. Just like general rights, such duties need not be exceptionless; young children are normally thought not to have such duties because they do not have the capacity to govern their behaviour so as to comply with them. The only thing that makes a right a right in rem is that the right correlates with a general duty as just defined, where 'correlate' has the following specific sense: a right in rem only exists if there exists a norm imposing upon every individual (again with possible exceptions) a duty whose violation would be a violation of that right. By parity of reasoning, a right in personam exists where there is no such norm. Applied to the four possible combinations of rights in rem, rights in personam, general rights, and special rights we get (leaving out mention of possible exceptions) examples such as:

i. A general right in rem: a right to bodily security is general, obviously, for everyone has such a right, and a right in rem because everyone has a duty not to interfere with my right to bodily security.
ii. A special right in rem: a property right in a tangible, whether in land or a chattel. The right is special as only the owner has (or co-owners have) the right, but in rem because of the general duty to comply with BPrN.
iii. A general right in personam: a right to the care of one's parents;[10] the right is general because all children have it simply in

[10] An autobiographical note: I came up with this example all by myself when a D.Phil. student at Oxford. I offered it as an example whilst sitting in on a B.Phil. seminar convened by Bernard Williams, when no one else could think of an example of a general right in personam. (I came later to understand this wasn't the brightest B.Phil. cohort, so the achievement is probably less than I fondly think it to be.) Williams immediately jumped on the example, pointing out that it didn't work the other way around such that people had general duties to look after their children, for not all people are necessarily parents, whereas necessarily all children do have parents. The reason I mention this is that fifty years earlier Kocourek,

virtue of being born, but in personam because there is no norm requiring all persons to take care of all children.

iv. A special right in personam: a contractual right is the obvious example here; it is in personam because there is no norm requiring all persons to discharge obligations under any contract that is formed when two persons exercise their powers to enter into a binding agreement.

What follows from this is that rights in rem cannot be specified because of either the numerosity or the fact that in principle the class of duty-owers may fluctuate by operation of law. It is only the fact that rights in rem correlate with general duties, that is, that the fluctuations occur only because people are born (or reach full age) or die, that makes sense of the scope of rights in rem. Oddly enough, Hohfeld recognizes this, but he doesn't see how it betrays his idea of a mutital jural relation. He says:

> It is not infrequently thought that the word 'general' is both appropriate and available to denote those rights, or claims, that are here called 'multital'. It is submitted, however, that according to the best usage the term 'general', as applied to a *jural relation*, indicates that the latter is one of a large class of similar relations residing *respectively in many persons*, i.e., people in general. For example, any *duty* correlating with a *multital right* would be a *general*, or *common*, duty. The right of person not to be struck by another is both multital and *general.*[11]

The last two sentences are, however, clearly false—Hohfeld is confusing the idea of a genuine right in rem, whose scope is such that it correlates with a general, common duty, with his own concept of a multital right. A multital right is a single jural relation that obtains between one right-holder and one duty-ower. It is the breakdown product of Hohfeld's analysis of a right in rem. Common or general duties cannot correlate with a single multital right. That idea is supposed to be the whole point of the analysis. The several distinct duties

in a sense, had beaten me to it; Kocourek 1919–20, 335–56. I say 'in a sense' because he seems to deny the generality of the child's right by saying further facts, such as the marital status of the father, are necessary to determine whether the child has a right to the care of the father. So the right, in so far as it is general, seems not to correlate with any duty; it merely sets the stage for that possibility, in which case it is not truly a general right.

[11] Hohfeld 1916–17, fn 20 (italics original).

correlative to an owner's series of multital rights are *similar*—the jural relations are 'companions'—not *common*, much less *general*. We shall return to the similarity point in 5.3.

Still, this does not mean that the concept of multital rights is, at this point in the examination, defunct. One could modify the definition as follows:

A multital right, or claim, (right *in rem*) is always *one* of a *class* (which at the limiting case could consist of only one member) of *fundamentally similar* yet separate rights, actual and potential, residing in a single person (or single group of persons) but availing *respectively* against all persons (i.e. living persons) (other than the right-holder herself).

But this weakens the analytic power of the distinction considerably. It doesn't so much explain the notion of right in rem as obscurely to trade on the idea of a general duty, the existence of which can only be explained by *a* (singular) duty-imposing norm, that is, BPrN.

5.3 General Rules and General Rights

We must now pass to what Hohfeld understands to be the consequence of treating rights in rem as multital rights. This is the view that BPrN, that is, that everyone has the duty not to interfere with property that is not their own, is misconceived, or rather, cannot be explained in terms of the correlativity thesis; the claim is that a right in rem cannot correlate with *a* duty imposed on all others not to so interfere. Rather, the right in rem can only properly be understood as a series of individual right–duty jural relations between the right in rem holder at one pole of the relation and an individual duty-ower at the other end. Hohfeld's argument for this proposition is found in this passage (forgive the long quotation):[12]

[I]t is submitted that instead of there being a single right with a single correlative duty resting on all the persons against whom the right avails, there are many separate and distinct rights, actual and potential, each one of which has a correlative duty resting upon some one person. Repeating a

[12] Hohfeld 1916–17, 742–4 (footnotes omitted, italics original).

hypothetical case put above, let us suppose that A is the owner of Blackacre and X is the owner of Whiteacre. It may be assumed further that, in consideration of $100 *actually paid* by A to B, the latter agrees with A never to enter on X's land, Whiteacre; also that C and D, at the same time and for separate considerations, make respective similar agreements with A. In such a case A's respective rights against B, C, and D are clearly rights *in personam*, or paucital rights. Surely no one would assert that A has only a single right against B, C, and D, with only a single or unified duty resting on the latter. A's right against B is entirely separate from the other two. B may commit a breach of *his* duty, without involving any breach of C's duty by C or any breach of D's duty by D. For, obviously, the content of each respective duty differs from each of the others. To make it otherwise C and D would have to be under a duty or duties (along with B) that B should not enter on X's land. Even if that were the case, there would be said to be three *separate* duties unless B, C, and D bound themselves so as to create a so-called joint obligation. In the latter case alone would there be said to be a single right and a single (joint) duty. Going beyond this direct analysis of the situation, it seems clear that the three respective 'right-duty' relations of A and B, A and C, and A and D respond to every test of separateness and independence. A might discharge B from his duty to A, thus (in equivalent terms) creating a privilege of entering as against A (not as against X, of course); yet, obviously, the respective duties of C and D would continue the same as before.

Point for point, the same considerations and tests seem applicable to A's respective rights *in rem*, or multital rights, against B, C, D, and others indefinitely that they, respectively considered, shall not enter on Blackacre. It is not a case of one *joint* duty of the *same* content resting on all - e. g., that B should not enter on Blackacre. Consistently with this view, A might, e. g., extinguish B's duty or, in other words, grant B the privilege of entering by giving 'leave and license' to do so. In such event, of course, the respective duties of C, D, E, and all others would continue to exist, precisely as before.

In order to see even more clearly that the supposed single right *in rem* correlating with 'a duty' on 'all' persons really involves as many separate and distinct 'right-duty' relations as there are persons subject to a duty, it may be worth while to reverse the situation somewhat, and consider, in anticipation of a more general treatment at a later point, the subject of duties *in rem*, or multital duties. Thus, e. g., X is under duty not to strike R, S, T, or any other ordinary member of the community. Are we to say that, as regards these many persons, X has but a single duty, and that, correlatively, there is but a *single* right held by R, S, T, and all the others? Manifestly not, for each one of these persons has a distinct and independent right; and any one of such independent rights might cease to exist without in the least affecting the others. If, e. g., R threatens bodily harm to X, R's right that X shall not strike him becomes thereby extinguished, and a no-right in R substituted; or, correlatively, in such contingency, X's duty to R ceases, and X acquires a privilege of self-defense against R. But such change in no way affects the entirely distinct relations existing between X and the various other persons involved.

A number of problems appear to arise if we take this passage at face value.

In the first place, as regards the independence of B's breach from a breach by C, D, or anyone else, this does not in itself tell against BPrN. The fact that B or C or D breaches a general norm does not in any way suggest or entail that E or F or G has breached the norm. This is true of rules in general. They only apply to fact situations in which they are engaged, and where the act of an individual engages a rule it is only engaged vis-à-vis that individual's act. The same moral applies to those jural relations where the waiver of one is not the waiver of another. If there is a general power to waive the duties of individuals in a class of duty-owers, then that power is only engaged when it is exercised in favour of one of the class.

In the second place, Hohfeld's mention of multital *duties* is not a help to his cause. To treat the duty of X not to strike R, S, and T as a 'multital' duty is to breach tenet 3 of the correlativity thesis.[13] The reason why the concept of multitality gets off the ground in the case of rights in rem is that the correlative duties of Y, W, and Z are 'fundamentally similar', and in the case of the duties here they are: if X is the owner of Blackacre, Y, W, and Z each have the fundamentally similar duty *to X* not to *trespass on Blackacre*. They are not identical because they cannot be breached by the identical act—only the act of Y trespassing on Blackacre will breach Y's duty not to trespass—but the act type is the same, and the duty in respect of that act type is owed to the identical person, X. But this is not so for multital duties as described. X's duty with respect to R is a duty *not to strike R*, her duty with respect to T a duty *not to strike T*, and so on. So conceived

[13] Chapter 3, 3.1.

as a set of multital jural relations, they only form a set, not through the identity of the right-holder as in the case of rights in rem, nor by the identity of the duty, but via the identity of the duty-ower, and employing a less stringent 'similarity' criterion (not to 'strike *others*') to group the duties together. In other words, they are only a similar act type because the *identity* of the right-holder is taken as irrelevant to their application. But, as Hohfeld emphasizes when focusing on the independent status of multital jural relations, the whole underlying outlook of HMP is that the identity of the pole-occupants in right-duty relations is essential to their nature. Hohfeld makes a distinct step away from this thesis when he acknowledges the possibility of multital duties framed in the way he does. Indeed, if the identity of the right-holder is irrelevant to the classification of a right sufficient to make it 'multital', then that is simply to admit the possibility of general duties such as that framed by BPrN.[14]

At this point it is worth reminding ourselves that Hohfeld's notion of similarity between rights 'intrinsically' considered does not distinguish rights based on their source. Here is the relevant passage:

Suppose that A is the owner of Blackacre and X is the owner of Whiteacre. Let it be assumed, further, that, in consideration of $100 *actually paid* by A to B, the latter agrees with A never to enter on X's land, Whiteacre. It is clear that A's right against B concerning Whiteacre is a right *in personam*, or paucital right; for A has no similar and separate rights concerning Whiteacre availing respectively against other persons in general. On the other hand, A's right against B concerning Blackacre is obviously a right *in rem*, or multital right; for it is but one of a very large number of fundamentally similar (though separate) rights which A has respectively against B, C, D, E, F, and a great many other persons. It must now be evident, also, that A's Blackacre right against B is, *intrinsically considered*, of the same general character as A's Whiteacre right against B. The Blackacre right differs, so to say, only *extrinsically*, that is, in having many fundamentally similar, though distinct, rights as its 'companions'. So, in general, we might say that a right *in personam* is one having few, if any, 'companions'; whereas a right *in rem* always has many such 'companions'.

If, then, the Whiteacre right, being a right *in personam* is recognized as a right against a person, must not the Blackacre right also, being, point for

[14] See Penner 1997c, 23, 25–7, where I aim at this point but fail to make it as explicit as I should have done.

point, intrinsically of the same general nature, be conceded to be a right against *a person*? If not that, what is it? How can it be apprehended, or described, or delimited at all?[15]

B's contractual duty to A to stay off the property of X is unital, because it has no 'companions'. But nothing stops X from also contracting with B to stay off Blackacre. (Perhaps B is constantly trespassing and, fed up, X contracts to pay B $50 each month he doesn't trespass). On Hohfeld's account, *this* contractual right, being owed to X, has the same 'intrinsic' content as does X's rights against C, D, E, and so on, so it does have lots of companions. Therefore this in personam right is also a multital right. So X would have two multital rights against B. Now imagine X, fed up with B's constant trespassing, gets a court order against B ordering B not to trespass. Is this another multital right? You might say 'no' because the duty imposed by a court order is a duty owed to the court, but you might also say 'yes', since X is the beneficiary of the duty and X has the right to enforce it against B by legal action. So plausibly X now has three multital rights against B with the 'same' content, considered 'intrinsically'. The point of these examples is, in the first place, just to show that the 'intrinsically considered' 'similarity' game is one that anyone can play, and you can make up the rules as you go along. But the second, more important, point is that it seems to give the wrong result—if the two latter 'multital' rights X has against B, the contractual right and the court order right, are multital rights on Hohfeld's analysis, and the first one definitely is, then his test for multitality fails to distinguish rights in the way that the law does. That is, it fails to properly distinguish rights in rem from rights in personam.

In the third place, let us note two further problematic features of HMP: first, understanding the right–duty relation or relations which characterize the duties people have in respect of the property of others in this way is, unlike BPrN, outlandishly epistemically onerous. In order to comply with one's duties, one must know the identity of each right-holder and each item of property he particularly owns. It also violates GFPN. In order to comply with the law, the identity of the owner and knowing whose property is whose is entirely inessential to complying with the norm.

[15] Hohfeld 1916–17, 723 (footnotes omitted, italics original).

HMP also illustrates the 'loss of understanding' problem of Hohfeldian analysis set out in Chapter 2, 2.4. It purports to explain or analyse a norm of general applicability as a series of special individual jural relations. The thought here is that even if we could spell out exhaustively all the multital jural relations in question, we would have no understanding of the law of property. Whilst the application of any Hohfeldian jural relation to the facts of a case would generate the correct result, it would be a mystery as to why it did so. The generality of BPrN is in fact obscured. Furthermore, by displaying these right–duty relations as multital jural relations, that is, as a series of rights in personam, one would naturally get the wrong normative signal. The law would have to be conceived as being concerned to establish a new normative relation every time property changed hands, every time someone was born or died, every time an individual property lost its identity through specification, and so on. It would be like saying that the rule of addition altered its character on each occasion that a new sum was calculated, because the set of applications would have changed, thus so would its sense or identity as a norm.[16]

As far as I can tell, Hohfeld, in the first passage quoted above, is essentially trading upon our linguistic intuitions when it comes to describing property rights, especially in cases where they are violated. Of course it is perfectly good English usage to say that Y owes X a duty not to interfere with his, X's, property, and that when Y trespasses he breaches a duty he owes to X, and that in doing so he violates X's property rights. But usage here does not point in only one direction. Not only can one say that everyone has *a* duty not to interfere with property not their own, but one can say that everyone has *the* duty not to interfere with property not their own. The fact that both are perfectly sound ways of putting the point strongly suggests that there is nothing in the logic of duties to require us to think of duties as necessarily individuated by the identities of the individual duty-owers and right-bearers. In other words, persons are individuated by their particular personal identities, but there is nothing in the logic of norms which suggests that the duties they owe need be individuated likewise.

[16] Kramer1998, 9, fn 2 says that Hohfeld's analysis is fully *compatible* with speaking of a right in rem, 'a single entitlement with indefinitely numerous applications', but I do not see how this compatibility is consistent with Hohfeld's insistence that a right in rem is *really* only a battery of rights in personam. If these rights in personam can only be identified by virtue of a right in rem, then they are not the 'freestanding' rights in personam that it was Hohfeld's intention to establish.

This is clear in the case of rules; no one would say that X has a duty to comply with *his* rule not to interfere with the property of others, whilst Y has a duty to comply with *her* rule not to do so, and so on with Z, W, and everyone else. We would say that X has a duty not to violate *the* rule against interfering with the property of others. The question is whether the 'independence' feature that Hohfeld points out in this passage accurately reflects the facts about the norms that constitute property law, and it is suggested that they do not unless one is also committed to the programme of expressing all norms *only* in terms of rights and duties that obtain between individuals. I can see no reason whatsoever to endorse that commitment.

5.4 Some Different Hohfeldian Perspectives on HMP

5.4.1 BPrN and the De Re/De Dicto Distinction

Let me begin this part by saying that by criticizing HMP, I do not deny that we all know that individual people and individual items of property are involved when we do or do not commit a trespass or do or do not negligently damage another's goods.[17] Of course we know that. My critique arises because I attempt to take Hohfeld's ruminations about the relationality of property rights to property duties literally. If Hohfeld was correct to say that rights in rem were to be understood as a series of rights in personam, and that rights are normative, then his multital jural relations must be treated as genuinely normative, that is, they enter into the guidance of the behaviour of those subject to them, which is a requirement of GFPN. This immediately leads to the question whether the norm-observer, the duty-ower in this case, is expected to know, or indeed be capable of knowing, the actual norm in question. In the general case[18] of Hohfeldian multital in rem duties this is laughable. To know that there is an owner out there, and that

[17] I had a first crack at disarming some of the arguments in this section in Penner 2013. I think I do a better job here.

[18] I was quite rightly criticized by Dorfman 2012, 576–7, for suggesting, Penner 1997c, 27, that a right in rem changes its character to a right in personam in circumstances where the duty-ower knows of the identity of the right-holder and the duty in question. What I should have said was that even in such a case, this knowledge is simply irrelevant to the application of BPrN; it adds nothing to shape or alter the duty in question.

this thing before me is (probably) owned, is to know nothing of the particular norm Hohfeld insisted governed the normative relationship, in which, for Hohfeld, the identity of the relata are essential features. If all Hohfeld meant was that the identity of the relata can be filled in as necessary, then his relata are identified *by the rule* which distinguishes such individuals out of the class of those subject to the rule when an occasion comes for the application of the rule (typically when it is breached); it is therefore the rule that is doing all the normative work.

This last point can be illustrated by Glackin's invocation of the de re/de dicto distinction in this context. He says:[19]

Consider the phrase 'the tallest boy in the class'; this picks out one determinate individual. But in semantic contexts such as belief and desire ascription or 'modal' claims about possibility and necessity, termed 'referentially opaque', such a phrase may be ambiguous. In the sentence 'Mary wants to kiss the tallest boy in the class', the phrase may refer to that specific person, or it may function as a general description that any number of others might have fulfilled in other circumstances. Suppose that Mary believes Henry to be the tallest boy; the sentence does not specify whether she wishes to kiss Henry in particular or whichever boy happens to be tallest (perhaps she is mistaken, and Henry is in fact marginally shorter than Ben, who slouches). If it is Henry alone whom she desires, the sentence should be interpreted *de re*, or as pertaining to the 'thing' identified by the phrase; if instead she desires the tallest boy regardless of who he may be, the sentence should be read de dicto, or as pertaining to the 'words' of the phrase itself.

Something of this sort, I take it, is at the root of Penner's concern. If I am granted a license in personam to walk Blackacre by its owner, I must have the ability to identify him, and the phrase 'the owner of Blackacre' should consequently be read *de re*. But if I am not granted such a license, I have, like everybody else, a duty in rem toward 'the owner of Blackacre', *whoever that may be* (i.e., read *de dicto*)....

The question here, which Penner appears to beg, is why I must have personal knowledge of somebody's identity in order to hold a right of or bear a duty toward them in personam. We might suppose that I must have such knowledge if I am claiming a special or exceptional right; ... This in no way entails that the rights and duties we assume in default of being specifically exempted—such as the duty to avoid trespassing on the property of

[19] Glackin 2014, 12–14 (footnotes omitted, italics original, my bold).

others—are any less in personam than the exceptional ones we are granted specifically. When Penner 'presumes' that we must know which owners (*de re*) hold what property in order to understand our in personam duties, he is helping himself to just what is at issue: the claim that an undifferentiated duty in rem cannot be reduced to a multitude of individual in personam duties.

Suppose that Mary, some years later, is out walking in the countryside. She happens upon Blackacre and briefly considers taking a shortcut across it. 'I had better go the long way around', she tells herself eventually, 'since I have a duty to Blackacre's owner not to trespass on the land'. Suppose further that Mary believes her old schoolgirl crush Henry to be the owner; nothing about the legal nature of the duty hangs on whether or not her belief is correct. Whoever the owner is, Mary bears an (otherwise) identical duty to that person not to trespass. **The distinction between *de re* and *de dicto* meanings can be problematic, but only in contexts of 'referential opacity', when the intended reference of the sentence may fail. Since the law does not traffic in such statements, the ambiguity identified by Penner cannot be legally significant**.

I must admit that I find some of this a little hard to follow. Rather than disproving my point, these considerations seem to confirm it. Consider the sentence in bold. Two things can be said here. The first is that nothing I have claimed has anything to do with some 'ambiguity' I have purportedly identified. On the assumption that all legal norms of the kind we are considering, that is, right–duty jural relations, are right–duty relations between two individuals, some apply de re, for example contractual norms,[20] and some *de dicto*, for example the basic exclusionary norm of property in so far as it relates X, an owner of Blackacre, to Y, a non-owner of Blackacre. The person at the right end of that norm is identified, to use Glackin's phrasing, 'by the words' of the relevant phrase, that is, 'the owner of Blackacre', and not by pertaining to a specific person or 'thing' the phrase was intended uniquely to identify. When an identifying phrase is used de dicto, it is used as an identifying description. Descriptions are a kind of rule, in the sense that they apply to whatever or whoever satisfies them, whether generally, or in the case of 'the owner of Blackacre', uniquely.[21]

[20] See again Glackin (2014) fn 51

[21] The sense of 'unique' here is not meant to be a 'single individual'. The rule uniquely identifies co-owners as well.

Secondly, if 'referential opacity' typifies certain beliefs, then so it does certain norms in the relevant sense. To embroider upon Glackin's example, let us say Mary sets up a kissing booth for charity, and Fred buys a ticket telling her that he wants her to kiss the tallest boy in the room. In order to determine the contractual norm with which she must comply, Mary must determine whether Fred's identification takes a de re or de dicto reading. By the way, this is not legally fanciful: it is the very stuff of contractual construction in certain cases.[22]

The point here is not to get hung up on the terminology of 'in personam' and 'in rem'. We could, if we wanted, say that all rights vis-à-vis others howsoever mediated are rights in personam. But we would still, to make sense of the law, have to draw a distinction between those rights 'in personam' in which the identity of the right-bearers and duty-owers is essential, and those rights 'in personam' for which it is not[23] for the purposes of complying with any relevant legal norm. My argument is that BPrN shows that what relates the rights of owners and the duties of others not to trespass is indirect, mediated by a rule. Moreover, I think this rule *establishes* these rights and duties. BPrN is a rights-conferring and duty-imposing rule, instituted in the interests people have in exercising their agency over material resources. This gives these rights and duties a particular kind of relationality, which I shall discuss further in the next section. Another way of putting this point: Hohfeldian jural relations are not referentially ambiguous—they do not admit of a de dicto reading since they explicitly relate the individual right-holder to the individual duty-ower. The question with respect to them is whether they are normatively operative, and my claim is that they are not because, (1) empirically, given their content, they are, in the general case, impossible to comply with since, in the general case, we have no access to that content, and (2) normatively, they are inert, since we would have no need of that content even if we did have access to it.

5.4.2 The 'Public Duty' Argument

As I have just mentioned, we owe the duty not to trespass to every person whose interests are protected by the imposition of BPrN, that

[22] For example, determining whether a sale of goods is a sale by description as opposed to a sale of specific goods.

[23] As Glackin 2014, 14 fn 51, seems to recognize.

is, everyone who owns property.[24] Thus besides being a duty-imposing rule, BPrN is also, at the same time, a right-conferring rule. We respect people's property rights by observing BPrN. We respect their rights *indirectly* via complying with the rule, rather than directly, by trying to comply with a Hohfeldian jural relation.

In *The Idea of Property in Law* I expressed BPrN in a way in which I now acknowledge is apt to mislead, as follows:

> We are under one duty to the plurality of property holders however their property is distributed amongst themselves.[25]

Such passages give rise to the thought that BPrN is a duty of public law, owed to some public collectivity.

Both Dorfman[26] and Essert[27] have argued that owing a duty to 'others in general', to the 'plurality of property holders', reduces the title-holder of property to a mere 'patient' or beneficiary of BPrN. And if that is so, there is no basis, at least no obvious basis, for the title-holder's having any particular standing to bring a claim against a trespasser. The injury committed by a trespasser, on this account, is an injury to the practice as a whole, or a general reduction of the good provided by people observing such a general duty, not an injury to the title-holder herself. On this reading my conception of BPrN denies the bilateral normativity, or bilateral relationality, that exists between the trespasser and the title-holder. Not only does the absence of this bilaterality make it mysterious why the title-holder is entitled to bring the claim for trespass, this absence also seems to take property rights out of the realm of private law in which, founded as it is on a notion of corrective justice, the bilateral relationship of the claimant and the defendant is an essential feature. It is common ground that merely being the beneficiary of someone's observing their duty does not ipso facto entitle one to bring a claim when that duty is breached. Non-party beneficiaries of contracts who suffer as a result of a breach normally have no claim, nor do non-title-holders who suffer as a consequence of a trespass to land.

[24] This section draws in part on Penner 2013, 257–9.
[25] Penner 1997c, 27.
[26] Dorfman 2012, 569–74.
[27] Essert 2013, 423–6.

Nevertheless, I think the sort of argument Dorfman and Essert are advancing reflects a mistaken understanding of private law. To see why, we can begin with an analogy to games.

A game might have rules regarding fouls, upon the occurrence of which the fouled player, or his team, might acquire a 'remedy', in the sense of being given some advantage in the game as a consequence. In this sense we could also frame the results of these rules in terms of rights and duties. When a foul occurs, that amounts to a breach of a duty, and the fouled player or his team has a right to a remedy. We could also say that players have a right not to be fouled. But returning to the game as a regime of rules, the fact that the rules are primary, and the players have a general obligation to play by the rules, does not make their compliance a reflection of some duty 'to the game' or 'to the practice' of playing. All the rules are there to further their interest in realizing, for themselves, whatever fun or other value there is in playing the game. There is no 'public' interest here. It simply does not follow from the fact that the rules do not explicitly relate players to each other on a one-to-one bilateral basis that the rules do not serve their individual interests as players and may therefore generate for them remedial 'rights' when a foul occurs.

More generally, a right-bearer is the beneficiary of a duty which was imposed in his interest. It does not follow that the duty was imposed *only* in his interest. It is just to say that the duty (singular) was imposed in his interest, amongst others'. This is true generally, by the way, of human or natural rights, and the rules which establish them.[28] A 'human right' to life is embodied in rules such as the rule prohibiting murder, and this rule is created in the interests of human beings. But the interest is generic. Nothing special about *you* or your *particular* interests *in your life* are relevant to the establishment or the application of the rule. You don't acquire any special status vis-à-vis other people because you fall within the class of those to whom the rule applies. HMP strongly suggests otherwise, and it is to be faulted for doing so. The same lesson is, of course, true in the case of any title-holder. Nothing about her personally is relevant to the establishment or application of the rule; nevertheless it serves and protects her interests because it was established, and is applied, to protect the interests of her and people relevantly identical to her, that is, all title-holders.

[28] I shall discuss the way in which the right to make use of material resources is a human or natural right in Chapter 8.

Essert asserts a particular notion of bilateral relationality[29] drawing upon Darwall's idea of 'second-personal' authority.[30] Say X steps on Y's toe. According to Essert, in response Y can make two sorts of claim: (1) Y can point out 'the general benefits of toes' not being stepped on'[31], that is, to some general value the general observance of which is to Y's benefit; or (2) a second-personal claim in which Y, as the person whose toe is stepped upon, has special standing to object. It is the standing to object which specifically, bilaterally, relates X and Y. This leads Essert to conclude that in so far as property rights are rights that relate individuals under private law, we each bear bilateral relations to each other as depicted by HMP.

I don't think this argument works. In the first place, it is not true that, in general, only the victim of a wrong has special standing to object to the transgressor's wrongful act. Parents, for example, often say things like 'stop hitting your sister'. It is true that, in general, only the potential victim has standing to license the would-be transgressor to commit the act, thus rendering it non-wrongful; but that second-personal standing to license does not indicate any special standing to observe or object to a transgression. Indeed, the whole point of the law, when setting rules such as the rules against trespass to the person or to property, is for *the law*, a third party, to object to such infractions. Of course, infractions occur in all sorts of circumstances, and for pragmatic reasons it often makes most sense for the victim of an inadvertent transgression to bring it to the attention of the transgressor. But I simply do not accept that a third party has no standing to point out the transgression. What wrong would she do either to the transgressor or the victim in doing so? In the case of a serious wrong, a third party would be morally obliged, *ceteris paribus*, to intervene.

The thought underlying the 'only Y has the right to object' thesis seems to confuse objecting to a wrong with the right to claim a remedy for a wrong. Just as only Y, in general, can license X to step on his toe, in general Y is the only one with a right to seek a remedy against X for doing so. In the first case we have the exercise in personam of a power, in the second case the prosecution of an in personam right of action against X. X and Y are brought together 'in personam' in the first case by the grant of the power, and in personam in the second case

[29] Essert 2013, 424–6.

[30] Darwall 2006, cited by Essert 2013, 424.

[31] Essert 2013, 424.

by the particular wrong having occurred. Neither of these cases establish that outside of these particular interactions the relations between X and Y are governed by second-personal pairwise Hohfeldian multital norms. In the first case the possibility of the interpersonal interaction is determined by the impersonal rule of law that empowers people to grant licences, and in the second case by the impersonal rule of law that prohibits trespass, BPrN.

These points are easily obscured if we focus, as Hohfeld does, and perhaps some proponents of 'corrective justice' do, upon the adjudication of disputes and the provision of remedies for wrongs. Private law in the first instance concerns the rights, duties, powers, and liabilities we have in respect of other persons and they have in respect of us just in so far as we are persons. Corrective justice, on the other hand, is that part of private law which concerns cases where things have gone wrong, where those rights have been violated, where those powers are purportedly validly exercised but in fact were not, and so on, where the appropriate legal response is the granting of claims to individuals, for example to compensation for loss, rather than to the community at large or to the state. The ideal world would be one in which there was no corrective justice, because nothing had gone wrong; such a world would still contain private law, that is all the norms whose observance, in the case of rights and duties, and whose rightful exercise, in the case of powers, would protect and facilitate the interests of people acting as purposeful agents. It should be perfectly obvious that corrective justice, however we understand it, is parasitic upon the primary structure of rights, duties, powers, and so on which exist prior to any violations or invalid purported exercises of powers. As Ernest Weinrib says,[32] '[Corrective justice] conceptualizes the parties as the active and passive poles of the same injustice (as the doer and sufferer of injury in Aristotle's account)'. This presupposes a rightful relation between persons prior to the particular wrong taking place; otherwise the act would not be an injustice. The rightful relation as regards title to property turns on rights in rem, rather than on Hohfeldian multital jural relations; that just is the structure of private law in so far as it deals with our rightful relations as agents with respect to the use of material resources. Rules such as BPrN show how we stand in a relation of *right* to each other; they determine our rights one to another, but such rules

[32] Weinrib 2012, 2. See also Ripstein 2016, 6–9.

are not *composed of* or *constituted by* those rights even though these rules reflect and are instituted to serve our interests. Nothing in the theory of adjudication or corrective justice has any power to upset that reality. Indeed, it underscores it, by addressing cases when a rule such as BPrN is transgressed.

One of the ways we can assuage Dorfman's and Essert's worry about forming a 'connection' between the breach of BPrN and the remedial rights of the particular owner who is wronged by the breach is by invoking what has come to be called the 'continuity thesis'. The 'continuity thesis' was first elaborated by Gardner in 2011.[33] This is the thesis that remedial rights reflect the same reasons which give rise to the primary duty that was breached. In tort law, my reason not to negligently injure you (which I shall discuss in the next section) does not cease to exist if I do in fact negligently injure you. If one of the reasons underlying the primary duty is that injuries can be painful, and that pain is bad, then that same reason is a reason to do what I can to assuage your pain afterwards. More generally, my reasons for not injuring you in the first place also give me reasons to ensure that, going forward, the new world is the world least incompatible with the world that would have existed (or continued to exist) had I not injured you at all. As to BPrN, if by trespassing against your property or acting negligently I cause damage to your property, by virtue of the continuity thesis I have a peremptory reason, a duty, to remedy the damage. Because such a duty, like the duty of BPrN, is recognized as being grounded in your interests (but not only your interests) as a property owner, you have a correlative right to that secondary duty being discharged.

None of the foregoing goes to deny that private law gives Y rights against X. It only denies that these rights all have the same relationality. The relationality of the duty not to trespass is mediated by a rule which generates rights and duties in rem. The relationality of Y's right to a remedy against X is mediated by the secondary rules which deal with infractions of the primary rule, which generates rights in personam when an infraction occurs. Both types of rule are in place to serve Y's interests but not, of course, only Y's interests. And none of this transposes Y's rights into the realm of public law.

[33] Gardner 2011, 28–50. Ripstein 2016, 234, provides a 'rights' version of the thesis, under which the right to a remedy is the same right as that which was violated. For discussion of my own views on the differences between their views and those of Rob Stevens, see Penner 2020, 261-2, fn.19.

5.4.3 The 'Duty of Care in Negligence' Argument

Dorfman draws sustenance for HMP from the structure of the duty of care in negligence. He says:[34]

> [T]hat norms can be impersonal and, at the same time, relational is an idea that figures prominently in the law of negligence, for example. The 'duty of due care' specifies a demand to exercise a reasonable amount of care. To this extent, it is highly impersonal, guiding the conduct of risk creators without relying on their prior acquaintance with potential victims. At the same time, the duty, at least since Cardozo's landmark decision in Palsgraf v Long Island R Co, takes a relational form. Rather than being owed generally to the world at large, it runs directly from each and every duty holder to each and every right holder with respect to each and every protected interest in the person or property of the right holder.

Fortunately, the duty of care in negligence cannot have the structure Dorfman claims that it does. This has been shown by Ronen Perry.

For the Hohfeldian right-duty correlativity to work, it must be reflected in every successful negligence action. A successful negligence claim must reflect the fact that at the time of breach the relevant duty, in Dorfman's terms, 'runs directly from' the tortfeasor to 'each and every right holder with respect to each and every protected interest in the person or property of the right holder'. But it needn't. For a claimant can establish tort liability against a negligent defendant even if

[34] Dorfman 2012, 571–572 (footnotes omitted), citing Palsgraf v Long Island Railroad Co 162 NE 99 (NY 1928) and stating, 'In this landmark decision, Cardozo CJ announced that the duty of care takes a relational form'. He does not provide a page reference. Addressing this passage, Essert 2013, 427, (footnotes omitted) helpfully points out a difference between the duty of care in negligence and the duty not to trespass against the property of others:

> 'Thus, the transferability [of property rights] that Penner points to seems crucial; the problem is not just that the bilateral normative position occupied by an owner is 'impersonal,' as Avihay Dorfman argues; it is that that normative position held by A today could just as well be held by B tomorrow. As Dorfman points out, there are many duties that we owe to others that are normally best conceived in impersonal terms, such as the duty of care owed in negligence to those within the ambit of the risk of one's conduct. But if we press on this, the two cases start to come apart. The difference between the negligence case and the property case is this: the duty in negligence is owed to an individual under a description which is impersonal ('person within the ambit of the risk of defendant's conduct at such-and-such time and place'), but the applicability of that description is invariant. Mrs Palsgraf is always going to be the person who was (or, in fact, was not) within the ambit of the risk of the conductor's careless conduct. But the description of the individual to whom the duty not to trespass on Blackacre is owed (i.e. 'owner of Blackacre') does not always necessarily describe the same person. As the discussion above shows, it can describe A today and B tomorrow. Property law thus seems distinctive in allowing the bilateral position held by the owner to be transferred to another.'

the claimant did not exist when the tort was committed, that is, when the standard of care was breached. Perry focuses much of his attention on cases of injury to infants where the tort occurred whilst they were in utero (and therefore having no legal personality) or prior to their conception, but his clearest example (to my mind) is found in the following passage:[35]

> [T]he Missouri Supreme Court criticized the distinction between substandard conduct committed after birth and before conception using the following hypothetical: D negligently constructs a balcony. Two years later, P1 and her one-year-old child P2 step onto the balcony, and it collapses injuring both P1 and P2. The court explained that it would be ludicrous to suggest that P1 had a cause of action against D, whereas no duty of care existed toward P2 because she was not conceived at the time of the negligent conduct.

Such examples can be multiplied. Consider the simple case of a negligently constructed wall built by P in 2013 adjacent to a public highway.[36] Anyone passing along that highway would be within the ambit of the builder's duty of care to ensure that the wall does not crash onto that public highway. Owing to its negligent construction, it crashes in 2018. Let us assume that the tumbling wall does the following: it seriously injures Q, a child born in 2016; it destroys the property of R, a company incorporated in 2016; and it destroys the property, a car manufactured in 2016, of S, a twenty year old. The fact that Q and R did not exist at the time of the breach is no bar to their successful action in tort against P, even though at the time of the breach P could have owed them no duty of care under the Hohfeldian analysis, for Hohfeldian jural relations only obtain between existing, specified individuals. Something that does not exist cannot be in relation to anything. So Q and R's successful claims breach the requirements of Hohfeld's correlativity thesis.

The property case is a little trickier, depending upon how one understands the Hohfeldian jural relation that expresses the duty of

[35] Perry 2009, 567 (footnotes omitted).

[36] The tort occurs at the time that the relevant duty of care is breached, though the damages may occur later, perhaps a lot later. The standard of care that applies is the standard relevant to the time of breach. For example, a failure to meet a standard of medical care is judged by the prevailing standards at the time of the purported breach.

care. A way of avoiding the conclusion that there is no duty owed to S at the time of breach is to say that P is in a jural relation not to trespass upon or negligently damage S's property, whatever his property happens to be. But this is not the way Hohfeld himself saw it. As the quotations from Hohfeld in the previous sections clearly show, the multital right X holds against B that B not trespass against Blackacre is framed in terms of trespassing, specifically, against Blackacre. That is why 'intrinsically considered' B's contractual duty to A not to trespass upon Blackacre is a companion right. So the right–duty jural relation between P and S that P not damage or destroy S's car did not exist at the time of P's breach of the standard of care. So this case is, taking Hohfeld at his word, on all fours with that of Q and R. These cases show that the law does not reflect Hohfeld's concept of right–duty correlativity.

Perry sums up the non-Hohfeldian characterization of the duty of care as follows:[37]

> First, a duty of care does not depend on the defendant's ability to identify the person ultimately injured; it is sufficient that the defendant can foresee harm to a member of a *generally defined class*. In other words, *foreseeability does not refer to a particular individual but to a certain type of persons*. Second, the existence of a time gap between the act and the injury does not preclude foreseeability. As put by the court in *Renslow*: 'a duty may exist to one foreseeably harmed though *he be unknown* and remote in time and place.' Justice Dooley, in a concurring opinion, emphasized that '[c]onduct which puts harmful consequences in motion and *injury to a foreseeable class* of persons as a direct result may be negligence for which responsibility may attach. That there may be a time gap between the wrongful act and the suffering is immaterial.'[38]

By the way, whatever the law's point of view happened to be on this, surely this is the right result morally speaking. It cannot morally be right that the perfectly foreseeable victims of my breach of duty, though not yet born or whose rights are not yet in existence, or people who will own property not yet in existence, are outwith my relevant moral concern when I choose to act in a way that will or might have

[37] Perry 2009, 568–9 (footnotes omitted, italics mine). The reference to *Renslow* is to *Renslow v Mennonite Hosp.*, 367 N.E.2d 1250, 1252, 1254–5 (Ill. 1977).

[38] *Renslow v Mennonite Hosp.*, 367 N.E.2d 1250, 1252, 1259 (Ill. 1977).

future consequences. If this were so an infant formula manufacturer could insulate himself morally from the harms he might even *know* will be caused to infants by embargoing the sale of the harmful formula for nine months (or ten months to be on the safe side). That cannot be right.

As far as I can tell, Perry concludes[39] that rights and duties do not necessarily correlate, and this presents a major challenge to the Hohfeldian correlativity thesis. I agree it does the latter, but I disagree that it does the former. All we need is a richer notion of correlativity, under which the correlation of the rights and duties of individuals are framed through general rules, and whose one-to-one correlation arises when those rules have been breached, as I argued in the last section. Because the rules for liability for tortious injury are rules, their application is not temporally bounded by the way Hohfeldian jural relations are; thus they can frame the correlativity of rights and duties in the cases Perry discusses with no problem.

One final point. As any reader of Hohfeld will know, he often refers to 'actual and potential' jural relations (Chapter 1, 1.3). Arguably, Hohfeldians might be able to save his correlativity thesis by wheeling in some machinery involving 'potentiality' to cover this sort of case. But as I stressed in Chapter 1, 1.3, one cannot just wave one's hands in this direction. If 'potential Hohfeldian jural relations' as a concept makes sense, it is for Hohfeldians to make that out. In the meantime the rest of us should just recline in the comforting knowledge that rules, as a matter of their nature, apply to future, that is, 'potential' cases, and that that is all we need to sort out a world in which the future consequences of our present actions have normative significance.

5.4.4 *Hurd and Moore on the Counting of Rights Violations*

Heidi Hurd and Michael Moore defend a version of HMP under the rubric of '*The Two Person Requirement of the Hohfeldian Analysis of Rights*'.[40] That requirement is that an individual does not have just one right to bodily integrity, but that 'there are as many rights as there are individual people holding them multiplied by the number of individual people against who they are held. That is a lot of rights.'[41] They suspect

39 Perry 2009, 580.
40 Hurd and Moore 2018, 315.
41 ibid., 315.

that for many, this fine grained individuation of rights is 'too fussy to be taken seriously'[42] but, as I hope the previous discussion has shown, that is not my objection. To repeat, my objection is that expressing our moral and legal relations one to each other as Hohfeldian multital jural relations in the case of something like our in rem right to bodily security is normatively otiose, and misleads our understanding. In any case Hurd and Moore contend that certain doctrines of the criminal law, which are also replicated in our moral understanding, show that the HMP correctly frames our rights against each other. It is my misfortune to disagree with Hurd and Moore about this.

They ask us to consider this case: 'One defendant with one shell of a powerful gun kills three victims.'[43] They then ask, 'how many times were how many moral wrongs done (equivalently, how many times were how many moral rights violated) in the [imagined scenario]?'[44]

Hurd and Moore answer this question in this way:[45]

> [I]t is not open to argue that more than one act-token was done (the unit of offense question), despite there being three distinct consequences of that act (viz, the three deaths). According to the overwhelmingly most plausible theory of act-token individuation, there was but one act here. Nonetheless, our law punishes that one act as having done three wrongs.

Since we are dealing with private law, I think I can transpose this case to a similar case of negligence, without undermining the force of Hurd and Moore's point. We could take the negligently constructed 'crashing wall' case from the last section as a parallel example: there is one wrongful act by P, that is, one breach of duty, but three distinct wrongs with three distinct victims, Q, R, and S, each of whom will have their own separate cause of action against P.[46] In the same way that one might say that the shooter in their example committed one criminal act that had three victims, like someone who explodes a bomb in a

[42] ibid., 316.

[43] ibid., 2018, 316. They consider a second case as well, also at 316: 'Three defendants with one shot apiece jointly cause the death of one victim.' Since I think the lesson they draw from this case is parallel with the one they draw from the first, I shall deal only with it.

[44] ibid., 316.

[45] ibid., 317.

[46] Hurd and Moore's claim may even be strengthened in the case of negligence law, because someone can be guilty for a negligent omission. It is hard to see how an omission could be more than one 'act', for it is not an act at all. Moreover, the same tortious act can violate two or more of the same individual's rights. See Stevens 2007, 199.

crowd killing three, one could say that P committed one tort, negligently constructing the wall, that injured three victims (one in their person, two in their property).

The lesson Hurd and Moore draw in support of HMP is set out in this passage:[47]

> If like us you think [the law, morally speaking, gets the right result in this case], then it must be that you think that moral wrongs are individuated by who suffers them and who does them; that the moral duties breach of which constitutes such wrongs are also so individuated; and that the moral rights correlative to such duties are individuated by who holds them and by against whom they are held. And this, of course, is Hohfeld's analysis too, now extended to morality as well as law.
>
> Explaining why it is that we should have these common moral intuitions is a tricky business. Surely most of the answer lies in the deontological nature of the most stringently obligating norms of deontic morality. A deontological view of ethics is person-specific in the senses that: (1) norms of obligation are directed to each of us individually, saying not, 'minimize duty-violations by yourself or others in your actions,' but rather, 'don't you here and now violate this categorical norm of morality;' and (2) rights are held individually, in the sense that each individual's right is separate from every other individual's right of similar content so that each right is to be respected, not traded off against other person's rights. This view of morality – often called an 'agent-relative' view but which could equally be called a 'victim-relative' view – seems to us to be the kind of morality definitive of the most stringent duties we owe one another. If this is right, our Hohfeldian intuitions about how to count rights and duties are on a solid moral as well as legal footing.

With respect, I do not see how this gives HMP any support at all. When Hurd and Moore say that a deontological view of ethics says to each of us, in (1), 'don't you here and now violate this categorical norm of morality', that is just what I have been saying: this norm makes no reference to any particular moral relationship one might have with one's victims, as HMP suggests. And (2), that 'rights are held individually', is, as I showed in 5.4.3, neutral as between HMP and the explanation of rights have presented here.

[47] Hurd and Moore 2018, 317–18 (footnotes omitted).

Indeed, I would suggest the very considerations Hurd and Moore concern themselves with raise a point against HMP. Returning to our distinction between results and consequences,[48] we understand the breach of a rule can have various consequences. The result of breaching a rule is that the rule is breached—P committed a breach of duty by failing to build the wall with due care—but it is the world that determines what the consequences of that breach will be. The norm applies, in co-operation with what happens in the world, to determine P's liability for a breach of it, whatever our ability to foresee its consequences. So a rule-centred conception of the breach of a moral norm, such as the one that I have been advocating, clearly handles the counting issue—how many rights were violated by someone's performing one act, committing one breach of duty. In the cases under discussion, three, because the breach causally led to the three rights violations.

It seems to me that the difference between Hurd and Moore and myself turns on an ambiguity in the word 'wrong'. On one reading, Hurd and Moore's, wrong equals the violation of a right. Because the shooter's one act violates the rights of each of his three victims, the shooter commits three wrongs by his one act. Under the influence of HMP's 'bilateral' or 'two person' thesis of jural relations, Moore and Hurd (revisiting part of the second quotation above, my italics) contend:

> ... moral wrongs are individuated by who suffers them and who does them; *that the moral duties breach of which constitutes such wrongs are also so individuated*; and that the moral rights correlative to such duties are individuated by who holds them and by against whom they are held.

My difference with Hurd and Moore lies in the italicized passage, which seems to me to be clearly false, not in all cases, but in the cases under consideration, that of the shooter and P. It is clearly false because of the way we, as a matter of moral intuition and common sense, individuate duties. Duties are individuated according to the act or omission they require, not by whatever consequences do or do not happen to flow from their breach, especially when the consequences are several, and are severally individuated as distinct harms,

[48] 5.1.

wrongs, or violations of rights. When the shooter, with intent to kill, fires his gun at his intended three victims, he breaches *the* duty not to commit such an act. Whether he succeeds, whether he misses or kills one, two, or three, will determine his criminal law liability, that is, for one or several counts of attempt, or one or two or three counts of murder, or some combination thereof. When P negligently constructs the wall, he has breached a duty of civil law in failing to take sufficient care in constructing the wall, however the consequences play out in the future as regards those who are injured by his negligence. In other words when we assess the *consequences* of the shooter's or P's breach, we will reveal how many rights were violated and in what way. In the scenarios under discussion, HMP insists that the shooter and P breached not one duty each, but three duties each, given that on HMP three separate right–duty jural relations were breached. If what I have said about the individuation of duties is right, this is plainly wrong. Moreover, if what I have said about the individuation of duties is correct, if each 'wrong' is taken to be a distinct *act (or omission)*, that is, a distinct failure, either by act or omission, to comply with one's duties, then HMP would seem to be contrary to the intuitions about the individuation of acts that Hurd and Moore seek to defend. In short, HMP can be shown to count rights correctly, but in these cases it counts duties wrong. I think I have said this before.

None of this seeks to show nor does show that a single act cannot breach multiple duties, even multiple duties owed to the same person, as our example of X, the owner of Blackacre, and B, the constant trespasser in 5.3 shows. Two of those duties were in personam (the contractual duty and the court-ordered duty) and the other was in rem, mediated by BPrN. My claim has been that analysing a breach of the duty of care in negligence or BPrN as ipso facto a breach of several duties just because it has as its consequence more than one wrong is incorrect.

5.5 Conclusion

There is not really much to say here by way of conclusion. I have considered a number of issues in and around HMP and the various technicalities of Hohfeld's characterization of a multital right. My aim was to dislodge the Hohfeldian Multital Picture of Jural Relations.[49] I hope to have shown that it is very much capable of leading us astray in our thinking about rights in rem, more specifically property rights in tangible things.

[49] In Penner 2013, 259–60, I presented a 'normative burden' argument which also sought to dislodge HMP. The basic idea was that there was a distinction between rights in rem and rights in personam that HMP obscured. Coming under a new multital right–duty relation as when, say, another individual is born, such that I now have one more duty not to interfere with a person's body, seemed not to impose the same sort of burden as when I acquire a new right in personam. For example, a genuinely new contractual obligation really does feel like a burden. But I now realize that whilst the intuition underlying the argument is suggestive, feeling burdened is obviously an empirical matter, and it doesn't work to illuminate the in rem/in personam distinction at the edges. If the population were small, the multital duties owing to one new person could feel burdensome, etc.

6

The Transmissibility of Rights and the Power to Transfer Title

6.1 The Alienability of Rights

It is generally understood that property rights are 'alienable', which is to say, transferable.[1] The most capacious term for the phenomenon by which A's right comes to be B's right is 'transmissibility'. The latter term best describes the phenomenon in question because property rights are not just transferable by the act of an owner, exercising his right to transfer title to his property to another, but also move from A to B by operation of law. For example, certain titles of A will pass by operation of law to his personal representative on death. In systems where a rule of inheritance obtains,[2] title passes by operation of law from the deceased to her heir on the former's death. Property of a company that is not distributed prior to the company's winding up will pass to the Crown as *bona vacantia*, that is, goods without an owner. Whether title to property moves because the owner exercised a power to transfer it to another, or whether title moves by operation of law, the idea underlying the transmissibility of a right is that B acquires the very same right that A had. The purpose of this chapter is to defend the sense of that idea against what, at first glance, looks like a weighty objection by Hohfeld.

[1] I explore the basis for this in Penner 1997c, ch. 5, 'The Objects of Property: the Separability Thesis'. This section of the book in part reprises, and in part develops, the views I expressed in Penner 2013.

[2] As used to be the case with land in England, and remains the case generally with property transmission on death in civilian jurisdictions.

Property Rights. J. E. Penner, Oxford University Press (2020) © J. E. Penner.
DOI: 10.1093/oso/9780198830122.001.0001

It is clear that Hohfeld did not accept the conceptual possibility of the transfer of rights, such that B gets the right that A had, as I previously noted in Chapter 1, 1.3. To remind ourselves: he places scare quotes around the word 'transfer' whenever he employs the term, and in the two passages in which Hohfeld considers the alienation of rights in rem he explains alienation as the extinction of the alienor's rights and the creation of a new and similar set of rights in the alienee. Thus, for Hohfeld, a 'transfer' of a right is not really a transfer at all, and so the lawyer's expression that title to Blackacre *passes* from A to B is, for Hohfeld, strictly speaking a solecism.

It is fairly clear why Hohfeld must adopt the extinction–creation model of transmissibility. It follows from HMP, his multitality picture of jural relations, discussed in the last chapter. What B acquires is not the identical set of multital jural relations that A had. For instance, one multital jural relation that B has is *A*'s duty to B not to trespass on Blackacre, and that is clearly a multital jural relation which A did not have when she was the owner. But the matter is much broader than this. Because jural relations have their relata—the people at either end of the jural relation—essentially, none of B's multital jural relations against C, D, E and so on have the same content as the ones A had. Prior to the transfer, these multital jural relations had A at the right pole, whereas now B is in that position. So it seems simply to follow from HMP that B can only have a right whose aggregate of rights is *similar*[3] to the one A held. Therefore, to the extent that HMP has substantial intuitive force, the extinction–creation model of transmissibility seems to follow from it, and this presents a serious objection to the idea of transfer, that B acquires the very right that A had, an idea that seems common to most people's, and to lawyers', understanding of property rights.

The strategy in this chapter will be similar to the one in the last. I shall have a look at different ways of understanding the transmissibility of a right, to poke holes in the Hohfeldian objection. The main definitional move I shall make is the following: as I explained in the last chapter, I agree that rights correlate with duties, but not on the one-to-one jural relation basis of HMP; so where B's right correlates with the *same* duty or duties that A's right has, B has an identical right

[3] As we saw in Chapter 5, 5.3, Hohfeld's notion of 'similarity' is, to say the least, underdescribed. I shall not pursue what criteria of similarity Hohfeld intends to be employed in this context.

to A's right. Once we have established the possibility that A's right and B's right have the same content, we can go on to ask whether B's right came to be his by a transmission from A, either by the exercise by A of a power to transfer, or by operation of law.

6.2 Can a Right Held by A be Identical to a Right Held by B?

As we have just seen, on HMP the answer to this question must be no, since jural relations have their relata essentially and B is not identical to A; they are two distinct individuals. Let us work first within the framework of HMP, and in so doing explore different ways to think about the challenge to the concept of transfer it poses.

What animates the idea that a right can be transferred is the idea that the transferee can stand in exactly the same normative position as the transferor did. So, with regards to transferable Hohfeldian claim-rights, the transferee is to be seen as being owed exactly the same duty or duties as the transferor. Can we identify such cases for the Hohfeldian, such that he is willing to allow an exception to the idea that jural relations have the identity of their relata essentially? I think we can. Let me start with a somewhat gruesome example.

Assume one of the incidents of title to Blackacre is that it passes by way of inheritance. Now consider the case where A dies giving birth to her first (and, obviously, only) child, B. At the moment A dies, B is born and inherits A's fee simple in Blackacre. Assume also that no one else is born or dies at the same moment. If we can individuate rights according to the identity of the performances or forbearances correlatively owed by the duty-ower(s), then in this case B succeeds to exactly the same aggregate of rights that A had, for B's rights correlate exactly to all the same duties that A's rights did, *for all the duty bearers are third parties*. That is, in this case, unlike the case in which A transfers title to Blackacre *inter vivos* to B, A *does not* come under a duty to B not to trespass on Blackacre upon B's acquisition of the right—A *dies* at the very moment the right becomes B's. And B is not released from any duty not to trespass on Blackacre when he acquires the right, for his right comes into existence simultaneously with his birth, so there was never a duty he owed to A not to trespass on Blackacre prior to his acquisition of the right. So the exact same constellation of duty bearers correlates with both A's and B's right, and thus this is a case of the transmission of the same right in rem from A to B. The question now is, can this sort of example be generalized? I think it can, but it is easiest to begin with an alienable right in personam, like the right to be paid a debt, and then consider rights in rem to tangible property like land and chattels.

There is a perfectly clear sense in which A's right to be paid £10 by C can be transferred or assigned to B, or is transmitted to B by inheritance, and so on, such that B acquires the very same right that A had. All we need show is that A, B, and any further successors, can benefit in the very same way when C discharges his duty. It is right to acknowledge the implications of this formulation 'benefit in the very same way' from the outset. Where a debt is assignable, the act C must undertake to discharge the duty will be different when the debt is assigned from A to B; in the first case, C must pay A, in the second, C must pay B. In view of this, if a right correlates with or is dependent for its sense upon the act necessary to discharge the correlative duty, then the right to be paid £10 by C does not endure through the assignment. Two things must be said about this. The first is that, as we have seen when discussing multital duties,[4] in so far as 'fundamentally similar' can be applied to different aspects of a jural relation in different circumstances, it does not lie in the mouth of the Hohfeldian to criticize one who focuses on certain but not all aspects of a jural relation to identify similarity or sameness. The second, much more vital, point, which we shall consider shortly, is that the relevant concept of similarity or sameness or identity when one is concerned with norms is a normative concept, not an empirical or physical one.

Carrying on with the example, then, C's payment of £10, this performance, is one that is capable of being performed, in principle, to the advantage of anyone, or at least to anyone who is entitled to receive payments. To show how this overcomes the 'C's paying A is not the same act as C's paying B' objection just canvassed, consider the case in which C is entitled to make payment by placing a £10 note at the base of Nelson's column in Trafalgar Square. Prior to A's assignment to B, A had the right to pick up the note, and afterwards B has. How is B's right any different from A's right, conceived of as

[4] Chapter 5, 5.3.

the right to pick up the note? Or take a case where C's duty is to do something that doesn't involve another person at all. Let us assume C has a contractual duty to walk from Kuala Lumpur to Penang, and that the corresponding contractual right is assignable. The duty, let us say, arose under a contract with A, who assigns this contract to B. B now has the legal right to C's performance, but the act that C must perform is the same, indeed identical, whoever has the correlative right.[5] These examples are not intended to restrict our sense of the identity of A's and B's rights to physical transactions, but only to make vivid the point that C's duty to deposit the note or walk to Penang can only be distinguished as different duties on the basis that any duty must be individuated (in part) by the identity of the correlative right-holder. Yet what we are trying to make sense of at this point is how a conception of a duty and its performance may not turn on the identity of the correlative right-holder, and these examples make it clear that we can do so. Moreover, these cases also provide the sense in which it is inherent to C's duty, in so far as it is a transmissible personal right—nothing I have said here would imply that any or all personal rights are in fact transmissible—that it is transmissible. The content of C's duty to pay £10, being something C can do to the advantage of anyone, is just what is involved in conceiving of a right *as* transmissible.[6] To say that C owes a duty to pay a debt which is assignable is just to conceive of the debt as being payable not only to the present creditor but, in principle, to anyone.

As regards rights in rem or multital rights in general, one can immediately notice that the preceding analysis applies just as well to any *individual* multital right. If A transfers Blackacre to B, then in respect to say, D, one of the multitude who owes A a duty not to trespass against Blackacre, as transferee B is the beneficiary of exactly the same duty that D owed to A, namely not to trespass on Blackacre. So whilst the preceding analysis would admit the transmissibility of multital rights in general, there remains the sticky problem of A and B themselves. Prior to the transfer, A was in a right–duty jural relation with B such that B had a duty not to trespass on Blackacre. That is gone after the transfer, to be replaced by a right–duty jural relation under which A owes B a

[5] I acknowledge that the contract here is one of personal service, a contract which is typically not regarded as assignable under the law. But the policy against assignments of such contracts does not undermine the point of the example.

[6] Penner 1997c, ch. 6.

duty not to trespass upon Blackacre. So the aggregate of jural relations B acquires has one jural relation that A didn't have—A's duty to B not to trespass upon Blackacre—and A had one jural relation B doesn't acquire—B's duty to A not to trespass upon Blackacre. Let's call this the switched places problem, or SPP. We shall come back to it in due course.

6.3 The Identity or Sameness Relation between A and B in the Case of Norms is a Normative Relation, not a Physical or Empirical one

We can now turn to the notion of identity or sameness as it applies to norms. But let's start with the quotidian concept of a dog to get an idea of what we're up to.

The word 'dog' refers to those creatures having the property of doghood. But no two dogs are the same in terms of all of their properties. Indeed no one dog is the 'same' dog in this sense at time t2 as he was at time t1. It is well beyond the scope of this chapter to identify how the property of doghood perdures in Rover despite various changes in him, for example, physical changes, but for the purpose of applying the word 'dog' to Rover (i.e. expressing that the concept of doghood applies to Rover) it is clear that some changes are irrelevant. They do not count to make the concept of doghood inapplicable.

So too, it is submitted, with rights. A right may persist, that is, its identity may remain unchanged, though the various normative incidents which go with having that right do not remain constant.[7] With regard to HMP, we can now raise the 'Fluctuation Problem' or FP. As regards title to Blackacre, the actual aggregate of multital jural relations is in constant flux as people are born or die. (The recognition of FP was implicit in the gruesome inheritance example set out above.) So A herself never has the same title to Blackacre from time to time if titles to Blackacre are individuated by the actual aggregate of jural

[7] I said something similar in an earlier paper about the way that certain legal interests remain the same despite their incidents changing; see Penner 2010a, 257–66. I should have cited Honoré 1959–60 there for providing a starting point for this argument, but to my regret failed to do so; I did acknowledge Honoré in Penner, 2013, 251.

relations in which A figures. Surely, however, this is a consequence any theory of the individuation of rights should want to avoid. No one wants to have a concept of 'title to Blackacre' that is constantly in flux in this way, such that A is constantly in the process of losing one title to Blackacre and gaining an entirely new one. At the very least one should say that the Hohfeldian characterization of titles to tangible property as an ever-changing set of jural relations between the owner and others is unmotivated. At the most, it shows that something must be wrong with a theory that forces such a conclusion.

But, happily, we are not forced to such a conclusion. Whatever one makes of the distinction between the essential and the accidental as regards the properties or features that make a thing what it is, clearly we rely upon some such distinction all the time when we make use of the concepts that we have. This is why we can step into the same river twice, why you are the same person you were yesterday despite the fact that many of the molecules of your body are different and that you are in a bad mood today but were in a good mood yesterday, why the steak that I cooked and ate was the same steak I bought raw at the butcher's. There is no sort of a priori reason, or at least none provided by Hohfeld or his supporters, that things are different in the realm of legal concepts. So there is nothing in principle obviously wrong in saying that a legal concept, a *technical* legal concept like the fee simple estate in Blackacre, has the content it has even though that concept continues to apply through time despite the fact that the configuration of Hohfeldian jural relations between the owner and everyone else constantly changes. Consider: if legislation were passed tomorrow which changed the limitation period for bringing actions for breach of contract, a Hohfeldian would have to say that by operation of law all the extant legally valid contracts had been abolished by legislation and replaced with other, similar though not identical, contracts. This is, quite clearly, just a conceptual fiat, and there is no reason to accede to it. This is not to say that legislation cannot produce a change of this kind. If, for example, legislation retrospectively made certain contracts illegal or unenforceable, or abolished the right to transfer a fee simple to anyone other than the Crown, then we might well *judge* that the contracts and fees simple in question were now, whatever we called them, different creatures. But it would be a matter of *judgment* which would not be foreclosed by the Hohfeldian's claim that there is no matter to be judged here since all of our rights are subject to this sort of fluctuation all the time.[8] So FP is disarmed.

These considerations also disarm SPP, for SPP is just a special case of FP.

SPP is only problematic if the following thought, which I am placing in the mouth of the Hohfeldian, is correct:

> Whilst, admittedly, for the reasons canvassed above, a right may persist through the change of some of its incidents, and this may be so even as regards the identity of its duty-owers (so the fact that some are born and some die does not mean that the owner of a fee-simple has 'a' right which continually changes its identity), there is something special about the fact that, upon 'transfer', the former right-holder is now one of the duty-owers, and one of the former duty-owers is now the right-holder.

The mistake here is to conceive of the power to transfer not as something positive that the law facilitates, but rather as a way of imposing a duty upon oneself and, correspondingly, to treat the right to receive by way of transfer (or by inheritance etc.) as a way of escaping one. But the right to property is not simply the absence of a duty not to engage with some particular tangible thing, for that would make me, you, and everyone else an owner of any unowned chattel or piece of land or any public land, like a public highway, which is nonsense. To have a right to tangible property is not merely to be free from a duty not to trespass, but to have the powers that go with that title, and to be subject to the incidents (the liability that it will pass to one's trustee in bankruptcy, and so on) that go with title. It is, of course, true that those who are involved in the actual transaction whereby their property passes to another have an historical connection to the property that was once theirs that any old third party does not. And people may feel keenly the loss of their property, not only, for example, on insolvency,

[8] The normativity of the sameness relation also illuminates the example of an assignable debt. It is a mistake to conceive of a duty as relating one-to-one with a particular physical act. Any act which discharges a duty counts. The relation of a duty with the act that discharges it is normative, not empirical or physical. If X owes Y £50, paying Y one £50 note discharges the duty just as paying Y five £10 notes does, as does X's ordering his bank to make an electronic transfer of £50 into Y's bank account. In the assignment case, C can discharge his debt by paying A, prior to the assignment, and paying B, following the assignment. Thus it is a genuinely realistic expression of C's duty, to which the correlative right is thereby entailed, to say that he has a duty to pay £50 to his creditor or any assignee of his creditor (or any subsequent assignee).

but when they transfer it themselves by contract or as a gift depending upon the circumstances, but the juridicial significance of this is, as far as the norms of property law go, nil. As far as those norms go A, someone who has transferred Blackacre to B, has exactly the same status of 'non-owner' as P, Q, and R, who have never had anything to do with Blackacre. Former owners have no special status as duty-owers once their property is no longer theirs. Their addition to the body of duty-owers is no more significant to the right than is the birth of a new person (or the coming of age of such a person) who now comes under a duty not to interfere with the property of others.

A couple of examples suffice to drive the point home.[9] When A falls under a duty not to trespass on Blackacre after he sells it to B, it is not *B's* duty not to trespass that A acquires. There is a transfer of the title to B, not a transfer of B's duty not to trespass to A. If, for example, B was A's licensee prior to the transfer, there would be no duty of B's to transfer. Similarly, if A only transfers to B on condition that B grant A an immediate licence to enter Blackacre, A will acquire no duty upon the transfer. So we can see an asymmetry between A's loss of his title and his acquisition of the duty not to trespass; the former is a *result* of the transfer—a transfer is not a transfer if title doesn't pass—but the acquisition by A of a duty is just the usual *consequence* or *effect* of A's losing his title, that is, the usual consequence of A's losing his title is that he falls under the general duty not to interfere with the property of others.

The last example could, indeed, be generalized without a different result. Say a statute was passed that entitled any former owner, like A, to a licence for a year over land that he transferred to B. A's transfer is still effective as a transfer for the duration of that year. A has given up the title, and B has acquired it; B is now entitled to license others, transfer the property on (according himself the same year-long licence), and so on. Transfers and the acquisition of a duty not to trespass simply do not go together as a matter of conceptual necessity.

Consider also A's making B a co-owner.[10] A's right to possession of the land is not altered by this transaction; he acquires no duty not to enter; what changes is that, not only has B no longer a duty not to trespass, but he acquires title to his undivided share of Blackacre.

[9] Rob Chambers suggested these examples to me.

[10] In England this would be pursuant to the power granted in section 72 of the Law of Property Act 1925.

The result of this transaction is A's having to share his title with B, but nothing about A's right to possession flows as a consequence.

All this is, so to speak, native to the very idea of transmissible rights. In the same way that in the case of an assignable debt the duty of C correlates from time to time with the right of whoever is the beneficiary of that duty, the duty owed by any individual in the throng of those who have a duty not to trespass on Blackacre is owed to anyone, from time to time, who will come to be its owner. The very idea of transmissibility is related to this idea of contingency—what is yours might as well be, and might come to be, not only mine, but his, hers, theirs, and so on. The fact that something you own might come to be mine, in which case I will typically no longer owe a duty not to trespass upon it and you typically will, is no reason not to think that the right that you had is precisely the right that I may acquire, rather the opposite. Consider this case: say I am some potentate of the realm who simply has no duty not to trespass on anyone's land. I have, one might say, an unlimited right to roam. Does that put me in a position whereby I own all the property in the realm, or cannot have property transferred to me? Of course not. Whilst I might have an unlimited right to roam, I have no power to license the property to others and no power to transfer it; the property will not go to my heirs on my death, nor will it go to my trustee in bankruptcy for the benefit of my creditors should I go insolvent.

Our conclusion is the following: Rights, one of whose incidents is that of transmissibility, are those rights whose identity is independent of the right-bearer, and this can be made sense of both for transmissible personal rights and transmissible rights in rem. In the case of assignable personal rights like debts or shares, the identity of the right *is* dependent on the identity of the duty-ower: the right to be paid £10 by C is individuated both by the duty to pay £10, and by its being C that has to pay it. In the case of property rights in tangibles, the right is independent in both directions; the fact that the class of duty bearers who have the duty not to interfere with the tangible property of others fluctuates (as does the class of persons who might receive the property by way of transfer, inheritance, and so on) does not mean that the right does not persist.

On this accounting, any specific multital right–duty jural relation not to trespass on Blackacre that arises between A and B following A's transfer to B is normatively inert. The reason why A has a duty not to trespass on Blackacre is not that he has undertaken not to do so to

B, nor that he has acquired B's previous duty to A not to trespass, but because he falls under the general rule, what I have dubbed BPrN, which requires people not to interfere with the property of others. A is subject to a duty-imposing rule, one the normative guidance of which is not to be conceived of as changing as he acquires particular property from others, or transfers his property to others.

The Hohfeldian may grant these points, yet still be unsatisfied, on the basis of the following consideration: A's titles to the rights in the examples are more complex than simply his right to C's payment of £50 or his right that D does not trespass against Blackacre. A's title both to the debt or to Blackacre comprises the incidents that the title is transmissible by operation of law on A's death or bankruptcy and his power to transfer his title (by assignment or conveyance).[11] Whilst A's right to the payment of a debt or his right that D, E, and F not trespass on Blackacre seem to be, in normative terms, identical for both A and B, the same cannot be said for these 'incidents of transmissibility'. In the case of transmissibility on inheritance, for example, different persons will inherit from A than from B if they were to die, and in the case of transfer, we know for certain that there will be one person to whom A can transfer the right that B cannot: B himself of course. Likewise when B acquires title, A will be a possible object of B's power to transfer, while that was simply not true when A held that power. To put the Hohfeldian point at its strongest, in the case of 'transmissibility incidents' the people at the liability pole seem to be essential relata if we are to individuate the power-liability relation successfully.

The solution of the sameness problem as it relates to these incidents of transmissibility requires us, finally, to re-visit the Hohfeldian characterization of legal powers.

6.4 The Legal Power to Transfer

We can start by considering several examples which nibble at the Hohfeldian intuition that transmissibility incidents have their liability-bearers essentially.

[11] There will almost certainly be other elements, such as A's power to waive his right or release C from the debt, a power to declare a trust over the right, a liability to account for the payment for tax purposes, etc.

As we have seen, when two parties are before the court the Hohfeldian analysis can be applied to characterize the dispute between the parties in terms of their either advancing or denying that one of the four jural relations obtains between them, or claiming some jural relation has been extinguished or has arisen by operation of law.[12] But once we consider relations between persons outside of a two-party dispute, a problem arises when we consider powers and liabilities. Call this the standing issue, SI. Consider the fact that I have the power to make a gift by deed by undertaking the relevant procedure (sealing, signing, witnessing, delivering, etc.) so as to create a document that the law will regard as passing title to my donee. As a matter of law, I can execute this deed of gift in favour of anyone, so my power to make a gift by deed is on the Hohfeldian accounting really an aggregate of power–liability jural relations that obtain between me and everyone else.[13] But let us say that a claim is brought that my deed is defective, so that the power was not properly exercised. Who has standing to raise this issue in court? It is clear that not everyone can; that is, it is clear that not everyone in a Hohfeldian power–liability jural relation to the donor can. In the normal case, it is usually someone who would otherwise have received or otherwise would have rights in the property in the absence of an effective transfer; for example, an executor, a secured creditor, or a trustee in bankruptcy. To the Hohfeldian this must seem puzzling. The people who can bring a claim regarding a defective exercise of a power are not those whose correlative liability to receive is wrongfully erased by the invalid exercise of the power but rather people whose (putative) right to the asset is not by way of the exercise of the power at all. We find the same in the case of wills. Although in principle anyone could be my legatee, not just anyone can challenge the validity of my will.

Consider also the way in which the law regards those who may take under a power of appointment under a trust, or those who are presumptive heirs, or those who are named legatees of a will, prior to an appointment being made, or the rules of inheritance operating, or the will being executed by an executor. In each of these cases, the law regards these individuals not as having any interest in the property in

[12] Chapter 3, 3.1.

[13] To simplify the discussion, I am assuming the Hohfeldian claim that power–liability relations relate persons; as we have seen, this is false: Chapter 4, 4.2. But I don't think the assumption affects the points in the text.

question, but rather as having a mere *spes*, or hope, of receiving. The trustee may in the end not appoint to anyone, the heir may die before his predecessor, the estate may have no property in it at the time of the testator's death for distribution to the beneficiaries under his will. These are cases where we *can actually identify* a list smaller than everyone alive as possible recipients, sometimes only a single individual, and yet the law does not regard the potential recipient(s) as being in a genuine legal relation, that is, having a legally cognized *interest* in the property of the owner which they might receive if the power were to be exercised, despite the fact that they are clearly in Hohfeldian jural relations with him.

The way to make sense of SI is to appreciate that the law conceives of the power to give or bequeath as a power to transfer *to someone*, not a power to transfer to named individual X, named individual Y, and so on. The same can be said of the rules operating in regimes of inheritance or on intestacy. The rules operate to transfer the property to whomever, at the relevant time, is indicated by the rules. As a result, *none* of the Hohfeldian liability-bearers has, in principle, a right of standing merely in virtue of such status. Rather the law chooses certain possible recipients of the property, which may not include any of the liability bearers, to have standing to challenge the power-holder's exercise of it.

On what basis, then, *do* certain people have standing in these cases? The basic rule is that those people who would otherwise take the property 'in default' of a valid exercise of the power do. These are the people who are regarded as having an interest (a defeasible one, certainly, since the power can be effectively exercised to defeat their interest) in the property. True it is that I am in a Hohfeldian jural relation with anyone on the planet who owns property, since they might give me some of theirs. But this does not put the two of us in a genuinely legal normative relationship of any kind, and this is clearly reflected in the rules of standing. Any legal action that just anyone brought challenging the validity of my deed of gift would be struck out for disclosing no cause of action. An owner is subject to a power-conferring rule by which he has a power to transfer property to others. There are no 'proto-exercises' of this power, to each and every individual to whom he might give, 'within the womb of this power' (in the same way, canvassed above,[14] that a competent adder does not have within

[14] Chapter 1, 1.3.

him all possible sums). The truth is that a gift *establishes* the legal relationship between the donor and the donee, as the donor and donee of a gift,[15] at the very same time as it extinguishes it: upon transfer the donee has the property and the donor is, correspondingly, in the converse but legally inert Hohfeldian jural relation of liability-bearer to the donee's power to make a gift himself. The very same is true of the power to enter contracts, of course. I have a power to enter into a contract with anyone about anything (barring illegal contracts), and so I am in Hohfeldian jural relations with everyone else with contractual capacity. But this is normatively inert in the law. And of course it is true that when contracting parties exercise their powers to create legally binding agreements, they then establish an aggregate of jural relations, an actual contract, that does indeed have legal normative significance. But until such time, there is no legal relationship at all.[16] In these cases all we have are unregulated liberties, liberties to exercise a legal power where the liberty is unregulated by law.[17]

These thoughts apply to the concept of a power the same ideas I employed in the last chapter to undermine HMP. Such considerations establish that it is *necessary* for workable normative guidance that certain aspects of private law are governed by rules, including power-conferring rules, in the way just sketched, and not in terms of multital Hohfeldian jural relations. To put it as simply as possible, the rule which confers the power *generates* the *class of recipients; the class of recipients* does not generate the rule. The class of recipients may fluctuate however much it does; the rule conferring the power, and the power the rule confers, don't fluctuate at all. Likewise, assuming it is possible to adequately describe the class of power–liability jural relations in play, the fluctuating *totality* of power–liability relations does not generate the rule; the rule generates the *class* of power–liability relations. Moreover, turning back to the interdependence of powers,[18] it is clear now why it is the case that exercising the power to transfer to one of the class extinguishes the power to transfer to anyone else—the rule is framed in terms of a power to transfer to one member (or several

[15] Which may of course be relevant for other legal rules, such as nemo dat or bona fide purchase.

[16] In the normal case. There can be cases of pre-contractual liability for, say, unjust enrichment, but then that liability does not arise through the exercise of the power to enter into contract, which is the subject of the discussion.

[17] Chapter 3, 3.2.

[18] Chapter 4, 4.3.

members) of a class, a feature of the rule that is inexplicable, and indeed obscured, by treating the Hohfeldian jural relations as constitutive of the legal norms at play.

Thus the power to transfer the fee simple estate is not to be understood to fluctuate with the number of possible recipients, as some are born and some die. Of course when a transfer is made only an identified individual or individuals will take, but that doesn't undermine the impersonal conception of the power. In consequence, in the same way as we can conceive of a right to be paid £10 by C as persisting through its transfer from A to B, we can conceive of A's power to transfer the fee simple to Blackacre *to someone* as persisting through the transaction in which A exercises that power in favour of B; B, now with the fee simple, has the self-same power to transfer it *to someone*, that is, not to make a *selection* from a class which now has a different member because A and B have switched places. The fact that now A is one of the individuals who might receive now that B, not A, has the power, is immaterial to our conception of the power, because the fact that A is a 'new' possible recipient because he is now no longer owner is no more material to the conception of the power than is the fact that D is a new possible recipient, having just been born. A, as former owner of Blackacre, has no special standing under the property norm as a new possible recipient by way of transfer; he is now just one of the multitude who come into being and pass away, through which comings into being and passings away the title to Blackacre, with its power to transfer, persists.

We are now in a position to 'theorize' the foregoing examples, relying upon the distinction between the results of the exercise of a power and the consequences that flow from that exercise.[19]

Recall the distinction elaborated by Ripstein and Sage between those cases in which A alters B's genuine normative relations with another or others, and those cases in which A merely 'changes the context in which B operates'.[20] A's opening up a shop next to B's may lure away B's customers, but A's doing so does not interfere with any legally recognized interest of B's, though clearly it changes the context in which B operates. Put in terms of powers, A has no *legal power* to ruin B's business by competing with him. On Hohfeldian terms, A and B are in a liberty–no right relation in these cases, which is to say that

[19] Chapter 4, 4.1.

[20] Chapter 3, 3.2.

A's acts are not regulated by law, and B is not regarded as having any legal interest with respect to A's acts.

And this explains why the power–liability analysis of the duty to transfer is misconceived on Hohfeldian lines. When X exercises her power to transfer Blackacre to Y rather than to W, this merely alters the context in which W operates. As we have seen from the examples above, neither Y nor W is regarded in the law as having any interest in Blackacre, despite the fact that according to the Hohfeldian analysis they are purported to be in the jural relation of power–liability with X as regards X's power to transfer Blackacre to them.

Both X's power to transfer Blackacre to someone, if exercised, and the operations of law by which title to Blackacre passes to his heir, if he dies, will result in a series of consequences. But none of these potential consequences 'entitle' any possible donee or presumptive heir with respect to Blackacre. The law conceives of them as merely having a hope, not an interest, in Blackacre, and the moral of this is that powers are not to be conceived as multital entities which reflect genuine legal relations between the power-holder and those to the benefit of whom he might exercise the power, or between the title-holder and those who might receive from him by operation of law. Hohfeldian jural relations, on this accounting, are explications of the consequences of, and nothing more than the explications of the consequences of, the application of general legal norms, in this case, of course, the norm that confers upon owners the power to transfer.

6.5 The Extinction/Creation 'Directional Abandonment' Model of Transfer

The power to transfer is a power to put someone else in one's shoes, normatively speaking.[21] It is the power to endow someone else with the normative position in which one stands. This is unlike making

[21] In Penner 1997c, 75–100, I distinguished two models of transfer, one of them being a 'directional abandonment' model, and argued that that model was a suitable framing of the transfer incident to a contractual exchange. In doing so I muddled together what I called the motivational ideas lying behind transfer and the 'mechanistic' aspect, or mechanism of transfer. I stand by what I said about the different motivations underlying exchanges, as opposed to gifts and what I called 'commanded' transfers. As the present text shows, however, directional abandonment is not a mechanism of transfer at all.

someone a co-owner, which in part duplicates the relation in which one stands to others. By transferring title, we typically transfer the normative position of a sole-owner to another. Where we transfer to others to take as co-owners, we also create a relationship between those co-owners, such as the relationship of joint tenancy over Blackacre. All of these powers, though not identical, reflect the transmissibility of rights subject to those powers, the idea that what is mine might just as well have been yours, his, theirs, and so on. Thus the power to transfer a right is a normative notion—it does not depend for its operation on any particular empirical performance, such as the 'delivery' of a chattel (or 'transfer of possession' of a chattel), though it may.

As we saw at the outset of this chapter, Hohfeld posits an extinction/creation model of transfer. Given that Hohfeld framed this in terms of a 'power to alienate', and that Hohfeld also acknowledged a 'power to abandon'[22], it seems plausible to me to attribute to Hohfeld the idea that his power to alienate is a power to abandon property so that another can take it up, by exercising his own power to appropriate unowned goods. I cannot think of any other attribution that coheres with his extinction/creation model. But whether this attribution is correct, it is necessary to conclude this chapter by showing why the directional abandonment model does not work, just in case it is the most plausible interpretation of Hohfeld's power to alienate.

Normatively speaking, the idea of a transfer is inherently relational, involving my putting you in my position vis-à-vis the right in question. Although the directional abandonment model relies upon two normative powers, the power to abandon and the power to acquire title to unowned property by taking possession of it (the 'power to appropriate'), the operation of these powers even in a coordinated fashion does not generate a true right to transfer. Directional abandonment followed by appropriation is essentially an empirical matter, a matter of empirical success. Try as I might to get you to obtain factual possession of the thing I want to transfer to you by my abandonment of it and your taking possession of it yourself, something can always, in principle, go wrong, so that you do not actually obtain possession of the object. You might fumble the hand-off allowing a third party to take possession and that third party would do nothing wrong by doing so—there's no wrong of embezzlement in a world where transfers

[22] Hohfeld 1913–14, 54, n. 90.

are conceived of as directional abandonments. And notice, no one would conceive of this third party as my transferee, despite the fact that exactly the same mechanism of abandonment and 'first appropriation' occurred. As a matter of the concept of 'abandonment' then, it cannot itself be directional; so however empirically workable (or not) 'directional abandonment' might be to mimic the normative relationship of transferor and transferee, it fails as a normative substitute, and so also fails as an 'analysis' of the transfer of a right.

Moreover, the directional abandonment conception of transfer is only conceived of *as a transfer* by analogy with the real thing. To put this thought another way, the 'power to abandon or extinguish' one's own right cannot, without a concept of *transfer*, be conceived as one element of a power to endow another with a right to what one has abandoned, the other part being the 'recipient's' power to appropriate unowned things. The operation of these two powers in the right circumstances provides a functional facsimile of the power to transfer, but it is only conceived as such because we have the real idea of transfer under our belts. Facsimiles only are facsimiles in relation to the real thing.

The directional abandonment model also has another very counterintuitive implication. It necessarily brings into play the nature and justification of acquiring rights by appropriating unowned things in every case of transfer;[23] indeed it abolishes the concept of 'justice of transfer', and Robert Nozick's second principle of justice in holdings[24] turns out to be otiose. Moreover, whatever one thinks about 'first' or 'original' appropriation,[25] it is awry to regard the justice of transfer per se as having a conceptually necessary dependency upon the justice of original acquisition in every case of 'transfer'; the intuitive view is surely that whilst the validity or legitimacy of B's right to the property transferred to him by A might well turn on the legitimacy of A's

[23] Parallel considerations arise in the case of novations—transfer now implicitly requires agreement between the duty-ower, the right-bearer, and the intended 'transferee'. It turns the transaction from one of a two-party transfer to one of a three-party contract. Thus it implicates our justification of contractual agreement, whereas transfers, for example gifts, are not necessarily contractual in nature.

[24] '(2) A person who acquires a holding in accordance with the principle of justice in transfer, from someone else entitled to the holding, is entitled to the holding.' Nozick 1974, 151.

[25] I am of the same mind as a few other scholars on this point, who do not regard the justification of first appropriation as particularly difficult. See Penner 2006b, 172–3; Penner 2018, 144–5; Gaus and Lomasky 1990; Feser 2005; Sage 2012.

prior right to it (i.e. B's right may be heir to the same infirmities as was A's right because B acquired the title to the property from A, and thus might perhaps turn on the legitimacy of *A's first appropriation* (or on that of a predecessor in the chain of title who first appropriated the thing in question)), the question regarding transfers is one about whether, and with what validity or legitimacy, B acquired his title by transfer *from* A. Indeed, the latter question would need to be determined prior to asking how any deficiencies in A's prior right affected B; for *only* if B's title *is* the title A had, that is, only if A effectively transferred A's right to B, should B be concerned with any deficiencies in A's prior right. If B's title is not A's, B should not be concerned with anything about it; rather he should be concerned only about the legitimacy of his own 'first' appropriation of the now unowned (having been abandoned) thing in question.

The importance to the law of property of genuine transmissions of rights is obvious. To take just one example,[26] lawyers distinguish between the case where a person acquires land as a successor in title from a previous owner by a conveyance and the case where a person acquires a title to land merely by taking possession of it, which (adverse) title may, by virtue of a limitation act, become the best or only title to the land following the extinction of the prior owner's title. In the first case, we identify the transferee as the successor in title to the transferor. In the second case, the adverse possessor acquires an entirely new title in the land (which he can, of course, transfer to someone else). The directional abandonment model of transfer cannot distinguish these cases, so as a model of transfer it is clearly wrong.

6.6 Conclusion to Part 2

It has not been my purpose in this part to assess or assail Hohfeld's general achievement, that is, the general efficacy or power of 'Hohfeldian analysis'. Our concern here has been with property rights, and what he said, or what we can infer he thought from what he said, about them. And in any case a philosopher's achievement is not to be measured by whether, in the end, what they said was right. It is to be measured by the extent to which their thoughts need addressing, because they raise

[26] See further Penner 2013, 244–5.

issues or problems which demand our attention. On that accounting, this part is a testament to the originality and importance of Hohfeld's thought, since the 30,000-odd words it contains have addressed his views relating to property in minute detail. Sadly, however, if the foregoing is correct, the following conclusion is warranted: nothing we know about property rights or the law of property is illuminated by the Hohfeldian analysis of jural relations; indeed much is obscured by it. To the extent it has been thought that Hohfeldian analysis worked a revolution in our understanding of property rights, this was a revolution that wasn't.

PART 3

The Form and Justification of Legal Property Rights

In this part, I consider the form and justification of property rights. My aim is not to set out any new theory of property rights, but unlike Parts 1 and 2 of the book, which have a kind of negative quality, this part is more positive. Here I shall develop and defend some claims from my previous work on property, addressing some of the developments in the literature that have taken place, especially in the last decade or so, that concern these claims.

Chapter 7 unpacks BPrN, the basic exclusionary norm that applies to tangible property which, along with the powers to license and alienate, characterize the tripartite title to tangible property. In particular, I shall show how it relates to the idea of use. I have already argued in Chapter 1 that the concept of possession does not help us explain the tripartite nature of title to property. As I said, possession is a working legal concept, though a rather vague one for which it is impossible to give any kind of analytic definition. It does its work in the explanation of 'transition cases', where title to property arises by acquisition of an unowned thing, by adverse possession, or in certain cases of transfer. But it does nothing to explain what it means to have title to tangible property once one has it. So although the right of exclusion that an owner has is sometimes thought to be explained by something like 'continuing' possession, it is not, so I shall dispense with any discussion of possession in Chapter 7. We shall see, however, that the related idea of occupation of land has significance for the law of nuisance. In a sense, then, this chapter defends my view that the 'form' of property in tangibles centrally concerns BPrN, a suitably elaborated 'exclusive' right to the tangible thing in question.

Chapter 8 concerns the justification of BPrN. Towards the end I shall argue that we do have 'natural' or 'pre-legal' rights to the use of things, and explain this in terms of what I shall call, by comparison with BPrN, the Basic Usufructory Norm, or BUsN, for short. But I shall spend most of my time on the Kantian theory of property rights, most thoroughly and convincingly developed by Arthur Ripstein. I choose this target because whilst there is a great deal about legal property rights on the Kantian picture I agree with, I do not accept its most basic groundings in Kant's Doctrine of Right. Yet I have given it the most concentrated attention since, to my mind, it has been the most significant development in the discourse concerning property rights and private law more generally in the last decade. In explaining my difference with this view I shall be expounding what has been called an 'instrumentalist' view of law in general and property law in particular, a view most closely associated with the private law writings of John Gardner.

The final chapter considers property in land. In my view, property rights in land, at least compared to property rights in chattels, are not very 'paradigmatic' of property rights. Rights in land are much more varied than rights in chattels or most kinds of intangible property. Because of that it is difficult, both historically and theoretically, to identify what 'ownership' of land consists in. This is not to say that we cannot apply our results from Part 1, namely our identification of the tripartite structure of title, to land. Rather it is to point out that because of its special features, title to land is everywhere adjusted, compromised, straitened, and complicated by a host of surrounding rules, some but not all of which have a public law character. The upshot of this is that land law, taken in its entirely, is a kind of 'law of the horse'.

7

Exclusion, Use, and Usability

7.1 BPrN: The 'Right to Exclude'

Let me begin here by recapping what I have already said about the right to exclude, and the way I framed it as BPrN, and then draw our attention to several platitudes about it which it is always well to bear in mind.

'The right to immediate exclusive possession of tangible property' is the counterpart formulation of the right correlative to the duty not to interfere with the tangible property of others, whether by taking it or using it without permission or by causing damage to it. Those duties are expressed in the tort law rules governing trespass, conversion, negligent damage,[1] nuisance, and so on. For purposes of abbreviation, I have called the norm prohibiting these wrongs against property 'BPrN', for the Basic Property Norm—The 'Property' Exclusionary Norm for Tangible Property. The torts in question are sensitive to the nature of the tangible property concerned, and cleave roughly along the distinction between property in chattels, or 'movables', and land, or 'immovables'. Unauthorized handling, occupation, consumption, destruction, dispossession, and keeping property from its true owner are all comprised in 'non-interference'. Each of these prohibitions does not apply to all things that are property. An apple can be handled, consumed, destroyed, and taken, and in the sense of taking we can dispossess the owner of it, but we cannot occupy an apple in any meaningful sense. Land can be occupied, but not, save in the case of

[1] For some considerations regarding how we should assess damages in cases of negligent injury to property, see Penner 2020.

Property Rights. J. E. Penner, Oxford University Press (2020) © J. E. Penner.
DOI: 10.1093/oso/9780198830122.001.0001

land next to the sea, totally destroyed, although fixtures, like buildings, walls and so on, which are regarded in law as part of the land, can be and, though it cannot be taken, an owner can be removed or excluded from the occupation of his land, and another can wrongfully take possession of it.

Ripstein helpfully categorizes wrongs as falling under two kinds or types: using and damaging.[2] When I use your property, I treat it as if it were mine, not yours. Elsewhere Ripstein frames this as my *usurping* your property.[3] In this respect by using or usurping your property, whether intentionally or not,[4] I make a sort of claim—the act expresses my regarding your property to be at my disposal. Damage-causing wrongs need express no such claim; I can, for example, damage your property by acting negligently or by causing a nuisance the effect of which in damaging your land I did not foresee. Whilst both kinds of wrong violate BPrN, by violating your exclusive right to your property, they do so in different ways.[5] Neglecting such a distinction, as Stern helpfully points out,[6] may lead us to mischaracterize BPrN as a 'right to exclude' under which all interferences with tangible property have the character of an individual's trespass to land, a wrongful entry into space. The truth, of course, is that BPrN is shaped by whatever duties in tort law give rise to valid claims one element of proving which is that the plaintiff had title to something. So from the point of view of BPrN, in so far as negligent acts may give rise to a valid claim to compensation for damage to one's property, the law of negligence is a component of BPrN. I shall depart in 7.2 from Ripstein's twofold classification of wrongs by suggesting a third kind of tort, an 'ouster' or 'deprivation' tort, and argue that it better reveals the tort of nuisance.

BPrN is independent of whatever remedies the law may provide for its violation, including self-help remedies.[7] An obvious example lay in the traditional common law as regards the different remedies for violations of (some) property rights in land and chattels, which gave rise to the distinction between 'real' property versus 'personal' property.

[2] Ripstein 2016, 43–51.

[3] Ripstein 2016, 234–5.

[4] As for example when I take your umbrella thinking it is my own.

[5] One act, can of course, constitute both wrongs, as for example when I throw a rock through one of your windows just because I like the way that glass smashes.

[6] Stern 2018, 46–50.

[7] Penner 1997c, 71–2.

Seisin (or possession) of the former could be regained from a wrongful possessor through the 'real actions', whilst in the case of the wrongful taking (conversion) of a chattel, the common law only gave money damages—you didn't get the 'real thing' back again. These differing remedies did not alter the deontic content of BPrN as it applied and applies to both. The norm as applied to a chattel is not 'take it but pay what it is worth'; the norm is 'don't take it', full stop.

Further platitudes concern the owner's liberty to make use of the property he owns, and its relation to BPrN. First, the notion of 'use' is, so to speak, 'inert' as regards the way BPrN applies.[8] It applies irrespective of the owner's actual engagement with his property. In this respect, to the extent that BPrN is seen to protect the owner's uses of his property, this use-right is merely a formal reflection of the duty upon others to exclude themselves in the relevant ways required by the law of torts. As Ripstein puts it,[9] 'the nub of a property right is that the owner *rather than others* gets to determine how the thing will be used'. That he in fact makes no such determination is irrelevant to the application of BPrN. BPrN continues to apply even if he has entirely forgotten about his ownership of something and would not miss it if it were taken.[10] This point is forcefully put in another way by McFarlane and Douglas in terms of Hohfeldian jural relations, which we noticed in Chapter 3, 3.2 above.

Another platitude,[11] already canvassed in Chapter 1, is that BPrN is framed in terms of a duty on non-owners not to interfere with the property of others. It is not framed in terms of interfering with an owner's 'use-rights', though as we shall see when we turn to nuisance shortly, the concept of a right to general 'usability' has been invoked.

Ripstein helpfully points out another platitude about BPrN,[12] which helps to show that it is not framed in terms of the uses an

[8] Arthur Ripstein corrected me on this point (Ripstein 2013, 160). At Penner 1997, 70, I elided the justificatory relationship between use and BPrN with the formal structure of BPrN. I shall defend the justificatory relationship in the next chapter.

[9] Ripstein 2013, 160.

[10] Of course an owner of land may lose it as a consequence of the adverse possession of another, and the adverse possessor is more likely to succeed if the owner has forgotten he owns something, but the legal grounds for adverse possession do not track the owner's intentions or lack thereof in relation to the land; it turns on his failure to exercise the remedial rights which protect his right to exclusive entitlement.

[11] See, for example, Ripstein, 2013, 161–78; Penner 1997c, 70–3.

[12] Ripstein 2013, 158–61.

owner can make of his property. The fact that someone else could make better use of your property does not mean that they have any entitlement to it.[13] The owner gets to decide how he will himself use his property, and also he must agree to any terms on which he will allow others, via the powers of licence and transfer, access to his property.

A different platitude relating to use is that general restrictions on the use of some things do not diminish the titles of those who own them. The standard examples are highway speed limits and the application of the law of murder that prohibits your killing someone with the knife you own. Neither of these rules diminishes your ownership of the car or the knife, even though they restrict their uses. The reason is that these norms apply irrespective of any ownership of the chattels in question. A thief who takes the car and exceeds the speed limit is liable just as the owner would be, and *mutatis mutandis* for his use of the knife.[14]

A final platitude is illustrated by an example. I want to stop you from competing in a horse race, from using your horse in a particular way. I can achieve my aim by smashing you up, or smashing up your horse (amongst other possibilities, such as falsely imprisoning you, or stealing your horse). Either way, problem solved. But my liability to you will not turn on my interfering with this use. It will turn on, in the first case, my committing a trespass to your person, and in the second case on my committing a trespass to your property. This shows that the law does not, in terms or per se, protect your liberty to use your horse as you will. My motive, *interfering with this use*, is irrelevant,[15] as is your perfectly sensible framing of your complaint as 'X wrongfully stopped me from competing in the race'. What matters is the 'by clause' that follows: 'X wrongfully stopped me from competing *by* φing', where φing identifies the relevant trespass, smashing me up or smashing up Black Beauty.

[13] Except in cases of necessity.

[14] For discussion of the way in which certain restrictions on what would normally be central dispositions of the property in question *may* be said to diminish the owner's property rights, see Penner 1997c, 100–3.

[15] It may be relevant for the criminal law, for example, for establishing motive or malice. The consequence of the wrong, my preventing you from competing in the race, is relevant for the determination of damages for consequential loss, under the head of 'loss of a chance'.

7.2. Use, Exclusion, and the Law of Nuisance

7.2.1 Nuisance: Essert's and Nolan's Accounts

A very orthodox statement of the tort of nuisance is this:

A private nuisance is an unreasonable interference with the use and enjoyment of land.[16]

In view of this sort of characterization, it is hardly surprising that commentators have characterized the tort as one which gives effect to the plaintiff's use- and enjoyment-rights in land. If the law puts me under a legal duty not (unreasonably) to interfere with the use and enjoyment of your land, it would seem to follow just as a feature of the correlativity of rights and duties that the rights in question are rights to the use and enjoyment of your land. It is the purpose of this part to show that this characterization of the tort is potentially misleading, and to offer a better interpretation of the law in this area, an interpretation which, while making necessary reference to occupation, needs to make no necessary reference to use.[17] On this interpretation, BPrN retains its character as a norm essentially concerned with exclusion, not use.

Before getting to that, two other characterizations of the tort of nuisance have to be raised and put to one side. The first characterizes nuisance law as the law of competing use-rights, or the law that adjudicates uses which come into conflict. From this perspective, the law can be seen as a private law form of planning or zoning law. From the economic analysis of law literature, the classic paper expressing this view was Ronald Coase's 'The Problem of Social Cost'.[18] For reasons I and others have explored elsewhere,[19] this is a fatally flawed

[16] *Winfield & Jolowicz on Tort*, 19th edn (London: Sweet & Maxwell, 2014), [15–1008], quoted in Nolan 2019, 72. See also the other statements cited there: all refer to use and enjoyment.

[17] My views in this part have been extensively shaped by Nolan 2011; Nolan 2019; Essert 2016; Merrill 1985; Ripstein 2016, 50, 136–84; and Smith 2004a, 2004b.

[18] Coase 1960.

[19] Essert 2016, 90–4; Penner 1993, 14–21; Smith 2004. Beever 2013 pursues a different 'competing use-rights' analysis. The essence of Beever's analysis, at 21, is that an action in nuisance will lie where the defendant's activity interferes with the plaintiff's use of his property and the plaintiff's use is 'more fundamental' than the defendant's use. However it is not clear to me that any clear criterion of 'more fundamental' is provided, and his application of this criterion to the cases, at 25–7, doesn't seem to generate one.

characterization of nuisance law for a number of reasons, but primarily and most obviously because it cannot explain the fact that nuisance is a tort, a wrong.

The second characterizes nuisance as a kind of boundary crossing, in analogy with the tort of trespass. It is of interest here, of course, because if the tort of nuisance is really some kind of version of the tort of trespass, it undoubtedly falls within the exclusionary force of BPrN. It has been most recently defended by McFarlane and Douglas.[20] Nolan dubs this the 'Physical Invasion View'.[21] For reasons given by Nolan and Essert,[22] I cannot see how this view can genuinely provide an account of the tort of nuisance; there are simply too many cases of nuisance which cannot plausibly be characterized as boundary crossings or physical invasions. To take just one example, obstructing a right of way is a paradigm case of committing a nuisance, the recognition of which goes back to the very beginning of the history of the action,[23] and it can, of course, be committed without any trespass on the relevant land.

We can now turn to two views of the law of nuisance which may be more fruitfully contrasted with the one I shall develop below. To set the discursive framework, here is the essence of my view: a nuisance is a wrong of indirect, or constructive, eviction or ouster. The absolutely clearest case of an actionable nuisance is one which makes an owner's occupation of the land physically impossible, where, for example, the defendant releases poisonous gas over the plaintiff's land, or where a right of way or access to a commons is obstructed, depriving the plaintiff of that very right—ousting them from their right, in other words.[24] Lesser nuisances 'evict' or oust the landowner of his right to occupy to lesser degrees. That is, in particular ways they restrict the owner's ability to occupy or access his land in deprivation of his rights. In my view the constant references to the use and enjoyment in the cases do

[20] McFarlane and Douglas 2013, 230–2. An earlier trespassory account was given by Epstein 1979; for critical discussion see Essert 2016, 87, 94–8.

[21] Nolan 2019, 79.

[22] Essert 2016, 94–8; Nolan 2019, 81–5.

[23] Baker 2002, 423.

[24] This is a shorthand. What the person is actually ousted from or deprived of is the *subject* matter of the right, not the right itself. So the landowner is deprived of access to or evicted from his land, or the right of way holder's access to the way is obstructed. Of course, sometimes my acts can actually extinguish your exclusionary rights, as when I actually kill you, or destroy or consume your property or use it in a way so that it accedes to other property, extinguishing any title in it. Deprived of or ousted from *the subject matter of the right* is my intended meaning, but it would be cumbrous to spell this out all through the text.

not show that the tort protects the use-rights of the owner, but are the best evidence or indicators of the relevant dispossession of the owner by the person creating the nuisance.

I am not going to proceed with a thumbnail sketch of the entire law of nuisance. I shall proceed on the basis that the reader has a passing familiarity with the subject. Of course the account I offer is erroneous if any of my claims in fact fail to line up with the actual doctrine, but so far as I am aware, they do not. Indeed, my claim will be that my view helps us better understand this doctrine.

For his part, Essert claims that the law of nuisance protects one's right to have a location in the world free from the interference of others, which he frames in terms of a 'normative refuge':[25]

> *[T]he law of nuisance sets the normative boundaries of the right of ownership by reference to the boundaries of the justification of the right in terms of a normative refuge.*

Since a refuge is something you occupy, so in keeping with my 'ouster' view of nuisance, I am sympathetic to the general thrust of the refuge characterization. Focusing as he does on the reciprocal *rights* of property owners, Essert asserts that the test of reasonableness sets a scope for those rights, not by adjudicating upon particular harms to a neighbour caused by one person's use of his land, but by establishing fair terms of interaction between owners given the fact that owners' activities will necessarily impinge upon their neighbours to some extent. With this I also agree. But it is right to identify a few wrinkles in Essert's account.

First, nuisance can be committed from a public highway or other public place,[26] so a non-owner can commit the tort, or rather, one can commit the tort without one's own property holdings being a relevant factor in the nuisance. I don't think this is a serious blow to Essert's account—he would just have to extend it to encompass this sort of plaintiff–defendant interaction,[27] which I imagine would be fairly straightforward. The second wrinkle is a little more troubling, perhaps. The idea of a refuge seems most fitting to describe residential properties, a place which secures privacy, intimacy, and so on, away from the public gaze. But as Essert knows, a nuisance can be committed against

[25] Essert 2016, 103 (italics original).

[26] For example, *Hubbard v Pitt* [1976] QB 142 (picketing outside the plaintiff's premises) and other cases discussed by Nolan 2011, 475–6; see also Neyers 2017.

[27] Interactions between owners of land and users of nearby public spaces.

an occupier of business premises open to the public,[28] locations which don't obviously attract the description 'refuge'. Even further from an obvious 'refuge' account would be non-possessory interests protected by nuisance law, like a right of way. It is hard to see how a right of way could be a refuge of any kind—the user of a right of way has to move along; she cannot just settle in the way and stay there.

So what is a nuisance, on Essert's account? It is an unreasonable interference with the plaintiff's '*control* over her own property'.[29] He also quotes, with approval, the formulation of the wrong given in *Appleby v Erie Tobacco*[30] that is, that nuisances are things that could, 'render property less fit for the ordinary purposes of life,' to which Essert adds (my italics):

> things that could *render empty* the plaintiff's *entitlement* to treat her land as a normative refuge.

It seems fairly clear to me that this account does not regard the tort of nuisance as one prohibiting any interference by the tortfeasor with a particular use or kind of use the plaintiff wishes to make of her land. Rather, the gravamen of the complaint is that the defendant has, to some significant extent, interfered with the 'habitability' or 'occupiability' of the land, rendering her entitlement to her land empty. What this amounts to is a rights deprivation, framed in terms of the defendant's having made the land unfit for occupation or possession in some significant way.

Nolan frames the tort in terms of depriving, to some significant extent, the plaintiff of the 'usability' of her land. My difficulty is understanding the conceptual work the notion of 'usability' is supposed to be doing. Clearly, one bit of conceptual work the term does is to distinguish Nolan's account from those which frame the tort as one that protects *particular* uses or kinds of uses by the plaintiff of her land,[31] and I agree with his account on this score. None of the cases, as far as I can see, make any reference to such a notion in terms, though as we have seen, the courts do refer to the 'fitness' of the land 'for the ordinary purposes

[28] *Sturges v Bridgman* [1879] 11 Ch.D. 852; *Bank of New Zealand v Greenwood* [1984] 1 NZLR 525, *Hubbard v Pitt* [1976] QB 142, which Essert 2016 cites at 91, 97, and 109 respectively.

[29] Essert 2016, 107.

[30] (1910) 22 OLR 533, para. 9; quoted in Essert 2016, 105.

[31] For example, Beever 2013.

of life'. The latter does sound like a kind of abstract 'usability' requirement, but it obviously needs unpacking: what are 'the ordinary purposes of life'? I suppose my differences with Nolan here turn on how such general, ordinary purposes, are elaborated in terms of usability.

Take also the typical right of way case, where A obstructs B's private right of way so B cannot access it. One *could* say that A has reduced or damaged the usability of B's right of way, but it seems clearer to me to say that A has (indirectly, that is without committing a trespass) merely *effectively deprived* B of his right.

Nolan's and my views may differ largely as a matter of semantics; rather than framing the wrong in terms of diminishing the 'usability' of the plaintiff's right, I would prefer to say that the plaintiff is simply being, indirectly but no less effectively, deprived of his right—not of a right to use or usability, but a right, in the case of ownership, to possess the land, and in the case of a right such as a right of way, of the right to take the route which the right confers upon him. The reason I say that our difference might be a matter of semantics turns on the reliance Nolan places upon Ernest Weinrib's Kantian explanation of the relation of property and usability.[32] Weinrib contends that from a Kantian perspective of right no private law could be such as to render the usable resources of the world 'res nullius'. No rightful private law could incorporate norms which imposed duties on everyone never to make use of things.[33] From this perspective, it seems to me that neither could any justified private law allow any individual unilaterally to make another person's property 'res nullius', by substantially depriving the owner of access to it or the liberty to use it. Whereas Nolan therefore draws upon Weinrib's thought to bolster his characterization in terms of usability, I can just as much draw upon it to frame the tort in terms of ouster—no system of justified private law could oust someone from any practical access to the subject matter of their right.

Rightly claiming the importance of including the law of nuisance in a full account of property rights, Nolan says this regarding nuisance cases such as an interference with a right of way:[34]

[T]he fact that the role nuisance plays in the protection of incorporeal hereditaments is such a problem for the physical invasion view of the tort

[32] Nolan 2019, 73, 80.
[33] Weinrib 2018.
[34] Nolan 2019, 86 (my italics).

serves as a useful reminder that theories of property need to be capable of explaining property rights of this kind, which clearly rest not on a right to exclude *but on (something like) a right not to be excluded.*

Of course, I agree. I just present the tort of nuisance in a more unified way than Nolan does, since I think the 'right not to be excluded', not to be indirectly ousted from the subject matter of your rights, is the entire foundation for the tort in all of its various instances, as I shall now explain.

7.2.2 Nuisance as an 'Ouster' Tort

So now let me turn to my own view. What do I mean by 'ouster', or alternatively, 'deprivation', and why is it wrongful? An act is an ouster if it prevents the owner from being in contact with the subject matter of his right. In the case of a right of way, it means preventing him in some way from accessing the way; in the case of ownership of land, it means doing something which indirectly yet significantly interferes with his rights to occupy or possess. As regards the tortfeasor himself, his act of dispossession or ouster of the true owner amounts to a kind of expropriation of the plaintiff's right. The tortfeasor's implicit claim is that *he* gets to choose the scope of the plaintiff's rights in her own land. To this extent he ousts the owner of her rights. This way of thinking about 'amenity' nuisance cases, that is, cases of noise, smoke, smells, and so on, is most clearly reflected in the curtilage principle, as enounced by Thesiger LJ in *Sturges v Bridgman*:[35]

It would be on one hand in a very high degree unreasonable and undesirable that there should be a right of action for acts which *are not in the present condition of the adjoining land*, and possibly never will be any annoyance or inconvenience to either its owner or occupier; and it would be on the other hand in an equally degree unjust and, from a public point of view, inexpedient that *the use and value of adjoining land* should, for all time and under all circumstances, be restricted and diminished by reason of the continuance of acts incapable of physical interruption, and which the law gives no power to prevent. The smith in the case proposed *might protect himself by taking a*

[35] *Sturges v Bridgman* [1879] 11 Ch.D. 852 at 865 (my italics).

sufficient curtilage to ensure what he does from being at any time an annoyance to his neighbour ...

The idea here is that if your activity is such as to require a surrounding curtilage so that you don't diminish the rights of your neighbours, it is up to you to acquire such land as to create the necessary curtilage. You have no right to bring your neighbours' land within this curtilage, expropriating it in fact so as to carry out your purposes.

I have used the expression 'expropriation'. What distinguishes the expropriietary, ousting, character of nuisance from expropriation in the usual sense, that of *taking*, is that the nuisance tortfeasor dispossesses the plaintiff from the subject matter of her right *without taking it himself*.

According to my view, the essence of these 'amenity' cases in nuisance is that the tortfeasor ousts the landowner *indirectly*, by acts *affecting her person*. Nolan characterizes these sorts of nuisance in this way:[36]

[T]he property tort analysis holds with equal force for all types of private nuisance, once it is appreciated that in cases involving noise, smells and so on the gist of the action is not the discomfort of those affected, but the *diminished utility of the land on which they live*—hence '[a] sulphurous chimney in a residential area is not a nuisance because it makes householders cough and splutter but because it prevents them taking their ease in their gardens.'

I think this is a rather odd way of putting it. The more obvious thing to say in such a case is that the owner of the sulphurous chimney has effectively evicted or ousted the plaintiffs from their gardens, 'prevent[ing] them taking their ease in their gardens', *by causing them this discomfort* any time they try to go into it.

Nuisance has a long historical association with the concept of ouster. As Baker points out,[37]

[Nuisance] was a wrongful disturbance of the enjoyment of real property, or of its appurtenances, or of rights over real property, *falling short of a forcible trespass or ouster.*

[36] Nolan 2011, 461 (footnotes omitted, my italics), quoting Newark 1949 at 489.
[37] Baker 2002, 422.

Unfortunately, as Baker clearly illustrates, one of the difficulties of sorting out what 'counts' as a nuisance arises because of the fact that, as a result of the indirectness of both nuisance and what we now call negligence, the assize of nuisance declined as actions for similar wrongs came to be actionable in 'case', that is, as actions for trespass on the case. So it was not until relatively recently that there was any particular analytic reason to designate a wrong as one of 'nuisance' rather than 'negligence'. All the litigant need know was whether the act in question was actionable in case. There was, in a sense, just a laundry list of wrongs which the action remedied. Some assize of nuisance cases were straightforwardly cases where the wrong was a deprivation of right. The plaintiff could get an order to get his right of pasture or right of way back again.[38] Another sort of wrong was the stopping up of a watercourse so as to flood the plaintiff's land. Here is a case which can, per Nolan, be described as a diminution of usability case, but it could equally be understood as a deprivation of right or ouster case. I cannot think of a better way of evicting someone from their land indirectly than by flooding it. Flooding literally puts the plaintiff's land (or part of it) *under water*. If that is not a case of constructive (indirect) eviction or ouster I don't know what is. The action on the case slowly supplanted the assize, which was 'put to an end' in 1601 when a clear dispossession or ouster case for which the assize was in part originally formulated, the wrong of enclosing a common, was held to found an action in case.[39]

Thus nuisance, along with trespass on the case, are the original 'indirect' torts. My claim is that the only sound way to distinguish nuisance from trespass on the case, or negligence, is that the former is a 'ouster' tort, whereas the latter is a damage tort.

It is not entirely clear why the association between nuisance and ouster has been lost sight of in recent theoretical and doctrinal investigations. It is not as if 'ouster' torts have been ignored across property law, in particular regarding civil wrongs concerning chattels. Consider unlawful distraint or distress and the action for detinue.

A landlord wrongs his tenant when he unlawfully distrains, that is takes possession of, his tenant's goods as a kind of security, typically for the payment of overdue rent.[40] No proof is required that the wrongful

[38] ibid.

[39] ibid., 426.

[40] Maitland 1909/1929, 355. The action of replevin allowed the tenant to recover the goods until such time as the lawfulness of the distraint could be determined.

distrainor of goods used them (if he did then he would also be liable for conversion) or that he damaged them. The gravamen of the wrong is that he unjustly deprived the plaintiff of his rightful possession. Detinue, the action against someone for 'wrongful' detention of goods, applies in any number of situations. Again, no proof of use or damage is required.[41] Although I cannot go into details here, I should also say the personal tort of false imprisonment has this form. Liability does not turn on damage to the victim, nor on any 'using' of him (as would be typical of a sexual assault). It turns on a deprivation of liberty.

Be that as it may, in the case of nuisance the 'ouster' angle may have fallen from sight because the land torts are now understood to be limited to trespass and nuisance, and so the character of nuisance is set against that of trespass, and analogies and disanalogies with trespass frame the discussion. When we think of the wrong of dispossession of land, the most obvious modern example is the case of the adverse possessor, and as against the owner, the adverse possessor's wrong is framed as that of trespass which is, in a way, correct. But she is *much more* than a mere trespasser. By taking possession as she does, she acquires her own title to the land, an exclusive right to the land which binds all others, and though it will not defeat the relatively stronger, prior title of the 'true owner' until the passage of the relevant period of time, the adverse possessor's intention must be adverse to the true owner—that is, her claim is only supportable give that as against the true owner the implicit claim of her act of dispossession is that she is denying the true owner's right, that is, it amounts to an act of ouster. That is what distinguishes her from a licencee in exclusive possession. Just as much as the adverse possessor, the licencee's possession gives rise to a title good against all others except for his licensor, but he does not hold adversely to the licensor. There is no act of ouster in such a case. Nothing shows better how modern jurists have lost sight of the wrong of ouster than when they classify a clearly dispossessory nuisance as an *actual* trespass. That was the holding in the US case of *Martin v Reynolds*,[42] a case in which a farmer was driven from his land by toxic gas.[43]

[41] Bridge 2015, 91–3.

[42] 221. Or 86, 342 P.2d 790, discussed at Merrill 1985, 30.

[43] Essert 2016, 112 fn 138 says that I suggested that cases of this kind 'amount to something similar to what is usually actionable in trespass (or ejectment)'. I don't think I suggested that trespass or ejectment were alternatives in this kind of case, but in case I did I was wrong to do so. I would have been wrong to do so because trespass and ejectment are entirely distinct

It might appear that my thesis is weakest in the amenity cases, and that the sulphurous chimney evicting people from their gardens is some special sort of case. But the classic examples of amenity cases involve fumes, smells, smoke, dust, etc., on the one hand, and noise on the other. Both are what might be called 'environmental' nuisances: they fundamentally affect the environment of the premises by affecting the persons upon it. They are both, if significant, clearly exclusionary. The former affect the ability to *breathe*. If I cannot breathe, or can breathe only with difficulty, you have indirectly but effectively excluded me from my land. In the case of smells, I can still breathe if I put a clothes-peg on my nose and only breathe through my mouth, but if that is the case, I would strongly submit that you have limited, not entirely but very significantly, my access to the subject matter of my right. Significant noise has a similar dispossessory effect. It can cause headaches, be enormously frustrating in terms of distraction, and so on. If you can literally get no sleep on your property then you will become ill and ultimately go crazy; in other words the noise will require you to leave. It is noteworthy that the early 'amenity' cases were framed clearly in terms of dispossessory sorts of interference: the 'unwholesomeness' of the air causing a risk of infection or otherwise threatening the health of the occupants.[44] This is why evidence that the effect on the individual is one which induces the land occupier to go out when it is happening is the best evidence that the act complained of constitutes a nuisance.[45]

Let me turn to a last class of cases, which have come to be called, unhelpfully in my view, 'affront' cases, which many nuisance scholars find problematic.[46] The relevant English decisions are *Thompson-Schwab v Costaki*,[47] which concerned a brothel, and *Laws v Florinplace*,[48] which concerned a pornography shop. The plaintiffs claimed that the citing of these businesses was a nuisance in a residential neighbourhood, and were successful at the interlocutory stage, the court holding that these

wrongs. I thought, and still think, such cases are not cases of trespass at all, but rather indirect ejectment, nuisance cases in other words.

44 Baker 2002, 429–30.

45 See, for example, *Tetley v Chitty* [1986] 1 All ER 663; *Kennaway v Thompson* [1981] QB 88; *Miller v Jackson* [1977] QB 966. See also Essert 2016, 104 fn 100, discussing *Esposito v New Britain Baseball Club, Inc.*, 49 Conn. Supp. 509, 512–13 (Conn. Supp. 2005).

46 See, for example, Beever 2013, 22, fn 30; Nolan 2011, 464–5.

47 [1956] 1 WLR 335.

48 [1981] I All ER 659.

businesses could constitute nuisances. I take the point that there can be no justification of these decisions on the basis that the residents merely objected to these activities because they might give rise to a decline in their property values. But whether or not made out on the facts, the *form* and *nature* of the complaint as grounding an actual nuisance can be defended. Essert[49] does so by saying that these cases can be seen as 'besetting' cases, along the lines of a picketing case—the plaintiff's having a right to a normative refuge means he should not be beset by others in close proximity to his land. I take a more straightforward view, which also shows why the cases are problematic on the facts.

One of the rights an owner of land has is the right to enter and leave his premises, as well as the public law right to make use of any public way in doing so. More crucially for these cases, the owner has a right to invite any other person to enter and stay on his land, and each of his licencees have the same public law right to make use of a public way in getting to the owner's house. As I read the judgments, a crucial factor in finding a triable case of a nuisance concerned the effects these businesses would have on the residential owners' licencees, in particular their children. The idea is something like these businesses make it impossible, or at least irresponsible, for parents to admit children to their premises, because the presence of these activities would mean that anyone getting there will be exposed to these immoral activities. This brings them in line with a picketing case such as *Hubbard v Pitt*. The problem with the 'besetting' was that the picketers were intentionally, and effectively, denying the plaintiff the right to invite others—customers in that case—onto their premises. Obviously, both the brothel and pornography shop cases, as well as the picketing case, raise serious issues regarding freedom of expression. So let me offer a hypothetical case, the case of 'the glass morgue',[50] which has exactly the same form but which doesn't raise any freedom of expression issues.

Let us say that a local council decides to privatize the performance of autopsies, and the defendant gets the contract. He rents premises in a parade of shops in a residential neighbourhood. Unfortunately, the

[49] Essert 2016, 108–9.

[50] This hypothetical case is a structurally identical variant of one that first occurred to me when Denise Reaume taught me torts in my first year of law school. That example was one of a 'glass abbatoir'. I have changed the relevant activity so as not to distract readers with the question of whether slaughtering animals for food should be defended as a socially worthwhile activity. I take it no one thinks that performing autopsies is not a socially worthwhile activity.

shop he rents has large glass windows which he does not black out or cover with curtains. Now the problem here is obvious—passersby, upon seeing an autopsy performed, will typically react either by fainting or being sick (and for my North American readers, this means 'vomiting'). Because it interferes with a public right of way, this will be a public nuisance, but it will also constitute a private nuisance to the other shopkeepers and to the nearby residents because it indirectly but very effectively interferes with their own right to leave and enter their premises, as well as with their right to invite (license) others to do so. There is no better way to make land unoccupiable than by making it hazardous or impossible to leave or to re-enter it, even if the 'making it hazardous or impossible' in this case is indirect, namely involving no trespass to the person[51] or to one's property. And I cannot imagine any court in the world not granting an injunction here, requiring the defendant to abate the nuisance, which would only[52] require blacking out the windows or putting up curtains.

7.2.3 Nuisance: The Supposed Damage and Fault Requirements

Is damage of some kind to the land an essential feature of the tort of nuisance? My view is that nuisance is actionable without proof of damage. Nolan disagrees, but our disagreement might again be superficial or semantic. Nolan thinks damage always accompanies the tort but this is because he defines damage as a diminution in 'usability'.[53] This, it is submitted, is not the way damage is conventionally understood in nuisance law. 'Damage' means physical damage to the land of some kind. In his 2011 paper Nolan discussed the damage requirement in nuisance in this way:[54]

Although it is also said (again reflecting the trespass/case distinction) that while trespass to land is actionable per se, private nuisance requires proof of damage, in practice this *notional requirement of damage* is synonymous with—and so adds nothing to—the requirement of substantial interference, which

[51] I accept that exposing, with intent, a person to something that causes them to faint or be sick might constitute a trespass to the person, but there is, I am assuming, no such intent here.

[52] By 'only' I am merely speaking common sense, not suggesting that a tortfeasor in a nuisance case can get out of abating the nuisance if doing so is costly to her.

[53] cf. Ripstein 2016, 137.

[54] Nolan 2011, 481 (my italics).

is where the real significance of the distinction between the two torts lies (there being no equivalent to this requirement in trespass).

In other words, the proof of damage requirement is essentially notional. We should therefore stop referring to it, as notional requirements are not real requirements.

Another issue concerns the concepts of unreasonableness and fault. We must not be bewitched by the formulation of the tort as an 'unreasonable' interference in the use and enjoyment of property rights, as Nolan correctly explains:[55]

A second terminological source of confusion is the use of the phrase 'unreasonable user' to describe the requirement of substantial interference. So long as it is understood that it is the *interference* which must be unreasonable, and not the *defendant's conduct*, no harm is done, but inevitably this distinction is frequently lost, so that we end up with a reference to 'the centrality to the tort of nuisance of the fault-based concept of unreasonableness' and the claim that no clear distinction can be drawn between negligence and nuisance, since in both 'the question is whether the defendant has acted reasonably'.

I would just modify this to say 'substantial interference' means a substantial deprivation of the plaintiff's rights, or 'an interference having a dispossessory character'. Dispossessing or depriving people of their property rights is unreasonable per se, just as is trespassing on someone's land.[56]

7.3 Conclusion

Exclusion, possession, and use are related concepts, and it has been the purpose of this chapter to vindicate BPrN in the face of a particular challenge. In Chapter 1, 1.2, with the assistance of Holmes, I dispatched the idea that BPrN turned on some notion of 'continuing' possession. This chapter primarily concerned itself with a particular corner of private law, the law of nuisance. I think it is a fair criticism of my

[55] Nolan 2011, 485 (italics original, footnotes omitted).
[56] cf. Essert 2016, 112–13.

previous work to say that when I discussed property rights in terms of the formal right of exclusion, BPrN, I neglected to consider in detail cases of ouster, and more particularly, the dispossessory character of nuisance. As my previous work on nuisance shows, I have always taken this particular perspective on the tort. The problem was that I didn't fully bring those thoughts together in explaining how nuisance figures in a complete description of BPrN, which is why I have spent so much time on it here. In short, I neglected the idea that part and parcel of the right to property was the idea that third parties were prohibited from *excluding me* from my property, even if they did not damage it or take it for themselves.

8

The Justification of Property Rights

8.1 Introduction

Recent work by Kantians, in particular Arthur Ripstein, has done us a great service in helping us to see the nature of the moral principles that relate us one to another, apart from institutions such as the law or the state. Some of those principles relate us in respect of our interactions with the external resources of the world. So I shall spend the bulk of my discussion on Kant's theory of property rights. I hope to point out the valuable insights of the Kantian account whilst at the same time explaining why, after reflection, I am not a Kantian about property rights. I shall then go on to consider my version of an 'instrumentalist' justification of legal property rights.

8.2 The Kantian Account of Property Rights

The account I shall provide here is mostly drawn from the work of Arthur Ripstein, in particular his path-breaking 2009 *Force and Freedom*.[1] I shall sketch the general shape of the Kantian account, focusing on those aspects to which I shall take exception below.

[1] Ripstein 2009. I have also learned a great deal from: Brudner 2013; Byrd and Hruschka 2006; Feser 2005; Ganesh 2018; Gardner 2016; Gregor 1988; Hodgson 2010; Katz 2011; Ripstein 2004, 2006a, 2013, 2015, 2016, 2017; Sage 2012, 2018; Shell 1978; Stone 2011; E Weinrib 2002–03, 2018; J Weinrib 2008, 2014; Westphal 1997, Westphal 2016, ch. 8; and Williams 1977.

Property Rights. J. E. Penner, Oxford University Press (2020) © J. E. Penner.
DOI: 10.1093/oso/9780198830122.001.0001

8.2.1 Private Right and the Civil Condition

As conceived in the Doctrine of Right, freedom is equal to self-mastery in the sense that, as a being able to set purposes for myself and pursue them, I am free when my choices are not determined by others.[2] This does not mean that my freedom is unconstrained by the existence of others. Their presence and their actions form part of the context in which I act, and therefore my choices may be limited by what others have chosen to do; they may stand in this particular spot so making it unavailable to me; they may eat that particular apple so I cannot. This notion of self-mastery is to be understood as independence from others in the sense that no individual is entitled to make choices for me *with respect to* my *means*, but others are under no obligation to provide a favourable environment for me to use those means. We shall return to the notion of means below, but for a start we can think of my means as my body and whatever external resources of the world (which I shall now just refer to as 'things', which includes parcels of land) that I have legitimately appropriated. As *my* means, no one else is entitled to make choices with respect to them. As far as the morality of right is concerned, I am a master of my means in the 'negative' sense that no one else is my master with respect to those means.

This notion of self-mastery as independence from the choices of others with respect to my means is not equivalent to the notion of autonomy popular in current political philosophy, which concerns being able to be an author of one's own life, having a range of worthwhile life plans to pursue. Ripstein points out the difference:[3]

Kantian independence is not a feature of the individual person considered in isolation, but of relations between persons. Personal autonomy contrasts with dependence on circumstance. Independence contrasts with dependence on another person, being subject to that person's choice. Independence is relational, and so cannot be predicated of a particular person considered in isolation. The difference is important from two directions. First, in principle a slave with a benevolent master and favorable circumstances could be autonomous in the contemporary technical sense. A slave could never be independent, because what he is permitted to do is always dependent on his master's choice or grace. Second, autonomy

[2] The next two pages draw upon Penner 2010b, 91–4.

[3] Ripstein 2009, 15.

can be compromised by natural or self-inflicted factors no less than by the deeds of others; Kantian independence can only be compromised by the deeds of others. It is not a good to be promoted; it is a constraint on the conduct of others imposed by the fact that each person is entitled to be his or her own master.

As Ripstein says:[4]

The idea of independence carries the justificatory burden of the entire argument, from the prohibition of personal injury, through the minutiae of property and contract law, on to the details of the constitutional separation of powers. Kant argues that these norms and institutions do more than enhance the prospects for independence: they provide the only possible way in which a plurality of persons can interact on terms of equal freedom. Kant's concern is not with how people should interact, as a matter of ethics, but with how they can be forced to interact, as a matter of right.

Ganesh helpfully describes the relation between these two realms of morality, 'right' or 'justice' on one hand, and 'ethics' or 'virtue' on the other, both in terms of the relations between individuals and those between nations:[5]

[T]he sole principle structuring right is the idea of 'external freedom'; that is, the ability to make choices with the means at your disposal in a manner compatible with a like ability on the part of all other persons to do the same. In contrast to virtue, all that is needed to fulfill duties of right is compliance with forms of interaction compatible with all persons making choices for themselves using the means they rightfully have. Whether or not the substance of a choice is ethically commendable is a separate and subsequent question. This why the Doctrine of Right comes before the Doctrine of Virtue: for Kant, one must first envisage the conditions under which freedom is assured for all persons forever—peace. Only then can we begin to talk about how to be a good person, because unless you are free, your choices are not yours to be praised or blamed for. This basic idea is illustrated by the remark that cosmopolitan right is simply the 'rational idea of a peaceful, even if not friendly, thoroughgoing community of all nations on the earth....' Peace is made between enemies, not friends. Afterward,

[4] Ripstein 2009, 14.

[5] Ganesh 2018, 163 (footnotes omitted).

they may go on to become friends, or they may not. Only after peace is conceived of is it worthwhile or even possible to think about friendliness, civility, or other supererogatory social graces between nations. Justice is the helpmate to virtue, not the other way round.

For Kant the law and the state concern relations of right, and right concerns that behaviour that can legitimately be coerced.[6] To have a right is to be justified in coercing another to respect one's freedom, one's self-mastery. The only purpose of the state is to provide the conditions in which rights can be made actual by being systematically, coercively, enforced.

8.2.1.1 The innate right of humanity In the state of nature, the notional or theoretical situation of individuals considered outside of the 'civil condition', that is, without there being in place the institutions of a right-enforcing state with legislative, executive, and judicial organs, the only indisputable right that we have is what Kant calls our 'innate right of humanity', the right every person has to be and to act as a self-directing creature. As Ripstein and Weinrib[7] both explicate the point, this is essentially equivalent to your right to your body, because your body *is you* to the extent that your capacity to set and carry out your purposes is concerned, and you are your body in the sense of the way that others' actions may impinge upon you as a purpose-setting and purpose-pursuing being.

Innate right is innate in two senses. We have already noticed the first: that the duty it imposes is seen to be conceptually necessary as soon as the (embodied) nature of my capacity for freedom is appreciated. It is innate, secondly, in that it is non-contingent. It comes into being for me if and when I do, and lapses on my death. It is not something that I acquire or can lose. So long as I exist, it does.[8]

[6] This is perhaps the most significant distinction between the morality of right, whose duties can be coercively enforced, and duties of virtue, which cannot, because the idea of coercing someone's will so as to bring their will in line with a good will is incoherent—a coerced will, that is, one reflecting external considerations not the person's own, such as a threat of coercion, cannot be a person's genuine will. In this respect will is like reason—there is no external coercion that could make someone actually believe that 2+2=5.

[7] Ripstein 2009, 40–2; Weinrib 2002–03, 804.

[8] This is not quite right, in so far as my right to my reputation, 'my good name', which is part of innate right, survives me. See Kant 1996 [1797], 73/6:291, 76–7/6:29. (References to Kant's *Metaphysics of Morals* will be to the page numbers of Gregor's 1996 edition, then to the AK pagination, for example: 73/6:291.) I thank Aravind Ganesh for bringing this point to my attention.

Innate right has several elements, but for our purposes here the relevant element concerns the right to the 'physicality' of our embodied nature. For Kant this aspect of innate right is the right of our embodied selves to occupy the space they actually occupy, no more and no less, and so innate right imposes a duty upon all others not to invade this space. Innate right prohibits not only our very bodies from interference, but as a collateral effect, protects our possession of those things that are actually within our grasp: innate right requires not only that you refrain from poking me in the eye, but also that you refrain from prising the apple from my grasp because in doing so you would invade the bubble of space that my body occupies. It is worth dwelling for moment on how radically austere this innate right to my body is.

As briefly alluded to above, the Kantian notion of right depends upon a clear conceptual distinction between acts which amount to the violation of a right, and acts which merely change the context in which a right-holder operates. The distinction may be empirically difficult to apply. A good example of the way this distinction arose and was dealt with in the common law concerned the development of the action of 'trespass on the case'. To use an old example,[9] if I throw a log at you, that is a trespass. But if I throw a log into the road which you later trip over, the law is faced with a question. Have I done something wrong, or have I merely changed the context in which you operate? In my defence, why can I not say you should just be more careful when you are out walking?[10] So trespass on the case concerned making fine distinctions between acts which violate another's rights and those which merely change the context in which the right-holder operates and, as we know, the current law of negligence has roughly drawn the line by settling on the idea that I am liable for those indirect injuries which arise as the result of the materialization of a risk I have 'unreasonably' created.

The importance of this distinction for present purposes is that in Kant's state of nature innate right only minimally works to secure our bodily right, in the sense of being free from the choices of others with respect to our bodies. On Ripstein's interpretation, in Kant's state of nature a wrong vis-à-vis another's body only occurs when a person

[9] *Reynolds v Clerk* (1725) 8 Mod. 272, 276, cited by Merrill 1985, 27–8.

[10] As late as 1880 Bramwell was reported as saying: 'If it was too dark for the man to see, he had no business to go there. If it was light enough for him to see, he had no business to stumble over the obstacle.' Baker 2002, 417.

actually pierces or physically impresses himself upon the surface of someone's body, because the principles of right as regards persons is conceived spatially.[11] Doing anything else merely changes the context in which the innate right-holder operates. Thus, in a state of nature it would appear that innate right only protects us from the *trespasses* of others—there is no notion of something like 'trespass on the case'.[12] So, for example, there is no violation of your innate right if I build a high, unscalable wall around you whilst you sleep, so that you later die of thirst or starvation.[13] Arguably, I could also lift and carry the bed on which you sleep and settle it gently in a river so it sinks and you drown. Whether I do wrong in doing this turns on the correct interpretation of Kant's claim that a person has a right to be where he is, 'where nature or chance, (*apart from their will*), has placed him'.[14] It might mean the coordinates in space that your body actually occupies, or just *some* space, and I only do wrong if I don't pierce or impress upon the actual bubble of your bodily surface. So long as I act 'indirectly' in this sort of way, I can make whatever choices with respect to your bodily means that I want. In that respect you are distinctly *not* 'not subject to any number of choices I might make with respect to your means'. I am not a good enough Kant scholar to understand precisely why Kant thinks that in the state of nature one's rights to one's bodily means is restricted in this way. I would only reiterate that if the very nature of a right is that it guarantees independence from the choices of others with regard to the subject matter of the right, then innate right does not secure that independence.

I should mention that this is not the only way to interpret Kant's account of innate right in so far as it relates to our bodies. Ganesh[15] suggests that 'my unscalable wall' and 'bed in the river' examples are wrong, for Ganesh reads Kant's claim that a person has a right to be where he is, 'where nature or chance, (*apart from his will)*, has placed him', must encompass two consequential rights. The first is a right to remain where one is, so one cannot be moved in the bed example; otherwise a person would have to be in constant motion. The second disposes of the unscalable wall example. If you can't be put in motion

[11] Ripstein 2009, 12.

[12] cf. Brudner 2013, 276–8.

[13] Although this is not an example discussed by Ripstein in his published work, he has acknowledged in private conversation that this example reflects the character of innate right.

[14] Kant 1996 [1797], 50/6:262 (my italics).

[15] Aravind Ganesh, private correspondence.

forever, neither can you be rendered immobile. As such, innate right also includes the right to move from one spot to another. Therefore, for Ganesh, building an unscalable wall around me does violate my innate right in my person, because it subjects all possible locations of my body to your unilateral choice. I would be entitled to resist this with force in a state of nature. In support of this reading Ganesh points out that Kant never mentions physical integrity in the 'bubble of space' sense—a sensible reading would frame our right to our bodies emphasizing that we are to be free of the choices of others with respect to it. Perhaps, but Ganesh seems to neglect whatever Kant meant by 'apart from his will' in the crucial passage, since on Ganesh's reading innate right includes a right to a person to move freely *by his own will.*

In any case, I used these examples primarily to show that there is a problem with finding a ground in innate right for indirect wrongs, trespass on the case-like wrongs. Ganesh admits that having rights to remain in place and not to be prevented from moving—essentially a right of voluntary movement—does not itself provide any way of getting to these indirect wrongs, like the log thrown into the road example.[16]

8.2.1.2 Acquired rights Beyond innate right, I may also acquire further rights in the state of nature. These rights, which Kant calls, naturally enough, 'acquired rights', are of three kinds: property rights (rights to tangible things); rights in or to others acquired through the formation of contracts; and rights in or to others arising because of relations of status, those of husband and wife, parent and child, and master and servant.[17]

A property right is a right in a thing which continues even though I am not in actual physical possession of it. Innate right protects my possession of the location I physically occupy, and so the mushrooms in

[16] In private correspondence Ganesh suggests that there would be no possibility of the wrong of negligent injury to one's body in the state of nature, because negligence is a violation of a kind of means akin to property rights, and one does not have property in one's body. Instead, negligent bodily harm becomes actionable only if we 'commodify' ourselves by entry into the rightful condition. The idea might be akin to the conception under Roman law, whereby a free person has no 'direct' Aquilian claim for negligent harm to the body, but instead must claim 'indirectly' under the *actio legis utilis Aquiliae*, which involves joining one's paterfamilias and claiming that by negligently harming your person, the wrongdoer violated your father's 'property-like' right in you. For an differenc characterization of the distinct normative bases of trespass and 'negligence', see Brudner 2013, ch. 6.

[17] See Kant 1996 [1797], 47–68/6:258–6:287.

my hand. The right to property protects the mushrooms I have sautéed when I set them down and start whisking the eggs for my omelette. Kant provides a kind of 'negative' justification for property rights: any normative regime which banned *in limine* my right to use something as mine (and your identical right to use something as yours) would sterilize a perfectly sensible way in which persons could set and pursue plans, turning such things into *res nullius*.[18] Weinrib puts the point in terms of 'usability'.[19]

Usability lies at the heart of the Kantian account of ownership. A regime of equal reciprocal freedom limits one person's action by the freedom of another. A thing, however, is devoid of freedom, and therefore imposes no limit on the action of the person using it. If this were not the case, then a person's action would be restricted by things rather than by the freedom of others. This would produce the self-contradictory situation in which something usable could not be put to use, even if using a thing were consistent with everyone's freedom and thus wronged no one.

For Kant, then, your rights are relational and negative; they concern the actions of others, prohibiting their acting so as to interfere with your means by damaging or usurping them, and you do not have any 'positive' rights in your property: no one else is under a duty to assist you in the use of your means, or to provide a favourable environment for their use. Finally, the function of property rights is essentially *allocative*. In order to have a regime of right which makes necessary reference to the concept of a person's own means, we have to know which means are yours and which are mine. That problem needs no solution in the case of the innate right to our bodies, but it does require a solution as regards acquired rights—there must be powers to acquire such rights, most relevantly here, a power to appropriate unowned things.

8.2.2 The 'Provisional' Nature of Acquired Rights outside the Civil Condition and the Assurance Argument

The next feature of the Kantian account has proved the most controversial, and has attracted a lot of concentrated attention from scholars.

[18] Kant 1996 [1797], 41/6:246. Ripstein 2009, 60–4; the same point applies to contractual rights: 'It would be an arbitrary restriction on freedom if a person could not make his person or powers available to others in cooperative activities.' Ripstein 2009, 64

[19] Weinrib 2018, 131 (reference omitted).

Although Kant presents the morality of right, both innate right and acquired right, as being fully *understandable* apart from any consideration of the state or a legal system, for Kant the morality of acquired right does not actually obtain outside the civil condition. We have to be very precise about what 'understandable' means here. First, the morality of right concerns the 'horizontal' relations between individuals, not the 'vertical' relations between individuals and the state. That is why it is 'private', as opposed to 'public' right. The nature of these relations is fully explicable, and fully explicated by Kant, as the necessary normative relations between people, people conceived as centres of rational freedom.

It might then seem to follow that this morality of right obtains in a state of nature, apart from any institution of the civil condition, simply because rationally free individuals are imbued with the capacity to recognize it, be guided by it, and judge acts to be rightful or wrongful in consideration of what it requires. But Kant thinks otherwise. The basic idea is that outside the civil condition, our rights cannot be *guaranteed* in a particular way. Try as individuals might with the best will in the world to observe the morality of right, they can only do so as individuals *unsystematically*. And, so the argument goes, an unsystematic regime of right is no regime of right at all, because it is in the nature of the idea of right, the idea of that branch of morality, that its realization must be systematic; an unsystematic realization of right is not a realization of right at all.

Kant's argument for this position is found in his famous 'assurance' argument.[20] The assurance argument, as expressed by the man himself, is as follows:[21]

When I declare (by word or deed), I will that something external is to be mine, I thereby declare that everyone else is under obligation to refrain from using that object of my choice, an obligation no one would have were it not for this act of mine to establish a right. This claim involves, however, acknowledging that I in turn am under obligation to every other to refrain from using what is externally his; for the obligation here arises from a universal rule having to do with external rightful relations. I am *therefore* not

[20] The next two pages draw on Penner 2010b, 94–6. At 96 I took the assurance argument to be valid for the purposes of the argument at hand. I was not accepting that it was, though I can see that the text might suggest otherwise.

[21] Kant 1996 [1797], 44–5/6:255–6: 256 (emphasis added).

under obligation to leave external objects belonging to others untouched unless everyone provides me with assurance that he will behave in accordance with the same principle with regard to what is mine.

Unfortunately, put this way, the claim that my obligations to others only exist because (note the italicized 'therefore') they assure me that they will respect their obligations to me seems to reflect no notions of morality or right whatsoever. Outside obligations that arise from mutual consent—obviously I have no duty to play chess with you, following the rules, if you have no intention of doing so yourself; what would be the point?—it is never a reason not to comply with a moral obligation that others refuse to comply with it. Two wrongs do not make a right, as they say. And if one had no true obligation to observe some rule, such as the (comprehended but in fact only provisional) 'rule' not to take another's property, then the assurance of others to 'play the game' would not ipso facto impose a duty upon me to do the same. Moral common sense tells us: (1) one wrong never licenses another wrong; (2) my relations with you are rightful or not irrespective of whether the moral relations that obtain between us are being observed in like cases involving third parties; and (3) outside of special contexts like games, contracts, and so on, morality is not a matter either of agreement or assurance. Morality is not *voluntaristic* in this way.[22] There is, obviously, something else going on if whatever Kant was trying to express is to be made sense of.

As elaborated by Weinrib, Ripstein, and Jeremy Waldron,[23] that something else is something like this: in the absence of a neutral authority, to which all must attorn, claims of right, one individual against another, fail to embody the equality of application of the laws necessary to a system of rights.

Ripstein[24] sets out the thought nicely in terms of three defects in the state of nature, and their solution by means of the institution of a legal authority. In the state of nature any claim of right I have can only be taken by others as valid in consequence of a law that applies to all; but

[22] Despite the language in which he frames the assurance argument, Kant elsewhere specifically denies the voluntaristic social contractarian idea that what is required is that everyone voluntarily makes undertakings either to others or to a state in order to create the civil condition: Kant 1974, 65; Kant 1996 [1797], 92–3/6: 315, 95/6: 318.

[23] Weinrib 2002–03, 808–10; Ripstein 2009, ch. 6; Waldron 1996, 1545–64.

[24] Ripstein 2009, ch. 6.

in the state of nature such a claim is unilateral in the sense that I have no authority to lay down the law for anyone else. Secondly, rights are just those norms that can be coercively enforced, so any claim of right is a claim to be able to coerce another. But in the state of nature, by what title does any individual validly enforce the law? Finally, if all of that were not bad enough, the application of any sort of right or norm requires judgement. In this sense, rights are indeterminate, and so the unsystematic enforcement of norms by individuals will lead to inequality in the enforcement of the law; it would be a recipe for the antithesis of justice: like cases would not be decided alike.

The solution is the institution of an impartial legal authority, with the power to legislate, adjudicate, and enforce laws laid down for all. In its guise as a legislator, the authority reflects the united will of the people, an 'omnilateral' will as opposed to the unilateral will of one individual purporting to lay down the law for others. As an adjudicator, the authority resolves the problem of indeterminacy by speaking with a single voice. The resolution does not require the law to be perfectly certain. That is impossible; what the impartial adjudicator obviates is each individual applying the law according to his or her own judgement, which leads to normative chaos even if each individual acts with the best will in the world. Finally, as an executive, the legal authority's enforcement assures all subjects of the law that their rights are equally protected, that is, subject to a regime of enforcement where all are treated equally, that is, from which no individual can excuse herself.

Waldron explains the assurance argument slightly differently, but to similar effect. Again, the essential thought is that no individual is entitled to coerce another to vindicate his or her rights. Rather, 'the paradoxical claim [is] that each person's doing what seems right to him is tantamount to that person's renouncing the concept of right altogether'.[25] The coercive enforcement by individuals of what they honestly and rationally believe are their rights cannot deliver an assurance either to themselves or to anyone else that their rights will actually be observed. Only an omnilateral will can use force in the name of all; a single individual's use of coercion to give effect to rights can only be perceived by the recipient of the force as the expression of a unilateral will.

[25] Waldron 1996, 1536.

Waldron then considers the obvious objection to this way of seeing things:[26]

Not so fast, you might object. Is it not possible for the will of a Kantian individual to be 'omnilateral' if the idea of universalisability disciplines that person's willing? (Isn't that, after all, exactly what judging things from the moral point of view is, according to Kant?) On this objection, it would be wrong to assert that an individual's acting on his own judgment in the state of nature amounts to a unilateral will governing matters that the common will ought to control. Instead, an individual acting on his own moral judgments in the state of nature already invokes universalization and thus transcends his unilateral viewpoint.

A little further on Waldron provides the riposte:[27]

To answer the question, we have to go back to the stubborn point that whatever rosy things we want to say about ... individual 'omnilateralist' thought, we cannot say that [it] will lead different individuals to converge on the same conclusion. The irremovable fact about individual moral reasoning is this: my universalisations are likely to differ from yours; my attempt to take everyone's point of view is likely to lead to a different conclusion from your attempt to take everyone's point of view; ... It is not inappropriate for force to be used to secure justice and right. But the point of using force must be to *assure* people of that to which they have, as a matter of justice, a right. If people use force to secure ends that are contradictory, then they rupture the connection linking force and assurance.

In short, on this reading of the argument, we can understand the insistence upon attorning to an impartial authority, an authority that applies to all, as a requirement that coercive enforcement of rights can only be just if systematic. We must all be playing the same game, not in the sense that the rights enforced are merely conventional, but in the sense that the coercive action cannot amount to the coercive enforcement of *rights* where the possibility, indeed the likelihood, is that a different version of the rights is enforced on each occasion of enforcement. To

[26] ibid., 1558.

[27] ibid., 1560 (italics original). cf. Westphal 2016, 171–2: 'No unilateral will can be entrusted, and so none can be permitted, to enforce principles of justice impartially; whereas "biased enforcement of justice" is oxymoronic.'

the extent that we conceive of justice as an expression of the equality of individuals, this state of affairs would generate the very opposite of equality under the law. It is a matter of equality before the law that our rights be the same. 'Decide like cases alike' is not, then, simply a criterion of legal rationality, but one of political equality.

Martin Stone has advanced a variation of the 'assurance' argument, though he doesn't frame it that way in terms. Stone argues that that aspect of morality which Kant calls 'right' is 'a sub-region of morality, one conceived to be proprietary to law'; and it is contrasted with the realm of virtue.[28]

Stone's basic claim, which is resonant with the explicit assurance argument, is that this area of morality is one which has specific features:

> [I]t is not because of any epistemic gap, but is in the very nature of the case that, in this area of morality, no account can be given, after a certain point, except through authoritative judgment and examples.[29]
>
> ...
>
> First, the precept, 'respect the other's possessions,' is an *a priori* moral precept. Its validity does not depend on any sources, save those (as it were) of God, pure practical reason, and so on. It is a specification of the still more abstract precept, 'give others their due,' external possession being one aspect of this 'dueness'; personal rights, like the right to bodily integrity, being another. Yet, second, the articulation of 'dueness,' being formally subject to conflicting claims, is necessarily mediated by, or structured in terms of, a principle of reasonable reciprocal forbearance; the right of one person must be compatible with the equal (or like) right of others. Third, what is reasonable in such reciprocal relations is, in principle, indeterminate. Morality might tell us *a priori* that we are bound to respect the boundaries of persons and property, but it affords us no way of deducing just what, in various circumstances, those proper boundaries are. Hence, the content of such rights must be spelled out through applicative judgments that are not deductively accessible. Fourth, such judgements cannot, consistently with the reciprocal form of right, be laid down privately: That would amount to a merely unilateral determination of right, the subjection of one person to the choice of another. So the realization of a regime of reciprocal right requires public sources, as grounds for private judgements, and public procedures where private judgements

[28] Stone 2011, 319.
[29] ibid., 333 (footnotes omitted).

conflict. In more familiar terms, 'do not take what belongs to another' finds application only by way of its articulation in a system of law. That is, it is to the law that we must resort to find out what exactly is required by respect for persons and their possessions.[30]

For Stone, this shows that private law is not a kind of 'applied ethics', or an applied moral theory. In the region of private right, morality is inseparable from law, because the judgment-applying function of the law is the only way we can access the relevant moral reality.[31]

It is important to notice what the assurance argument, on any of its variants, does not entail. The fact that enforceable property rights do not exist in the state of nature, and are dependent for their very existence on entry into the civil condition, does not make them into a part of public law, whereby the state ipso facto acquires rights in the property of its subjects, to redistribute them or in any other way take advantage of them.[32] The assurance argument, if valid, does not have as a consequence the transformation of property rights into a kind of public right, or a right to the state's largesse in granting rights to resources to individuals, rights that might be subject to modification in view of the state's purposes. Although only assured by a neutral public authority, property rights remain firmly in the realm of private right.[33]

Kant concludes that in the absence of a law-giving, law-enforcing state, that is, in the state of nature, acquired rights are 'provisional'. We appreciate the sense of these rights, but because of the lack of guaranteed, omnilateral application, they are 'not real', not real in the sense they are not really rightful.

In view of all of this, Kant holds that individuals are under a positive duty to enter into a civil condition in order to establish fully a regime of right including, of course, property rights.[34]

[30] ibid., 336–7. 'Judg(e)ment' is spelt differently in these two passages.

[31] ibid., 341. cf. Brudner 2013, 45–51.

[32] See Waldron 1996, 1566; Ripstein 2009, 154–5. For contrary views, which space precludes me from pursuing here, see Westphal 2016, 166; Brudner 2013, ch. 2.

[33] This assertion is vigorously contested by Brudner, 2013, ch. 2, in particular 73–87, on Kantian textual grounds. On Brudner's understanding of the omnilateral legislative and adjudicative will, which is an institution of public law, property rights and contractual rights are provisional in the sense of merely being presumptive, and yield to the omnilateral will whenever the omnilateral will regards them as outweighed by other public law considerations.

[34] Kant 1996 [1797], 86/6:307–8.

There are two last parts of the Kantian picture of rights in a state of nature I must set out. The first concerns the acquisition of property rights. Kant treats this as a specific case of the assurance problem.[35] According to Kant, when I appropriate property I impose a duty on all others not to interfere with the thing I have just appropriated and, so the argument goes, this would amount to my determining the rights of others. In the same way as enforcing rights outside the civil condition amounts to my 'laying down the law' to others, appropriating property is laying down the law in the sense of my unilaterally fixing everyone else's duties with respect to this particular thing. So any rightful power to appropriate property is only conceivable as one which is granted to all subjects of the law by way of legislation by the state.

The second part of the picture is the obligation to enter into the civil condition. Kant holds that those who cannot avoid coming into contact with others are obliged to enter the civil condition, and they 'do wrong in the highest degree by willing to be and to remain in a condition that is not rightful.'[36]

Summing up: the reality of the morality of right depends upon three factors 'of relation', so to speak: our relation to ourselves, our relation to the external world, and our relation to others. First, we are embodied creatures. Second, as Weinrib points out above, things cannot be made 'res nullius' as a matter of principle; so long as unilateral appropriation can be made rightful, things must be appropriable; otherwise things, which have no purposes or agency that could conflict with our own, would block our own agency. Third, in certain circumstances we will have to run into each other, and therefore cannot maintain our freedom, our independence from the choices of others, just by keeping our distance from them. When we can keep our distance from others, we can ensure that there is no *empirical* possibility that we could interfere with their means.

[35] Arie Rosen has suggested to me that because Kant frames his assurance argument in terms of rights to external things, it is not merely a specific case of the assurance problem, but its source, as it were. Another way of putting this is to say that it is the problem of property rights which leads to the problem of life outside the civil condition, and the civil condition, solving the assurance problem, solves the problem of property rights. It seems to me, however, that for Kant all acquired rights face the same assurance problem—with regards to contractual rights, Kant frames the problem in terms of the basis upon which my statements can bind me (Kant 1996 [1797], 30–1/6:238), though I agree the problem is more vivid for property rights in things just because these are rights in rem.

[36] Kant 1996 [1797], 86/6:308.

Incidentally, regarding this third factor of relation, there is nothing in Kant's account of private right itself, so far as I can see, to suggest that that there is any ground for *preferring* the civil condition to the empirical state of affairs in which we maintain our independence by keeping our distance from each other. We can, however, manufacture a Kantian reason to prefer the civil condition, which is that one might say that the resources of the world are not just material things, but also other people, who we can take into our means by entering into contractual relations with them.[37] In order to acquire this form of acquired right one will necessarily need to come into contact with others, and so the civil condition generally expands the scope of our possible means, for only in the civil condition can we take other people's means into our own.[38] On the other hand, there is a countervailing Kantian consideration. The possibility of taking other people into our means opens up not just an *empirical* possibility of exploitation, but its *conceptual* possibility; so without contract, there can be no fraud, for instance. So entering the civil condition not only expands the grounds of right, in terms of expanding what might be our rightful means, but correlatively expands the grounds of wrong. I don't see anything in the Doctrine of Right to help us ponder this sort of thought. In any case where, because of the force of empirical circumstances, we cannot help running into each other we must enter the civil condition. Plausibly, that is the empirical state we occupy, so keeping our distance is not an option. But it would seem that there could be a choice here about what laws we install. It seems to me to be equally available for a state just to install a regime of tort law, ensuring that others don't damage or usurp our bodies and our acquired rights to things, but not to install a law of contract at all.[39] This would amount to a world of exclusive, usufructory property rights, in which we would need a power to first acquire things, and rules about abandonment, but we would have no need for a power to transfer or a power to license. Arguably, this is the normative shape of the morality of right that, based upon certain of

[37] On contractual rights as 'means', see Ripstein 2009, ch. 5, especially at 109, 124, 127–8, 134.

[38] The fact that we cannot take others into our means unilaterally, as we can with material things, is not to the point.

[39] There is a third kind of acquired right, one of status, which is pretty much inescapable, given the relations between parents and children, but installing this right has no bearing upon whether we install a regime of contract.

Kant's ideas in the Doctrine of Right, Kant might have found to be the case in the state of nature, as we shall see at 8.3.1 below.

Finally, the Kantian claims, on the basis of the assurance argument, that right *cannot be implemented in any way that reflects right* outside a civil condition, *despite our understanding of right and wrong outside the civil condition*. So it would seem that no genuinely moral principles can be cited by which we could actually judge our or someone else's action outside the civil condition. So this is not the Lockean claim that a civil condition, or entry into a state, better *empirically* protects or gives effect to our moral rights. It is the claim that justifications of right, of moral right, of any kind, are simply *conceptually* unavailable to us outside the civil condition. Now this is a very strong claim, under which the Kantian holds that outside the civil condition, we live in a lawless state. 'Lawless' does not mean the absence of a legal system—what it means is that the moral law, in so far as we are discussing the morality of right, that morality which secures our freedom from the choices of others with respect to our means, *has no claim upon us*, except as regards the one innate right of humanity. At first glance this would seem absurd, for it essentially denies those living outside the civil condition of an aspect of their *rationality*, that is, their ability to choose and act in reference to what the morality of right requires of them. Nevertheless, this is Kant's view, and others have ably tried to defend it. At 8.4.1 I shall argue that these defences are unsustainable.

But first let me pause to point out those principles of right that Kant's account elucidates and with which I agree. First, I agree that the structure of private right is relational and 'negative' in the sense explained above. I also endorse Ganesh's claim that, for the reasons he gives, the morality of right is prior to the morality of virtue or ethics. And third, I accept the point that applying the morality of right requires judgment in actual cases.

8.3 'Internal' Criticisms of the Kantian Account

I now set out my criticisms of the Kantian account. These criticisms aim to be 'internal' in the sense that they seem to point out difficulties in making the Kantian account hang together in a persuasive fashion.

In other words, they aim to show that certain Kantian arguments do not work on their own terms, or involve contradictions.

8.3.1 Kant's Claim about Omnilateral Authorization for Acquiring Rights to Unowned Things Neglects his own Distinction between Interfering with the Means of Others and Merely Changing the Context in which They Operate

This criticism is straightforward and we owe it to Sage.[40] The idea is disarmingly simple. Recall the distinction between interfering with the choices of others with respect to their own means, and merely changing the context in which they operate. The Kantian claim is that by initially acquiring an unowned thing, I impose a new duty on all others, a duty not to interfere with that thing because I have taken it into my means. But on what basis, by doing so, have I interfered with the relational nature of Kantian right? On what basis do you found your claim that I should not have taken it? Clearly, I have done you no *wrong* by imposing this duty upon you, so that cannot be the explanation. That is, prior to a thing's acquisition by someone, no one has a *right* to it. That simply follows from the fact that it is unowned. So how can the non-owner's complaint be framed?

Well, it would seem that the only way that the claim can be made out is to claim that I have removed a possible object of your choice from the environment that we share. I have made a choice that restricts yours. But this sort of restriction is something that Kantian right is rightly blind to. For this restriction is nothing more than changing the context in which you operate—and you have no Kantian right that others cannot change that context. So, as Sage points out, the complaint has no Kantian basis.

But hold on, you may say, the one thing we know for sure is that by taking some thing up as my means, I exercise a normative power which creates a new duty upon you not to interfere with it. And that is equivalent to my laying down the law for you. However, the notion of a 'new duty' here is problematic.

The problem arises in this way. If we frame the duty not to interfere with the property of others as a series of duties we owe to any individual with respect to each item of their property, then it follows that a new duty arises each time someone appropriates anything. In our

[40] Sage 2012, 130–6; Sage 2018; see also Westphal 2016, 164–5, 176.

discussion of the Hohfeldian multitality thesis, HMP, in Chapter 5 we noted some problematic features of this concept of rights in rem. But the one pertinent here is the 'individuation' problem. If we take the 'new duty' view to be actually, not just fancifully, true of the nature of property rights, then we obscure the nature of BPrN as a general norm which itself defines our rights in property (as regards the duty not to interfere with the property of others). For the most part, the norm doesn't require determining how many things you own when you own a basket of apples or a pound of salt. In many contexts the very inquiry would be senseless.[41] Furthermore, as we have seen BPrN embodies the negative and relational form of Kantian private right, but it doesn't itself fluctuate as particular people are born or die or as things are appropriated, destroyed, and so on. It would seem then that the power to appropriate lies, in a sense, *within* BPrN, for properly formulated BPrN, states: Do not interfere with the property that has been appropriated by others.

More importantly, however, reflecting as it does the negative and relational nature of property rights, a Kantian cannot just ignore this conception of BPrN and property rights, and unilaterally choose the one-by-one duty formulation necessary to found the 'laying down the law for me by imposing a new duty upon me' complaint. That choice has to be motivated. And as Sage shows perfectly well, on Kant's own terms with respect to his distinction between the violation of rights and the mere alteration of the context in which a person operates, it is not motivated on Kant's own conception of freedom; indeed Kant's own conception of freedom militates against it.

Of course, Sage's solution to a problem that Kant seems to have created for himself won't work if there is some genuine Kantian version of the common ownership of the earth. If that is the situation that prevails in the state of nature, then it is certainly arguable that any appropriation by any individual would need some sort of sanction by everyone else, and this sanction might possibly only be provided by the state's legislating some sort of power to do so. For his part

[41] When you steal a match from my box of twenty matches, you steal one match. But if you steal the whole box, the law doesn't sit down and puzzle over whether you have stolen one thing, a box of matches, or twenty-one things, the individual matches and the box. Only a crazed Hohfeldian mutitality-minded prosecutor would proffer twenty-one counts of theft in such a case.

Ganesh denies that property is available for appropriation on just these grounds:[42]

For Kant, land before original acquisition is not *res nullius*: others have just as good a claim to it, which cannot be extinguished by unilateral occupation or specification. If you try to exclude others from a plot of land on the basis that you have labored on it and grown enough apples to feed them, they may justifiably reply that they care not for apples, and—even if they did—that it was not your place to decide that they will have apples.

This is a somewhat curious passage. In the first place, the passage in the Doctrine of Right Ganesh cites[43] does not to my mind support the claim that land before original acquisition is not '*res nullius*' in one of the senses of '*res nullius*', that is, not presently unowned, that is, communally owned in some way; in this sense '*res nullius*' means unavailable for appropriation because it has already been in some sense rightfully occupied. But as we have seen, the concept of *res nullius* for Kant is the not the idea that a thing is somehow owned in common by all persons, so unavailable for appropriation by someone else, but the idea that a thing *could not come to be owned ever by anyone*. Second, the second sentence, whilst correct, is irrelevant to the justice of first acquisition. All that matters for first acquisition is that you get to the unowned thing first and take it into your possession, however that is done with respect to the kind of thing that is in question. You don't have to justify your first acquisition to others in any way, and so whether or not they accept some such Lockean justification concerning your labour or some welfarist argument about how your appropriation might benefit them is entirely irrelevant on the Kantian picture. The only objection to your appropriation of this thing that a person is entitled to make is that it was *his already*. This is the respect in which Ripstein depicts Kant's theory of acquisition as 'boring'.[44] Taking possession of something is all that is required—one needs no further fussy theory about labour or added value or anything else.

One final point. Sage rightly points out that this complaint generalizes to all other acquired rights,[45] and to all other cases where a

[42] Ganesh 2018, 182 (footnote omitted).
[43] ibid., 2018, 182, fn 122, citing Kant 1996 [1797], 52–3/6:265.
[44] Ripstein 2009, 90.
[45] A similar point is made by Brudner 2013, 69–70.

person merely changes the application of the innate right they clearly have by changing their own location. As to the former, if I hire Fred as my full-time employee, I have denied you the possible choice of doing the same, and for good measure, if right is spelled out to regard inducing the breach of another contract as a tort, then by making this contract with Fred I do create a duty in all others. As to my innate right, when I choose to stand in this spot I also remove from you a possible object of choice, so though I don't lay down a new law on the assumption that whilst my innate right is one right that applies to me wherever I happen to be, my liberty to move around has the ongoing effect of denying you possible objects of choice—to stand in the places that I do. It follows, then, that not only do all the powers to acquire acquired rights need to be legislated, but so also does innate right itself, which is the one right Kant clearly claims to need no legislation; that is one of the senses in which the right is *innate*. Maybe, for a revisionist Kantian, they all do require legislation. But if that is so, then it would seem that Ganesh is right and there really is a kind of common ownership idea working here, and importantly, not only common ownership of the earth *but of all people in it*, for on the Kantian picture of private right, other people just are nothing more than possible means for me, possible objects of my choice, though unlike things they are not subject to my unilateral choice. But just because the acquisition by contract of your performance as part of my means requires agreement between you and me, that does not make the acquisition *qua* acquisition any different. Acquisition of any kind alters the range of possible objects of choice for everyone else.

8.3.2 Usufructory Right

The last example concerning innate right reveals something else that is interesting. It shows us that the rights to things we recognize need not be full property rights of the kind Kant defends. What kind of right is it that I have as regards my liberty to move about, in so far as it protects my right to a location in space? It would seem that this is a kind of usufructory right.

A usufructory right[46] has the following features: it is a kind of right of occupation that is limited by the *actual* uses a person is making of

[46] 'Usufructory right' as it is understood in the philosophical literature, not 'usufruct' as understood in civilian legal systems. For a general introduction to use or usufructory rights, see Penner 1997c, 68–9. cf. Westphal 1997, 151–2; Westphal 2016, 146–9.

some thing. It gives no title, or right, that is unlimited in time; the right to the thing in question lasts only so long as that person is using it. Second, it gives the right-holder no right to transfer the right of use once she has finished using it. Finally, it is not in principle exclusive. Two or more people can make use of a thing so long as no prior use by the first user is interfered with. In so far, then, that the right to one's location is protected by innate right, the right has a usufructory, not a 'proprietary' character, where by 'proprietary' I mean a right that is acquired and has the negative, relational character of property rights, under which the individual uses one might make of something have no bearing on the existence or the quality of the right. This latter is clearly the kind of right Kant understands rights to things to be.

If this is correct then Kant's implicit denial of a usufructory right to things seems to have something of the quality of fiat. Ripstein frames Kant's objection to usufructory rights in this way:[47]

> Kant argues that it would be inconsistent with right if usable things could not be rightfully used. The ability to use things for your purposes could be satisfied through a system of *usufruct*, in which things are borrowed from a common pool for particular uses. However, because of the way Kant conceives of the relation between having means and setting ends, permissibly using things is not enough to extend your freedom; it would merely enable you to succeed at some particular purpose or other. Freedom requires that you be able to have usable things fully at your disposal, to use as you see fit, and so to decide which purposes to pursue with them, subject only to such constraints imposed by the entitlement of others to use whatever usable things *they* have. Any other arrangement would subject your ability to set your own ends to the choice of others, since they would be entitled to veto any particular use you wished to make of things other than your body.

There seems to me to be a flaw in this argument to the extent that it amounts to an argument, rather than merely a statement of what Kant asserts. The last sentence simply does not follow from the preceding ones. Usufructory right does allow a person to have things available to her '*fully at her disposal*'. The difference between usufructory right and

[47] Ripstein 2009, 19.

property right is simply the boundary each draws on what is available and what is not. Under usufructory right, something is available to you so long as it is not actually being used by another, or your proposed use of it does not interfere with theirs. So it is simply false that a system of usufruct 'would subject your ability to set your own ends to the choice of others, since they would be entitled to veto any particular use you wished to make of things other than your body'. Indeed, a system of usufruct is *less* restrictive of rights than property is. Under either system, your freedom is limited by the choices of others, in the former by their choice to use something not being used, to that extent making it unavailable to you, in the latter by their choice to appropriate it, making it *entirely* and *permanently* unavailable to you. Later in the book Ripstein says this:[48]

> Perhaps a consistent theory of the temporary right to use a thing could be made to depend on acquiring it by using it. The theory of property cannot.

That is true. Usufruct and property are different kinds of rights. Kant is wedded to the idea that rights to things should be property rights. But as far as I can tell it is only by stipulation that this is required by the underlying concern to maximize freedom conceived as independence of the choices of others with respect to the means that are available to you and which you can bring within your purposes.

Let us also notice that the idea of a usufructory right is not ruled out by Kant's notion of 'intelligible' possession, rather the opposite—it seems prima facie to counsel a system of usufruct, not property. For Kant, intelligible possession is what explains why one has a right to some thing when it lies outside one's grasp, outside one's actual, 'empirical' or 'phenomenal' possession, as with the sautéed mushrooms one sets down before turning to the rest of the omelette preparation.

Nothing in the nature of intelligible possession per se suggests the right need be an exclusive, time-unlimited right, under which appropriation is necessarily intended to lead to permanent, exclusionary, possession. Kant seems to think there are only two options here: (1) a right based on innate right which is not so much a right of possession but a right to bodily enclose a thing, for example by grasping it; and

[48] Ripstein 2009, 104.

(2) a 'full-blown' property right which is necessarily unlimited. But in fact 'intelligible possession' itself suggests otherwise. Modelled on the notion of possession itself, even intelligible possession imports no requirement that the right it secures be permanent and entirely exclusionary. It suggests rather the opposite—it is only yours even as a matter of intelligible possession in so far as you are actually, currently making some 'intelligible' connection or choice with respect to the thing, for example, in choosing to sauté the mushrooms to use in an omelette. To put the point most strongly, recognizing A's intelligible possession *just is* the recognition of A's agency in respect of the mushrooms even though they are not in her immediate physical ('empirical') possession. One appreciates or cognizes that when A set the mushrooms down she did not abandon them—they continue to figure in her apparent plan to make an omelette. So intelligible possession as an idea is not only an *inadequate* basis for exclusive, permanent property rights—trading on the notion of possession it actually points against them, for possessing something as an agent is only ever a manifestation of *actual choice* with respect to some thing, to bring it within one's *means* for some purpose or other, not all possibility of choice.

I shall defend later in this chapter the idea that the only rights to things we are generally *morally* entitled to (apart from any legally instituted permanent, exclusive property rights when, in fact, their legal institution turns on good moral reasons) are usufructory rights.[49]

[49] I must now notice two other claims about Kantian use or usufructory rights. Westphal (Westphal 1997) argues, based upon a fine-grained analysis of Kant's argument for property rights in the Doctrine of Right, that the most Kant can claim is that only usufructory rights are justified in the state of nature, and he fails to succeed even in doing that. Not being a Kant scholar myself, I am unable to say whether all of his arguments work. I am, of course, happy to welcome whatever support he provides for the position I have set out in the text. But a couple of further points. Westphal bases part of his argument on a BOR-like interpretation of Honore 1961 (Westphal 1997, 146–9, 158–9). Thus to the extent that he faults Kant for failing to see that 'eigentum', or genuine property rights, can have an integrated structure, like the tripartite nature of title set out in Chapter 1, I would disagree. Secondly, Westphal defends his claim about the justification of usufructory right not by drawing upon Kant's discussion in the Doctrine of Right, but by drawing upon other Kantian sources, in particular invoking a particular 'universalizability' test, a 'Contradition in Conception' test (Westphal 1997, 165–82). By contrast, my own view aims at what I think is the best Kantian conception of a private right to things, that is, usufructory right, referencing only what Kant says in the Doctrine of Right. In this Katz 2011 is, I think, an ally. At 137–42 she argues convincingly that the preservation of an individual's independent capacity for choice requires no more than that a first appropriator is given priority in determining the use of the appropriated thing, a kind of usufructory right, in my view; see 8.5.

8.3.3 The Problematic Characterization of our Right to our Bodies under the Innate Right of Humanity

The point here is a simple one, to which I have already adverted in 8.2.1.1. Although innate right is meant to continue in force after entry into the civil condition, it is not clear how it is, or becomes, part of a general structure of private right in which my body becomes part of my means, along with my property, that is subject to a BPrN-like norm that protects it, particularly against negligent injury.

Kant, quite rightly, wants to deny that our relation to our bodies is a kind of property relationship, that our bodies are something we use in the way we use our property. But this nature of our being embodied—that our agency and setting purposes for ourselves is only realized through the actions of our bodies—is translated into Kant's 'physicality' element of innate right, the right to be where we stand. That is all fine and good if the concern is just with the embodied nature of our agency. It is clearly true that if others did no wrong if they could by any means extinguish our very physical presence on the earth then human agency per se could not have any rightful existence. On this view of the right to our bodies, as we saw in 8.2.1.1 only direct trespasses to the body count as wrongs. And if *this right* is the one which is made secure by entry into the civil condition, then the civil condition would itself be required to institute a right of this form—it would mean not only that the law would be required to institute a right against trespass to the person; it would also mean that the law would be barred from instituting a right not to be negligently injured. It would be barred from developing a law of negligence in so far as persons' bodies were concerned. In short, this formulation of innate right, a right to be merely physically present in the world of others, makes no room for the negative and relational character of a right to our bodies as a proper element of our 'means'.

Consider again Kant's conception of 'means'. Kant wants to end up in a place where the negative and relational right that others do not make choices with respect to our means is a structurally identical right in so far as our rights to our bodies and our rights to our property is concerned.[50] BPrN, in other words, should be mirrored by a similar norm reflecting our permanent, exclusive, right to our bodies. In particular, indirect destruction, which protects property rights through

[50] Ripstein makes much of this structural similarity; Ripstein 2013, 175–6.

the laws of negligence, should be mirrored by a duty not to negligently injure the bodies of others.

Even though our bodies are the site of our agency for ourselves *and others*, in setting out our innate right to humanity in so far as it is a right to our bodies, Kant seems to ignore the 'and others' aspect of this. That is, nothing of our potential agency 'in the world' vis-à-vis others seems to be relevant for anyone's behaviour in so far as innate right is concerned. We are, on this construction of innate right, simply movable vessels whose only innate connection to the world is to the physical space we occupy.[51] Now why is that, and where is the argument for that thought? It depends on focusing upon the 'internal' aspect of our bodily agency, our relation to our bodies as the sites of our agency, whilst ignoring the externality of our agency, its effects in the world beyond our bodies. We are not just embodied, but have the power of motion, and when we move intentionally one can, I think, say with perfect Kantian propriety, that I have made a choice with respect to my means,[52] and if someone blocks my way that could in principle be an interference with such a choice. For Kant, however, blocking someone in the state of nature is fine; we simply cannot move them ourselves. The suggestion here is that Kant stipulatively restricts the rights that derive from our embodiment in the state of nature to the right to our physical bubble in space. Now I suppose a Kantian could reply in this way: the innate right of humanity, though founded in the fact of our embodiment, is not really a right to our body as part of our means, about which we should be independent of the choices of others. It is *just* a right to our location, because only by having *some* location in space can I be at all. But if our embodiment per se does not entail that our body constitutes, along with our acquired rights, one of our means as regards others, then how are we to understand where this relation of ourselves to our bodies, such that they *do* form part of our means *in the civil condition*, come from? It is not an innate relation. The structure of innate right in the state of nature denies that. But it is not an acquired right either. So in the state of nature our body is not conceived of as a means, but entry into the civil condition magically makes it so without

[51] This thought is bolstered by our previous thought that the only wrong that one person can do vis-à-vis another's body is trespass, to which the coercive right to enforce one's rights is to physically interfere with the 'agressor'. Ripstein 2009, 176–81.

[52] Which includes here taking part of the world, the location I move to, as also part of my means, in the same way I do when I pick up an apple.

explanation or justification. I suppose the Kantian could say that for Kant, innate right is not really part of 'private' right at all, or not part of private right in the same way that our bodies as 'means' for others is. Private right concerns our means, and for private right it is just understood that our means includes our bodies as well as our acquired rights. Innate right is something entirely different. But that, of course, just raises another problem, which is what that different 'realm' of right is. But whatever the answer to that is, we still haven't anything to help us to locate a source in Kant for the claim that once we enter the civil condition our right to our bodies is now to be conceived as an element of our means, protected by a BPrN-like norm.

8.3.4 The Structural Distinctions between Innate Right and Acquired Rights Does not Sustain the Imperfect Right/Provisional Right Distinction

As we have seen, for Kant there is no moral reality to our acquired rights outside the civil condition because the assurance argument tells us so.[53] The basic idea, you will recall, is that in the absence of an 'omnilateral' will that systematically enforces with coercion the rights that we have, individuals can only apply what right requires in the way that they see it. It would seem, at first glance, that exactly the same problem arises with respect to innate right, the right to coercively enforce your right to stand where you are. Ripstein fully appreciates this problem,[54] yet argues that whilst this makes innate right 'imperfect' outside the civil condition, it is not 'provisional' in the same way that acquired rights are. Unfortunately, it seems that our 'at first glance' judgement is correct here, and the imperfect/provisional distinction is a distinction without a difference.

In the first place, Ripstein acknowledges that the problem of individual judgement in conditions of indeterminacy so emphasized by

[53] Much of the discussion here is anticipated by Brudner 2013, 70–4. Where I disagree with Brudner is in his thought at 67, that for Kant innate right has the 'implicit' consent of the omnilateral will prior to entry into the civil condition. I do not see how there could be such a thing under the Kantian framework, for the civil condition is constituted by the omnilateral will or, reciprocally, the civil condition via its institutions constitutes the omnilateral will. In other words there seems to be no room for the omnilateral will's giving any kind of *implicit* consent, as opposed to explicit, legislated or adjudicative consent, to anything.

[54] Ripstein 2009, 176–81.

the assurance argument arises just as much in the case of the innate right as it does with acquired rights. Ripstein gives the following example:[55]

If I shout loud enough to startle you when you stand on the edge of a cliff, but I do not touch you, do I wrong you?

Cases of this kind could be multiplied. Is shouting at you so my breath parts your hair a minor trespass? Is shining my torch in your face so that you blink and squint a trespass? What counts as a trespass is just as indeterminate in any number of cases of innate right as it is in cases of your acquired rights.

But the more worrying problem is that Ripstein fully admits that the indeterminacy is equally relevant to the 'reality' of innate right outside the civil condition in respect of the right to coerce, and this comes up especially in cases where one person 'enforces' her innate right in the face of what she takes to be the aggressive action of another. As Ripstein puts it:[56]

[J]ust as the question of who is an aggressor in a state of nature can be answered by nothing other that what seems good and right to the person defending himself, so, too, these higher-order constraints that require there be only one justified defender can only be applied by the parties themselves. It is thus a structural feature of the situation that it is possible for each party to believe, in good faith, that the other is the sole aggressor. They each make inconsistent claims of right. However, once they have made inconsistent claims of right, there is no answer, apart from what seems good and right to each of them.

Yet Ripstein maintains that this does not render innate right merely provisional. He says:[57]

The imperfection of the right to self-defence does not, however, render that right merely provisional, because it is a conclusive authorization to coerce. Your right to repel those who invade the space occupied by your body does not require an omnilateral authorization. It is imperfect because it is not

[55] ibid., 176.
[56] ibid., 178.
[57] ibid., 179.

an authorization under universal laws, since any such authorization would have to be a member of a necessarily consistent set.

As far as I can tell, however, what makes it a 'conclusive' authorization is just that Kant says it is.[58] It is not clear why there could not be a similar conclusive authorization with respect to acquired rights. The assurance argument seems to apply to them equally and for identical reasons. Innate right is conclusively *innate*, because it is *not acquired*. That is so. But innateness in this sense is entirely orthogonal to the issue of whether or not its coercive enforcement suffers from the same frailties in the state of nature as the enforcement of acquired right does. Nothing in its innateness in this sense bears on the issue of unsystematic enforcement. Ripstein concludes by discussing the power of the state to bring innate right under universal law, that is, omnilateral legislation which solves the structurally identical assurance problem for innate right. Here is the relevant passage:[59]

> Thus although there is no direct argument from the innate right of humanity to the creation of a civil condition—no civil condition could be mandatory if acquired rights were impossible, because nobody would have standing to force another into one—systematic enforcement of acquired rights generates the state's authorization to make law with respect to innate right.

With respect, I do not see how this works or is relevant to the question whether innate right and acquired rights are imperfect or provisional. The idea here is that the provisionality of acquired rights is the reason for the existence of the civil condition, but that having been established, the omnilateral legislative institution acquires a power, not mandated by any provisionality of innate right in the state of nature, to regulate innate right anyway. It is not explained how this is can be so. If the right is real, however imperfect, in the state of nature, the

[58] Peter Chau points out that one element of the innate right to humanity is the duty of rightful honour: Kant 1996 [1797], 29/6:236, Ripstein 2009, 161–2, and suggests that the right of self defence, though imperfect, does not directly implicate the duty of rightful honour, whereas, as Ripstein puts it, at 162: 'my rightful honor demands that I only refrain from using what you possess if I have assurance that you will do the same for me'. All I can say in response is that I don't see how distinguishing the 'assurance' of innate right from acquired rights, on the basis that one implicates rightful honour and the other doesn't, addresses the issues raised in the text.

[59] Ripstein 2009, 181.

state's being conceived of as having a power to solve the provisionality problem of other rights does not support, much less entail, its having a different power to solve the *imperfection* problem of a genuine, *non-provisional* natural right, that is, innate right. So that way of justifying the regulation of innate right is, I think, foreclosed. So the Kantian, it seems to me, is on the horns of a dilemma. The only problem omnilateral legislation is empowered to address is the assurance problem, that is, the non-systematic use of coercion outside the civil condition. I have argued that there is no sound distinction between imperfection and provisionality here. So taking up that argument is one horn of the dilemma—the Kantian would have to re-configure the distinction between innate and acquired rights so that the assurance argument applies to them both. The second horn of the dilemma is to hold firm to the idea that innate right is, though pretty wildly lawless—imperfect if you will—in its coercive implementation by individuals, nevertheless not provisional, and therefore not subject to the assurance problem. In that case the omnilateral will has no standing to regulate it by legislation, for the only thing that gives standing to the omnilateral will is its function in assuring rights that are provisional in the state of nature.

8.4 'External' Criticisms of Kant's Account

Here I shall consider the linchpin of Kant's account, the assurance argument, and try to show why the argument doesn't work despite the best efforts of those who have tried to make sense of it. This is not because I can show that there is some kind of internal inconsistency in Kant's position, but rather that it is wrong whether internally consistent with his other views or not. Kant seems to claim that morality, or at least the morality of right, embodies or requires a kind of *fairness*. But, as I hope to persuade you, morality has nothing to do with fairness. Or rather, it makes no sense to ask whether morality is fair. Morality just is what it is, and fairness doesn't enter into it. I then move on in 8.4.2 to the issue of co-ownership, and suggest that Kant's account provides insufficient resources to makes sense of it.

8.4.1 Critique of the Assurance Argument

If we recall Kant's own formulation of the assurance argument, the sort of claim that seems to be being made, which is typical of a sort of child's claim about the application of rules, is that unless the same rules are being applied to everyone, then applying the rule in any particular case is *unfair.*[60] It is this sort of thought which seems to lead to the emphasis assurance argument defenders place, as we have seen, on the idea that rights are only rights when their coercive enforcement is 'systematic', or to put it another way as Ripstein does, that their rights form a 'consistent set'.[61] And it is true, I think, that the notion of 'fairness' does come into play when we are concerned about the moral legitimacy of a legal system. But it seems to me that morality itself, the kinds of considerations that go to determining our categorical obligations *apart* from the law, or in a 'state of nature', has nothing to do with fairness as it seems to be understood by the proponents of the assurance argument.

The basic thought is that what moral rights[62] we have is not a matter of distribution, fair or otherwise. Underlying the concept of an undistributed right or power, in particular what we might call a 'natural' right, is that one's having such a right is not the result of a distributive *choice*, in the sense that a society could, whilst complying with basic moral requirements, deny anyone that right. Of course this does not mean that everyone agrees on what these 'natural' rights may be. The point is rather that the considerations that go to justify the recognition of such rights do not turn on the idea that they reflect a fair or just allocation of rights amongst persons.

One way in which moral rights can be thought of as distributed rights is on some kind of contractarian model, under which our rights owe their existence to our ability to agree on some set of rights and liberties that we can all equally hold. I don't think I can do better than Otsuka in addressing this sort of distributive or allocative model of basic rights: [63]

A contractualist device such as Rawls's original position that constructs principles of justice out of the self-interested choices of individuals who have been placed behind the 'veil of ignorance' will fall short of generating principles that reflect the existence, importance, and stringency of

[60] The first few pages of this part draw upon Penner 2018, 138–44.

[61] Ripstein 2009, 165.

[62] By rights I mean to include powers, such as the power to enter into agreements or the power to appropriate property.

[63] Otsuka 2003, 5–6 (footnotes omitted), citing Rawls 1971, chs 1 and 3, and Scanlon 1998, 153.

natural rights of self-ownership. It will fall short because, when it comes to our convictions regarding the circumstances in which it is unjust to harm others, we are moved by a variety of ethical considerations that are far too subtle to be captured by any such contractual device that reduces the choice of principles to a procedure of self-interested choice in conditions of ignorance. A contractualist device such as Scanlon's that endows the parties to the contract with the ethical motivation to arrive at principles that are unreasonable to reject might, by virtue of endowing them with this motivation, ensures that the parties arrive at those principles that give natural rights their due. But this greater accuracy in choice of principles of justice is bought at the price of a reduction in the usefulness of the contractual device as a means (distinct from ordinary forms of moral reasoning) of arriving at the right principles of justice. Although we can figure out what people would choose in their self-interest in conditions of ignorance without engaging in ordinary forms of moral reasoning, the same cannot be said regarding principles it would be unreasonable to reject. In order to determine which principles would be unreasonable to reject, one cannot avoid engaging in the familiar sort of moral argumentation ...

This thought regarding 'the familiar sort of moral argumentation' can be fleshed out, I think, by drawing upon the 'value theory', most thoroughly explored by Raz[64] and Gardner.

Gardner develops the idea in terms of 'basic responsibility'. He writes: [65]

Basic responsibility is what it sounds like. It is an ability. More fully, it is the ability and propensity to have and to give self-explanations in the currency of reasons. The ability and the propensity are but two sides of the same coin. As beings who are able to respond to reasons we cannot avoid being disposed to respond to them. There is nowhere to hide from them. ...

Basic responsibility, I suggest, cannot be assigned or allocated by anyone. There is no normative power, by the exercise of which anyone can add to or subtract from it. That is not because it is impossible for any of us not to have it. Some of us lack it altogether. Well, actually, that depends on who counts as 'us'. But assuming we mean 'human beings', we might doubt the basic responsibility of very young children, those with advanced forms of

[64] Raz 1990.

[65] Gardner 2017, 11–13.

dementia or severe mental illnesses, and those in comas. Surely basic responsibility is entirely lacking in at least some such cases? Yes, and that is already a matter of regret. Human beings ought to be answerable to reasons. That is part of their human ergon, to use the Aristotelian term, sometimes translated as 'function' but perhaps better as 'destiny'.

The basic idea is that we are 'valuing' creatures. We respond to or react to or understand facts, including facts about events and human actions, *as reasons*. We see the world, in part, in terms of values (physical pleasure, social and aesthetic values, and so on) that we have reason to realize, and also in terms of disvalues (pain, actions which we regard as cruel or debased or pointless), which we not only have reason to avoid but also have reason to prevent. Reasons underpin rights and duties in a straightforward way on this perspective; X has against Y a right to q if the value of q gives rise to a reason for action which is 'categorical' in the sense that it prevails over Y's otherwise innocuous plans to realize values. Y cannot push X out of the way, thus interfering with X's right to bodily security, in order to hasten himself on his way. Very roughly, X's interest in bodily security is of a strength and stringency such that it imposes a categorical (which is not to say absolute) duty on Y not to infringe it.

If this way of looking at things is right, then the idea that our natural rights are a matter of distribution or allocation is awry. We have the natural rights we have because of the kind of creatures we are. We have these rights as against each other (aberrant circumstances aside) because we are all capable of recognizing the values and disvalues the world presents us with and responding accordingly in our practical reasoning, that is, in reasoning about how to act. Natural rights, then, are undistributed rights.

It is worthwhile pointing out that on a spatial distributive model of rights it would seem to be to my advantage to have the greatest liberty to do whatever it occurs to me to do, irrespective of whatever values *or disvalues* my acting realizes. But that is misconceived. It is not to my advantage to have the liberty to punch you on the nose, take your life, or steal your goods, however much I might mistakenly *want* to have such freedom of action available to me. On the value theory I am endorsing, one has no (rightful) liberty to realize disvalues; equivalently, one can have no right to such a liberty. A duty not to assault or kill others is not, on this account, a normative *burden* of any kind, since one rightly appraised of the values and disvalues out there should have no interest in pursuing such actions in the first place.[66] Of course, given the sort of person I might be, the absence of such liberties, or contrariwise, the presence of such duties 'not to', could chafe, for example, psychologically. I might be naturally careless or have a quick temper or be alienated from others, and so on. But my psychological dispositions are obviously not to the point.

On a non-distributive reading of our moral rights, then, the reason we all have the *same* rights has nothing to do with the 'consistency' or 'compatibility' of my rights with the rights of others but merely reflects the fact that *we are all relevantly the same creatures*, that is, are relevantly the same in terms of what we can demand of each other in terms of the requirements of morality. We have the same rights because we are all tokens of the same type of intrinsically valuable being. Of course one could put the idea of 'same' rights in terms of 'equal' rights but the danger of doing so should now be obvious: 'equal' suggests a division or distribution, in particular a distribution that should be judged according to whether it is 'equal', or *fair*.

The assurance argument's concern with the systematic coercion of right is, to my mind, just a reflection of this 'distributive fairness' thought. Take a homely example:

> MUM: Eden, stop hitting your sister!
>
> EDEN: Why?
>
> MUM: Because it hurts and it is wrong to hurt other people.
>
> EDEN: But my friend Freddie hits his sister all the time!
>
> MUM: What Freddie does doesn't matter. Even if Freddie does something wrong it doesn't make it all right for you to do it.
>
> EDEN (A PHILOSOPHICAL PRODIGY): But Kant says that I do no wrong unless some neutral legislative authority exercising an omnilateral will makes it the case that all wrongs are systematically coercively prevented when that is possible, or systematically remedied after the fact.
>
> MUM: Go to your room.

Mum is, in my view, clearly right here. She is asking lovely young Eden to appreciate the reasons that apply to his action, what makes it wrong

[66] This point is not to be confused with Hart's point when criticizing Rawls 1971, that the contours of our liberties could vary upon what might be called ethical considerations, about the sort of lives people see as better in some ways—for example, some 'tougher' types might be glad to endorse a broad freedom of expression in which, for example, defamation was not prohibited, leaving the response to defamation to be more expression. See Hart 1972–73, 545–52. See also Mendus 2008, 309–13; Rawls 2005, Lecture VIII.

in this instance. But when moral considerations fail on their own to keep the peace, she invokes authority, that is, the law. Her authoritative relationship with her son is only invoked when Eden is being a captious little Kantian. Mum is a good instrumentalist. Eden's mistake is the same mistake made by anyone whose response to a claim based on morality is 'who says?'. They have made a conceptual error, because anyone making a moral argument is *not* purporting to 'lay down' the law for anyone. Morality just has these requirements, not different in kind from any other aspect of our responsibility to account to reason, no different in basic kind from being faulted for not complying with basic logic. It is our native responsibility to reason that is being invoked, not some legislated structure of rules. So Waldron, in the first quoted passage in 8.2.2, was right, and his riposte wrong.

Another way of putting this point is that there is no such thing as 'rule of morality' considerations which correspond to 'rule of law' considerations which Eden is trying to invoke here. The law does indeed involve any manner of questions of fairness, because law is an artefact and the rule of law considerations are specifically there to ensure that the rule is a rule of law, not a rule of individual human judgement, 'a rule of law, not of men' to use the traditional sexist formulation. Kantian assurance argument advocates have simply made a mistake on this point: they look at the unequal enforcement of morality outside of the law as raising 'rule of law' considerations which are simply inappropriate. In other words, morality *as such* has no 'authority structure', so it cannot answer to authority structure considerations like those associated with the rule of law.

As regards the variation of the assurance argument provided by Stone, as far as I can tell he simply says that moral determinacy is casuistic in the realm of right, casuistic in the non-pejorative sense that our understanding of what right requires means considering individual cases and aligning them with others. There is an innocuous reading of Stone, and a pernicious one, which we can see by considering a different case of judgement, judgement in the case of the natural sciences. First, the innocuous reading. No one, I think, would argue that discovering truths about the natural world is conceptually dependent upon certain social structures, even though the accumulation of scientific understanding is historically path dependent. On the other hand, it may be that scientific reasoning is very much suited to a kind of collective enterprise, in which findings and experiments are tested and theorized by individuals organized around social institutions whose aim is to do that very testing and theorizing. Likewise, I should say, with the morality of right. Our current best understanding of what the morality of right requires is a matter of our intellectual history. And it may be that institutions like the law profession, legislatures and courts, and law faculties, were instrumental in making whatever progress along those lines we have made. But this observation does not supply the needed argument, which is that in the absence of the law profession, courts, and so on, our judgements about what the morality of right requires are so meaninglessly indeterminate that right is somehow conceptually unavailable to us. That would be the pernicious reading of Stone's idea.

Two final points about the problem of indeterminacy and 'laying down the law' by individuals. First, if there is anything problematic about indeterminacy in human reasoning, there is no such thing as a democratic, institutional, or other 'structural' cure for it, a fact to which any lawyer will be more than willing to attest. We do try, with things like legislation and the doctrine of precedent, *artificially* to constrain the *effects* of indeterminacy. That is, after all, one of the main instrumentalist claims about what the law is for. How well it works is a matter of empirical assessment. And it is, of course, not without moral consequence. Imposing rules and systems is intended to make the law apply more determinately so as to get people closer to the morality that otherwise binds them. Kantians, of course, know this. Even for the Kantian the institutional, whether legislative or judicial, determination of a matter of judgement never insulates it from criticism from the moral point of view. It is perfectly fine for a Kantian to claim that the law has made a wrong turning, determining the law in a way which is inconsistent with right as they understand it, criticizing, for example, those who would decide cases in tort by reference to considerations of economic efficiency. The ominaliteral will cannot by legislation or adjudication ipso facto cure the indeterminacy of judgement so as to make any such judgements it provides morally, rather than merely legally, legitimate.

Second, it seems to me that Kantians are making a mistake about the nature of determinacy which Wittgenstein worked hard to expose, in my view successfully. It is not the case that because indeterminacy is possible in many cases that all cases are indeterminate. If this were true, any kind of normative human life would be impossible. We could not work within the norms of language, for instance (another area of human nature and life which, like morality, is not legislated). As Baker and Hacker, explicating Wittgenstein, put the point, the *possibility* of doubt if we were to try to apply a norm in another, possible, case does not mean that applying the norm in *this case*, when we know exactly what the norm requires, is doubtful.[67] So it would seem that the determinacy problem, especially as it is so relied upon in the assurance argument, is overstated.

To conclude: a moral right does not depend upon its being 'guaranteed' in the way the assurance argument would require. It is wrong to think that guaranteed enforcement is constitutive of something's being a matter of right. Locke was correct—enforcement and assurance are empirical concerns, albeit important ones, not conceptual ones. Those empirical concerns are the main reason why, for the instrumentalist, the law as an institution exists.[68]

8.4.2 Mine, Yours, but no Place for Ours

Outside of status rights, rights to 'domestic society', which concerns spouses, parents and children, and heads of a household and servants, Kant's morality of right is relentlessly individualistic. As someone who has previously written that,[69] given the social nature of human beings, the idea of co-ownership is *prior* to the notion of individual ownership, I fear this is a point on which Kantians and I are bound to disagree. I shall not reprise that argument here but the basic idea is that certain kinds of cooperative activity between people cannot be framed along contractual lines, where I achieve my individual purpose and you yours by exploiting, albeit consensually and rightfully, each other's means.

This non-contractual co-operative activity, typically cases of sharing and giving, cannot be fractioned into particular benefits to particular individuals, because I can share interests with others, and I can be interested in the interests of others, something that is obvious in the case of family members and friends, but is also so of teammates, colleagues, and so on. These are 'horizontal' relations, as between private law actors, not vertical relations between individuals and the state, so

[67] Baker and Hacker 1984, 114.

[68] For an argument that something akin to the assurance argument has distinct traction in the case of criminal law (particularly regarding punishment, a kind of coercion), see Penner 2019a, text to n 11.Peter Chau has suggested to me that for the Kantian, it is coercion itself, at least in the case of property rights, say of one individual resisting another who attempts to trespass on her land, that brings in requirements of fairness, or what I have called rule of law values. I suppose I would just say that I don't think coercion per se has this sort of magic.

[69] Penner 2006b.

prima facie if they involve relations of right then a rightful private law must find room for them.

Taking full account of this kind of co-operative activity explains why the use of property in these circumstances, whether real property rights to actual places or spaces, or personal property interests in things like bottles of wine, provide a location or a site or the means for the unfolding of this sort of activity; rights to the realization of shared values of this kind must be actual ownership rights, for these kinds of uses are, by their very nature, creatively open-ended, in that they depend upon a continuing interaction of interests the particular course, success, or failure of which cannot be spelled out in advance. The point is not that social uses serving shared interests in this way are too vague to be defined—contractually negotiated rights and duties too can be more or less vague. The point is rather that the values that are created cannot properly be allocated through a system restricted to individual rights protected by correlative duties.

The result is that property devoted to this kind of co-operative activity must inherently be 'co-owned', and the uses by individuals only loosely defined. The necessary rights and duties of co-owners are the rights to: (1) a kind of *common* ownership—the right of each to access all, with general understandings as to the sort of conduct that is permitted and expected, and the right and duty to participate in the joint exploitation of the property for the benefit of all; and (2) co-*ownership*, that is, the right of the benefit of BPrN vis-à-vis all others. Those who are not co-owners are subject to the duty not to interfere with the thing in question per se, for only by 'keeping off' is space provided for a realization of value. Incidentally, this is, roughly, the normative situation which we find in common law legal systems regarding the co-ownership of land.[70]

These considerations, to my mind, provide one of the many persuasive instrumentalist justifications for instituting property, a justification which points out how the open-ended right to the use of property may serve values (the sharing of interests) which simply cannot be accommodated if only individual rights to specified values in things are permitted. And it quite nicely undermines the individualistic taint which has attached itself to ownership, at least amongst legal and political philosophers. It also, I think, reflects a great deal of common sense, for it must be the case that there are very few hermits, and furthermore

[70] See, for example, Claeys 2019, 59–61.

that most others would regard it as a gross mischaracterization to say to them of their property that they hold it only for what they individually can get out of it.

As far as I can tell, Kant has no theory of co-ownership or collaborative agency, and has no resources to provide one. For Kant, human interaction can only be conceived of as a rightful division of means. If co-ownership is a part of the law and cannot easily be squared with the 'division of means' idea, then this is a theoretical deficiency.

One last point on non-individual rights to things. On Ripstein's reading of Kant, there can be no such thing as a common or public right outside the civil condition—as I understand him, not even *provisionally*. As I understand him, all public spaces such as roads can only exist by virtue of legislation.[71]

For Ripstein it seems to be essential to the concept of property rights that all land could be privately appropriated, if his discussion of roads is anything to go by. Ripstein rightly argues that a system of private property that allowed utterly unfettered appropriation could result in individuals being literally imprisoned in their landlocked properties. They would be dependent on other owners to allow them to leave and enter their land. But Ripstein argues not that the necessity and validity of public spaces like public ways are conceptual aspects of a valid regime of property rights conceived independently of the state, but that they are rather the creation of the state, as part of 'a system of public provision',[72] not part of the private law of property per se:[73]

[Other theorists] represent a road as if it were a natural free space, on which everyone is entitled to go as he or she pleases. The state is then depicted as an extrinsic agent that steps in and places limits on this natural freedom, for the sake of overall convenience.... [This] raises the question of just what sort of arrangement we are being asked to imagine. Are roads like the high seas, uninhabitable zones that are available for all to traverse? Or are they somehow a residue of the original commons, the bit of land that has not been appropriated? Neither model has much to recommend it. The first, 'high seas' reading requires the roads be uninhabitable; if this assumption is dropped, it turns into a version of the 'commons' reading, which conceives of the road as simply unowned, in which case anybody who wants to could

[71] The next two pages draw upon Penner 2010b, 100–1.

[72] Ripstein 2009, 250.

[73] ibid., 249.

come along and claim it as his or her own property. Perhaps the 'commons' reading can be modified to conceive of the road as a sort of residue left over from private appropriation, subject to some sort of Lockean proviso to guarantee the sort of access that roads provide. If so, then its residual status requires rules of use and access ... Although the details of those rules need to be fixed by a public authority, that there are such rules constitutes the system of roads. Neither model provides any way of thinking of the road as a free space which the government steps in to restrict.

It is not as though the road is already there, and then the rules are subsequently imposed. The road and the public rules regulating it come as a package.

I agree with the last paragraph, except for the word 'public', as in 'public rules', as for Ripstein this means 'state' rules.

Ripstein's error, as I see it, is to confound the idea of 'unowned, but used', with the idea of 'available for appropriation'. It is not the case that 'simply unowned' entails 'anybody who wants to could come along and claim it as his or her own property'. Ripstein argues forcefully that a regime of property rights would be self-defeating, would imprison owners, if rights of way could be appropriated. So why does the same not go for conceiving natural limits to the rightful power to appropriate so that roads or ways that are in actual use (as well as other public spaces, like open pastures and forests, use of which is continually made) are literally off-limits for appropriation? One might wish to ask the appropriator who disagreed, 'How did you *get* to the land you have appropriated in the first place?' The public space preceded the private, necessarily so. So, *pace* Ripstein, both historically and conceptually the soundest view is that roads and public spaces are not a 'residue', space *left* after private appropriation, but rather communally used and occupied space that was not available for appropriation by anyone, spaces that provide the necessary spine supporting private appropriations.

Perhaps the greatest injustice in the history of the institution of property rights was that institution's abuse by the powerful to appropriate lands which, while not 'owned' in the strict sense, were certainly occupied and used. Anyone with any sympathy at all for commoners whose lands suffered enclosure, or with the concept of aboriginal or native title, understands this point.[74]

[74] For a possible Kantian endorsement of this general point in relation to international law and colonialism, see Ganesh 2018, 185–6. For a discussion about how takings akin to enclosure continue to this day, see Upham 2018.

8.5 From Usufruct to Property

As I have argued elsewhere,[75] a right to exclude for any reason, or no reason at all, has no moral value per se. Indeed the recognition of such 'dog in the manger' rights has a positive disvalue. This is something upon which instrumentalists concerning property—Henry Smith is a good example[76]—agree. On the instrumentalist perspective, exclusionary property rights, rights defined by BPrN, can be justified, not as a matter of conceptual necessity in light of the structure of private right on a Kantian account, but because they protect human agency with respect to our use of things.

Property, as with other acquired rights, protects an individual's *means*, so there is an internal justificatory relationship between exclusion and use on this account. This requires us to consider the idea that a particular appropriation could be a wrong in rem, that is, a 'horizontal' wrong having nothing to do with the state, but a wrong against indefinite others.[77] The roads case, discussed at 8.4.2, stands as a case of illegitimate appropriation because it is a kind of expropriation—taking something not available for appropriation because others have rights in regard to it that make appropriation wrongful. The other is wrongful destruction or sterilization. Destruction is of course related to consumption, but wrongful destruction concerns the taking away of future use, removing something as a means from the realm of means without justification. It seems to me that this can be a wrong in rem. I don't think, for example, that the destruction of significant cultural objects or the poisoning of land needs to be conceived as a wrong against a collective, or a group, or a state, though for obvious reasons the degree of harm may be different depending upon one's 'identity'. It can be an wrong in rem to others per se. Sterilization, though related, need not involve destruction, though I suppose one could say that destruction as a form of 'elimination' is a subset of sterilization. By sterilization I mean an appropriation either with the intention never to use something, or in respect of a subsequent failure ever to make use of something, to subject it to some actual choice. This is to use the right to appropriate to render some thing, '*res nullius*' in fact. This is

75 Penner, 1997c, 70–1.

76 Smith 2012b.

77 It would be a further matter to determine which of those others would have standing in law to enforce a remedy to such a wrong.

also a wrong that no rightful system of private law could countenance. The attentive reader will notice that these in rem wrongs of appropriation mirror the structure of the bilateral torts enumerated in the last chapter—use- or usurpation-based wrongs, damage/destruction-based wrongs, and deprivation-based wrongs.

From this perspective, the basic moral norm governing our use of things is what I shall dub the Basic Usufructory Norm with respect to tangible things, chattels, and land, or BUsN for short: Do not interfere with the lawful uses that others are making of things. This account meshes, in a way, with Katz's characterization of ownership as the right to 'set the agenda' with respect to the thing in question.[78] Although I shall not consider her account in detail, the basic idea is that, under BUsN, the lawful user who first makes use of something that was previously not being used by anyone—a person I shall dub the 'First User'—acquires a right to carry on using it and has the benefit of BUsN. In that sense the First User sets the agenda for the thing, by making uses by others which are incompatible with her use off-limits. But the usufructory right of the First User is not, in principle, fully exclusionary in the way that a property right is. A third party is not disentitled from using the thing in question so long as his use does not interfere with the owner's first use. So, for example, the third party does no wrong by crossing through the first owner's orchard so long as he does not damage the fruit trees or in any other way interfere with the first owner's use of the land as an orchard.

Having said all this, there are numerous instrumentalist considerations that weigh in favour of the law's introducing exclusive property rights, protected by BPrN. I shall only mention here a few of the most obvious ones.

First, some things, most obviously things we consume like food, are more or less 'one-use' things. Protecting the usufructory is more or less tantamount to protecting a property right in them. To the extent BPrN is more easily complied with than BUsN, it makes instrumental sense to apply BPrN to goods of this kind.

Second, and perhaps the most overwhelming argument for instituting BPrN rather than BUsN, is BPrN's epistemic cheapness. As explored in great detail by Merrill and Smith from a transaction costs perspective,[79] and by me in more homely terms, BPrN is a

[78] Katz 2008.

[79] See, for example, Merrill and Smith 2000, 38; Merrill and Smith 2001a, 809–51; Smith 2002, 2009b.

'bright line' rule which, to use Kantian terminology, allows us to know where we stand vis-à-vis each other much more easily than trying to judge whether any particular usufructory right is justifiable in terms of protecting a legitimate use. Whether in all cases current rights to things deserve this blanket protection is an ongoing question, in particular in relation to objects of cultural significance, as I have mentioned above, or in relation to land, the subject of the next chapter.

A third issue concerns privacy and sociability. Property in land, but not only in land, is quite rightly a means by which one of the ways in which we stand to each other—our relations of intimacy and our general gregariousness—can be organized. Residential property in land, in particular, provides a space for privacy and intimacy, and both public spaces and privately owned yet sociable spaces, such as pubs, cater to our general gregariousness.

This brings us finally to the two powers of title, to license what would otherwise be a trespass, and to transfer title to the property itself. I have already spoken about giving and sharing at 8.4.2. In my view, using the powers of title to share and give respond to certain relationships in which individuals share interests, whereas contractual licences and transfers do not, and so need a second, independent, element of justification, the justification of contract itself.[80]

8.6 Conclusion

Occasionally I think of myself as a kind of impossible theoretical chimera, a Kantian instrumentalist.[81] As this chapter shows, I have found some of the Kantian picture of property entirely persuasive, as I pointed out at the end of 8.2.2. In particular, I think Kantians get this right about the morality of private right: the morality of private right is negative and relational. By securing our (not absolute) independence from the choices of others with respect to our means, private rights secures our basic individual agency; it lets us know how we stand as agents in relation to each other. Only once that is established can we make ethical judgements about the choices we make, for only once

[80] Penner 1997c, 74–5, 87–97; Penner 1996b; Penner 2014a.

[81] At other times a Hegelian instrumentalist. See Penner 1997c, ch. 8. As I mentioned in n. 1, my thinking about several of the issues in this chapter owes much to Brudner 2013.

that is established can we understand the choices to be genuinely ours. This is as much to say that I am not an instrumentalist about morality.

Accepting all that, however, does not undermine in any way the instrumentalist perspective on the law. The law, on this perspective, even private law, must always answer not only to the morality of private right, but to a host of other considerations. Is the law working efficiently? Is it effectively bringing us closer to observing the morality of private right? Has it judged the relative urgency of different private law claims well, and devoted its energies accordingly? And so on. But, as I hope to have persuaded you in my discussion of the assurance argument, the dependency relationship does not go the other way round. The morality of right is not, as a matter of the force or application of its claims upon us, dependent upon the law.

9

Rights in Land

9.1 The Recurring Issue

Over the course of the last five years or so when I presented draft chapters of this book, but in particular Part 1, I was frequently invited to consider whether the tripartite structure of title really made sense of our ownership rights in land. Think of all the other aspects of what might be compendiously referred to as 'land law'—the law of landlord and tenant, the historical listing of buildings, zoning or planning law, environmental regulation, and so on. Doesn't all this law make our ownership of land so much more complicated than the picture of title to land, as a tangible object of property, that I present? Doesn't the existence of laws of this kind detract from that picture?

There is a short answer and a long one.

The short answer is 'no'. *To the extent* our private law relationships as against others with respect to land is primarily shaped by the tripartite structure of title, then land counts as kind of property, something that can be owned. To say this says nothing about the scope of public law limitations of that right, nor about private law limitations, as I shall discuss.

The longer answer, which will take up the rest of this chapter, concerns the question whether land, given its particular features, is a very *suitable* object of ownership. To make a point clear to my audience: that I advance a theory of property rights, and have explained the way in which they can valuably structure our interpersonal relations, does not make me a general *proponent* of property rights, insisting upon instituting them whenever they can frame our interpersonal relations with respect to some thing, land in particular.

Property Rights. J. E. Penner, Oxford University Press (2020) © J. E. Penner.
DOI: 10.1093/oso/9780198830122.001.0001

9.2 Particular Features of Land

Compared to goods, land has a number of special features. This is a partial list, and I trust the reader can generate some more of her own. I hope that everything I shall say in this part is uncontroversial. My aim is just to set out a number of features of land which complicate any kind of land law.

1. Even before the Westphalian settlement, land has been closely associated with territory and jurisdiction.[1] It is no surprise then, that public law has always taken a special interest in rights to land.
2. Land is immovable, as any refugee will tell you, and for this reason the law governing land ownership will be that of the jurisdiction in which it is situated. That's why there are no choice of law rules for land title transactions.
3. Rights in land are extremely malleable, as any acquaintance with the history of English land law reveals. As I have said elsewhere,[2]

   > Immediately after the Conquest, the rights in land were not property rights. Such rights were not freely alienable, not inheritable, nor could they be left by will; all manner of services were attached to them; and they were extensively personal in that they were intended to reflect personal bonds of loyalty.... Indeed, in legal terms one can define feudalism as that state of affairs in which there is no property in land, but rather that rights to land are specifically intended to reflect an individual's status, or 'office' in the political, economic, and legal order.

   Though feudal land law is an excellent illustration of the point, the variety of rights in land make the point much more general. Consider, for instance, aboriginal title, rights of commons and of way, the estates system, nomadic rights, and so on.[3]
4. The landed surface of the earth, as the natural home to which we have evolutionarily become suited (though not equally for all parts of the globe, obviously), is also our environment, which

[1] See, for example, Miller 2011.

[2] Modified slightly from Penner 1997c, 151–2.

[3] As Upham 2018 suggests, rights in land are particularly susceptible to the forces of 'creative destruction' which Schumpeter thought characterized capitalism.

spans differently across different plots of property. No single owner's land is its own environment in this sense.

5. Whilst it is true that some chattels can last forever, and we treat some, such as works of art, to ensure that they do, most chattels have lives of a certain duration, either because they are consumed, or because they wear out. Not so with land. Leaving aside such issues as encroachment by the sea causing erosion, land lasts forever. But this is not to say that land cannot be 'destroyed' in the colloquial sense that it can be made unsuitable, or even dangerous, for future occupation or use. Think of the strip-mining of coal or the Alberta tar sands.
6. Land has some natural boundaries, and these can restrict the way in which parcels of land can practically be delineated as plots of land that can be owned, but in general ownership of land requires the imposing of artificial boundaries.
7. Land is contiguous, in the sense that, natural boundaries aside, plots of land will abut each other. Since public or common rights to land are native to regimes of rights in land (8.4.2) there will always arise issues of access, intersecting private and public rights to land.[4]
8. Rights to land necessarily, even if only in terms of rights of way to get to the land, depend upon infrastructure. Of course the infrastructure today is typically much more complicated than the simple provision of public roads. This is not to say that certain kinds of chattels do not depend for their usefulness on elaborate infrastructure—think of your mobile phone—but rather that this is native to property in land. Partly in virtue of this fact, the libertarian idea that property grants 'independence' from others is generally spurious in the case of land.[5]

These features ramify in a number of ways, but let me just mention a few. First, the value of land varies enormously with its location in a way having basically nothing to do with whether the owner improves the land or not, or its basic use value (as a residence, or a shop, whatever). Because humans are social creatures, and because land requires

[4] To take one example, for a fascinating exploration of the way that US authorities, in giving effect to the 'public trust' and similar doctrines, struggled with fitting the notion of public ownership into the model of individual or corporate or state ownership, see Rose 1994, ch. 5.

[5] Penner 2009, 196–7.

infrastructure to support it, the neighbourhood and political jurisdiction in which a plot of land is situated will extensively affect its value. Second, because land is immovable and requires infrastructure, collective or community infrastructural endeavours, such as building roads or railways, will typically be beset by 'hold-out' problems, which is why states have powers of expropriation (aka 'eminent domain'). Thirdly, and most importantly, the use of land by an owner will inevitably have effects that outlast his ownership, not only in time, but in space. Any use of land has an environmental impact. No land is an island, environmentally speaking.

9.3 Public and Private Constraints upon Land Ownership

In view of all the considerations raised in the last section, it is not surprising that rights in land are extensively regulated beyond the regulation of implementing a regime of private property in respect of them.[6] There should, of course, be extensive public regulation of land use, and sporting my lefty environmental credentials for a moment, I think we regulate land use far less than we should. But a question sometimes arises whether any limitation upon or modification of the basic rules of title, in particular the power to license or transfer, are a matter of public law. I want to suggest that they are not.

Consider rent control legislation. There are two ways of looking at this. One is to say that this is a public intervention in the market to achieve public goals, such as, I suppose, a more efficient market in housing. The other is to say that this is an adjustment of private rights—the *basic* rights of title and contract are adjusted because, in this context, regulating the relations between landlords and tenants via these basic rights alone leads to interpersonal injustices. We intervene in the market here because this market reveals itself to be beset by inequalities in bargaining power, information asymmetries, unconscionable exploitation, and so on. Whether the legislation is seen to advance a goal of public justice, or one of private justice, or both, is a

[6] See also Penner 1997c, 100–3. In Chapter 7, 7.1, I already mentioned restrictions that apply to the use of things irrespective of who owns them, which are not germane to the present discussion.

matter of judgement, of course. All I want to insist upon is that legislative deviations from a strict regime in which our personal interactions with respect to things is governed by the tripartite nature of title does not necessarily take us into public law, or more vaguely, 'distributive justice'.[7]

Judges, as we know, also impose similar deviations, deviations which become part of private law. To take two obvious examples: (1) equitable intervention in the law governing mortgages in land, over time creating the 'equity of redemption', which adjusted the rights of mortgagors and mortgagees to prevent the exploitation of the former; (2) the intricacies of landlord and tenant law.

The long and short of this is simply to point out that a property theorist of my stripe is not committed to the idea that, however illuminating the tripartite nature of title is in explaining one of the ways in which our interpersonal relations are structured, that is, or indeed must be, the whole story. Of course it is not, for it is not exhaustive of the content of interpersonal, relational, justice.

9.4 Conclusion: Duties in Rem, the Right to Enclose, and the 'Common Ownership' of the Earth

In Chapter 8, 8.5, I mentioned wrongs in rem, a wrong a person can commit by expropriating, destroying, or sterilizing property. The wrong is in rem, and counts as the breach of a duty in rem, because it is owed to all our fellows. The environmental degradation of land is an obvious example. Unfortunately, as it seems to me, making sense of this kind of duty is often framed in terms of our 'common ownership of the earth'.[8] I shall conclude this chapter by suggesting that this framing is not helpful. In the same way that we do not own our bodies, we do not own land. To express a thought often associated with aboriginal concepts of land, the land is part of us, or the land 'owns' us.

The ideas at play here can be elaborated with the example of enclosure. Land can be 'enclosed' for any number of useful purposes. One

[7] My account therefore differs in important respects from that of Austin 2018.

[8] For an illuminating recent discussion, see Olsthoorn 2018.

can fence a garden patch to keep the rabbits out, or fence a pasture to keep the sheep in. One can build walls or plant hedges to maintain privacy, or set up windbreaks. But there is no general right to enclose land, and so exclude others from it. Rousseau got it more right than wrong when he said:[9]

> The first man who, having enclosed a piece of ground, bethought himself of saying 'This is mine,' and found people simple enough to believe him, was the real founder of civil society. From how many crimes, wars, and murders, from how many horrors and misfortunes might not any one have saved mankind, by pulling up the stakes, or filling up the ditch, and crying to his fellows: 'Beware of listening to this imposter; you are undone if you once forget that the fruits of the earth belong to us all, and the earth itself to nobody.'

The question is, what construction should we place on the notion of 'belonging' Rousseau invokes in the last sentence. One, of course, is ownership, some kind of 'common ownership'. But since in the case of tangible things like land we cannot own what we cannot possess, ownership, common or otherwise, is unavailable for describing our relationship to the earth, for the earth cannot be possessed, only bits of it from time to time.

The thought is this:[10] Consider Locke's idea that the earth is given by God to man in common. Sitting here in Singapore, is it churlish to think that God made a poor job of giving me a right (in common with all others, of course) to Australia? The bottom of the Pacific Ocean? Mars? The unspoken premise behind the concept of common ownership is that I as an individual, simply by existing, have some normatively significant relation to every piece of matter in the universe concerning the realization of its value, a relation that all others must acknowledge and respect. The implausibility of this is obvious as soon as it is stated. Any sensible characterization of what is *owned* by 'common owners' involves the summation of what each has actually possessed, and what underpins any possible normativity in respect of my relationship to things which I myself have never possessed is the fact that other people have possessed them, and that I, by virtue of my relation to those other people, may through them have some normative

[9] Rousseau 1913, 192.
[10] Modified from Penner 2006b, 172–3.

relation to those things. This is, we may say, the basis of usufructory right, a right in relation to a thing by which our interpersonal relations can be structured. But this has nothing to do with 'ownership' of the earth.

So what is our relationship to the earth, such that enclosure generally is prima facie wrong? This would need a lot of spelling out, which I cannot do here, but I think it would require the theoretical development of the idea of 'home'. The earth is our (common) home, and no one should be entitled to take away or destroy our home.

A Conclusion of Sorts

Where have we got to? As the title of the book indicates, this has been a re-examination of a number of issues that I think are vital to our comprehension of property rights. I am conscious of the fact that this book, taken as a whole, is somewhat 'bitty' or fragmented. I have addressed a number of distinct issues, and my purpose has not been to advance or defend a comprehensive theory of property rights. But let me just recapitulate some of its themes.

Both Parts 1 and 2 can be seen as an outworking of what I called in the Preface my 'rules fundamentalism', the idea that general norms structure and explain the individual right–duty (or power–liability etc.) jural relations. If there is a guiding principle here, it is the idea that attempts to understand or explain property rights which start from these person-to-person jural relations get things the wrong way round. Underpinning this thought are the following ideas:

- That no system of private law can be exhaustively represented only by the enumeration of interpersonal jural relations;
- That jural relations are analytically and normatively inert;
- That jural relations are just the outputs or instantiations of the application of general impersonal rules;
- That corrective justice is parasitic on the structure of general norms which pre-exist and determine the nature and consequence of any instance of their violation.

The general structuring norms of property together give us the tripartite nature of title. One element of that, what I called BPRN, the basic property exclusionary norm for tangible property, was the focus of

Property Rights. J. E. Penner, Oxford University Press (2020) © J. E. Penner.
DOI: 10.1093/oso/9780198830122.001.0001

Chapters 5 and 7, whereas the powers of title, in particular the power of transfer, were examined in Chapters 4 and 6.

All of this, you might say, was the ground-level, structural work, which I built upon in Chapters 8 and 9. Chapter 8 examined the perennially fascinating subject of the justification of property rights, on which issue I criticized the Kantian position and defended an instrumentalist one, whilst Chapter 9 addressed the suitability, as I put it, of organizing our rights to land around property rights.

As the reader can probably tell, I could write about property endlessly, but heeding Shakespeare's thought[1] that a surfeit may spoil the appetite, I shall say no more.

[1] Twelfth Night, Act 1, Scene 1:

If music be the food of love, play on;
Give me excess of it, that, surfeiting,
The appetite may sicken, and so die.

Bibliography

Austin, L. (2018). The Public Nature of Private Property. *Property Theory: Legal and Political Perspectives*. J. Penner and M. Otsuka. Cambridge, Cambridge University Press: 1–22.

Baker, G. P. and P. M. S. Hacker (1984). *Scepticism, Rules & Nonsense*. Oxford, Basil Blackwell.

Baker, J. H. (2002). *An Introduction to English Legal History*. Oxford, Oxford University Press.

Baron, J. B. (2014). 'Rescuing the Bundle-of-Rights Metaphor in Property Law'. *University of Cincinnati Law Review* **82**: 57–101.

Beever, A. (2013). *The Law of Private Nuisance*. Oxford, Hart Publishing.

Biasetti, P. (2015). 'Infinite Regress and Hohfeld: A Comment on Hillel Steiner's "Directed Duties and Inalienable Rights"'. *Ethics* **126**: 139–52.

Block, N. (1997). 'Anti-Reductionism Slaps Back'. *Nous* **31**: 107–32.

Bridge, M. (2015). *Personal Property Law*. Oxford, Oxford University Press.

Brudner, A. with J. M. Nadler (2013). *The Unity of the Common Law*. Oxford, Oxford University Press.

Byrd, S. B. and J. Hruschka (2006). 'The Natural Law Duty to Recognise Private Property Ownership: Kant's Theory of Property in his *Doctrine of Right*'. *University of Toronto Law Journal* **56**: 217–82.

Chang, Y.-c. and H. E. Smith (2012). 'An Economic Analysis of Civil versus Common Law Property'. *Notre Dame Law Review* **88**: 1–55.

Claeys, E. R. (2018). 'Use And the Function of Property'. *American Journal of Jurisprudence* **63**: 221–58.

Claeys, E. R. (2019). 'Property, Concepts, and Functions'. *Boston College Law Review* **60**: 3–72.

Coase, R. H. (1960). 'The Problem of Social Cost'. *Journal of Law and Economics* **3**: 1.

Cohen, F. S. (1935). 'Transcendental Nonsense and the Functional Approach'. *Columbia Law Review* **35**: 809–49.

Cohen, F. S. (1954). 'Dialogue on Private Property'. *Rutgers Law Review* **9**: 357–87.

Cohen, M. R. (1927). 'Property and Sovereignty'. *Cornell Law Quarterly* **13**: 8–30.

Corbin, A. L. (1919–20). 'Legal Analysis and Terminology'. *Yale Law Journal* **29**: 163–73.

Corbin, A. L. (1921). 'Terminology and Classification in Fundamental Jural Relations'. *The American Law School Review* **4**: 607–14.

Coval, S., J. C. Smith, and S. Coval (1986). 'The Foundations of Property and Property Law'. *Cambridge Law Journal* **45**: 457–75.

Cullison, A. D. (1967). 'A Review of Hohfeld's Fundamental Legal Concepts'. *Cleveland State Law Review* **16**: 559–73.

Darwall, S. (2006). *The Second-Person Standpoint: Morality, Respect, and Accountability*. Cambridge, MA, Harvard University Press.

Dickey, A. (1971). 'Hohfeld's Debt to Salmond'. *University of Western Australia Law Review* **10**: 59–64.

Dorfman, A. (2012). 'The Society of Property'. *University of Toronto Law Journal* **62**: 563–607.

Dorfman, A. (2014). 'Private Ownership and the Standing to Say So'. *University of Toronto Law Journal* **64**: 402–41.

Douglas, S. and B. McFarlane (2013). Defining Property Rights. *Philosophical Foundations of Property Law*. J. Penner and H. E. Smith. Oxford, Oxford University Press: 219–43.

Epstein, R. A. (1979). 'Nuisance Law: Corrective Justice and its Utilitarian Constraints'. *Journal of Legal Studies* **8**: 49–102.

Epstein, R. A. (2011). 'Bundle-of-Rights Theory as a Bulwark Against Statist Conceptions of Private Property'. *Econ. Journal Watch* **8**: 223–35.

Essert, C. (2013). 'The Office of Ownership'. *University of Toronto Law Journal* **63**: 418–61.

Essert, C. (2016). 'Nuisance and the Normative Boundaries of Ownership'. *Tulsa Law Review* **52**: 85–120.

Feser, E. (2005). 'There is No Such Thing as an Unjust Initial Acquisition'. *Social Philosophy and Policy* **22**: 56–80.

Finnis, J. (1972). 'Some Professorial Fallacies about Rights'. *Adelaide Law Review* **4**: 377–88.

Fodor, J. A. (1974). 'Special sciences: The Disunity of Science as a Working Hypothesis'. *Synthese* **28**: 97–115.

Fodor, J. A. (1997). 'Special Sciences: Still Autonomous after All these Years'. *Nous* **31**: 149–63.

Ganesh, A. (2018). '*Wirtbarkeit*: Cosmopolitan Right and Innkeeping'. *Legal Theory* **24**: 159–90.

Gardner, J. (2011). 'What is Tort Law For? Part 1. The Place of Corrective Justice'. *Law and Philosophy* **30**: 1–50.

Gardner, J. (2014). Some Rule-of-Law Anxieties about Strict Liability in Private Law. *Private Law and the Rule of Law*. L. M. Austin and D. Klimchuk. Oxford, Oxford University Press: 207–23.

Gardner, J. (2016). 'Private Authority in Ripstein's *Private Wrongs*'. *Jerusalem Review of Legal Studies* **14**(1): 52–63.

Gardner, J. (2017). 'The Negligence Standard: Political Not Metaphysical'. *The Modern Law Review* **80**: 1–21.

Gaus, G. F. and L. E. Lomasky (1990). 'Are Property Rights Problematic?' *The Monist* **73**: 483–503.

Glackin, S. N. (2014). 'Back to Bundles: Deflating Property Rights, Again'. *Legal Theory* **20**(1): 1–24.

Gregor, M. (1988). 'Kant's Theory of Property'. *Review of Metaphysics* **41**: 757–87.

Grey, T. C. (1980). The Disintegration of Property. *Nomos XXII: Property*. P. J. R. and C. J. W. New York, New York University Press **XXII**: 69–85.

Halpin, A. (1985). 'Hohfeld's Conceptions: From Eight to Two'. *Cambridge Law Journal* **44**: 435–57.

Halpin, A. (1991). 'More Comments on Rights and Claims'. *Law and Philosophy* **10**: 271–310.

Halpin, A. (1996). 'The Concept of a Legal Power'. *Oxford Journal of Legal Studies* **16**: 129–52.

Halpin, A. (1997). *Rights and Law - Analysis and Theory*. Oxford, Hart Publishing.

Halpin, A. (2003). 'Fundamental Legal Conceptions Reconsidered'. *Canadian Journal of Law and Jurisprudence* **16**: 41–54.

Halpin, A. (2017). The Value of Hohfeldian Neutrality When Theorising about Legal Rights. *New Essays on the Nature of Rights*. M. McBride. Oxford, Hart Publishing: 1–30.

Harris, J. W. (1986). Ownership of Land in English Law. *The Legal Mind: Essays for Tony Honore*. N. MacCormick and P. Birks. Oxford, Clarendon Press: 143.

Harrison, R. (1982). 'Transcedental Arguments and Idealism'. *Royal Institute of Philosophy Lecture Series* **13**: 211–24.

Hart, H. L. A. (1972). 'Bentham on Legal Powers'. *Yale Law Journal* **81**: 799–822.

Hart, H.L.A (1972–73) 'Rawls on Liberty and its Priority' (1972–1973) *The University of Chicago Law Review* **40**: 534–55.

Hart, H. L. A. (1982). *Essays On Bentham: Jurisprudence and Political Philosophy*. Oxford, Oxford University Press.

Heller, M. (2008). *The Gridlock Economy*. New York, Basic Books.

Hodgson, L.-P. (2010). 'Kant on Property Rights and the State'. *Kantian Review* **15**: 57–87.

Hohfeld, W. N. (1913–14). 'Some Fundamental Legal Conceptions As Applied In Judicial Reasoning'. *Yale Law Journal* **23**: 16–59.

Hohfeld, W. N. (1916–17). 'Fundamental Legal Conceptions As Applied In Judicial Reasoning'. *Yale Law Journal* **26**: 710–70.

Holmes, O. W. (1963). *The Common Law*. Boston, Little, Brown and Company.

Honore, A. M. (1959–60). 'Rights of Exclusion and Immunities against Divesting'. *Tulane Law Review* **34**: 453–68.

Honore, A. M. (1961). Ownership. *Oxford Essays in Jurisprudence*. A. G. Guest. Oxford, Clarendon Press: 107–47.

Hudson, S. D. and D. N. Husak (1980). 'Legal Rights: How Useful is Hohfeldian Analysis'. *Philosophical Studies* **37**: 45–53.

Hurd, H. M. and M. S. Moore (2018). 'The Hohfeldian Analysis of Rights'. *The American Journal of Jurisprudence* **63**: 295–354.

Kant, I. (1974). *On the Old Saw that Might be Right in Theory but it Won't Work in Practice* (trans. E. B. Ashton). Philadelphia, PA: University of Pennsylvania Press.

Kant, I. (1996) [1797]. *The Metaphysics of Morals*. Cambridge, Cambridge University Press.

Katz, L. (2008). 'Exclusion and Exclusivity in Property Law'. *University of Toronto Law Journal* **58**: 275–315.

Katz, L. (2011). 'Ownership and Social Solidarity: A Kantian Alternative'. *Legal Theory* **17**: 119–43.

Katz, L. (2018). Legal Forms in Property Law Theory. *Property Theory: Legal and Political Perspectives*. J. Penner and M. Otsuka. Cambridge, Cambridge University Press: 23–37.

Kim, J. (1992). 'Multiple Realization and the Metaphysics of Reduction'. *Philosophy and Phenomenological Research* **52**: 1–26.

Kocourek, A. (1919–20). 'Rights In Rem'. *University of Pennsylvania Law Review* **68**: 322–36.

Kocourek, A. (1920–21). 'The Hohfeld System of Fundamental Legal Concepts'. *Illinois Law Review* **15** 24–39.

Kocourek, A. (1921). 'Reply to Paper of Professor Corbin'. *The American Law School Review* **4**: 614–16.

Kocourek, A. (1928). *Jural Relations*. Indianapolis, The Bobbs-Merrill Company.

Kramer, M. H. (1998). Rights Without Trimmings. *A Debate Over Rights*. M. H. Kramer, N. E. Simmonds and H. Steiner. New York, Oxford University Press: 7–111.

Kramer, M. H., N. E. Simmonds, and H. Steiner (1998). *A Debate Over Rights*. New York, Oxford University Press.

MacCormick, N. (1977). Rights in Legislation. *Law, Morality, and Society*. P. M. S. Hacker and J. Raz. Oxford, Oxford University Press: 189.

Maitland, F. W. (1909, 1929 Reprint). *Equity, Also The Forms of Action at Common Law: Two Courses of Lectures*. Cambridge, Cambridge University Press.

Mendus, S. (2008). Private Faces in Public Places. *The Legacy of HLA Hart: Legal, Political, and Moral Philosophy*. M. Kramer MH et al. Oxford, Oxford University Press.

Merrill, T. W. (1985). 'Trespass, Nuisance, and the Costs of Determining Property Rights'. *Journal of Legal Studies* **14**: 13–48.

Merrill, T. W. (1998). 'Property and the Right to Exclude'. *Nebraska Law Review* **77**: 730–55.

Merrill, T. W. (2011). 'The Property Prism'. *Econ. Journal Watch* **8**: 247–54.

Merrill, T. W. (2012). 'The Property Strategy'. *University of Pennsylvania Law Review* **160**: 2061–95.

Merrill, T. W. and H. E. Smith (2000). 'Optimal Standardization in the Law of Property: The *Numerus Clausas* Principle'. *Yale Law Journal* **110**: 1–70.

Merrill, T. W. and H. E. Smith (2001a). 'The Property/Contract Interface'. *Columbia Law Review* **101**: 773–852.

Merrill, T. W. and H. E. Smith (2001b). 'What Happened to Property in Law and Economics?' *Yale Law Journal* **111**: 357–98.

Merrill, T. W. and H. E. Smith (2007). 'The Morality of Property'. William and Mary Law Review **48**: 1849–95.

Miller, D. (2011). 'Property and Territory: Locke, Kant, and Steiner'. *Journal of Political Philosophy* **19**: 90–109.

Mossoff, A. (2003). 'What is Property? Putting the Pieces Back Together'. *Arizona Law Review* **45**: 371–443.

Munzer, S. R. (1990). *A Theory of Property*. Cambridge, Cambridge University Press.

Munzer, S. R. (2011). 'A Bundle Theorist Holds On to His Collection of Sticks'. *Econ. Journal Watch* **8**: 265–73.

Newark, F. H. (1949) 'The Boundaries of Nuisance'. *Law Quarterly Review* **65**: 480–97

Neyers, J. W. (2017). 'Reconceptualising the Tort of Public Nuisance'. *Cambridge Law Journal* **76**: 87–115.

Nolan, D. (2011). 'A Tort Against Land': Private Nuisance as a Property Tort. *Rights and Private Law*. D. Nolan and A. Robertson. Oxford, Hart Publishing: 459–90.

Nolan, D. (2019). The Essence of Private Nuisance. *Modern Studies in Property Law Volume 10*. B. McFarlane. Oxford, Hart Publishing. **10**: 71–88.

Nozick, R. (1974). *Anarchy, State, and Utopia*. Oxford, Basil Blackwell.

Olsthoorn, J. (2018). Two Ways of Theorising 'Collective Ownership of the Earth'. *Property Theory: Legal and Political Perspectives*. J. Penner and M. Otsuka. Cambridge, Cambridge University Press: 187–213.

Otsuka, M. (2003). *Libertarianism without Inequality*. Oxford, Oxford University Press.

Page, W. H. (1921). 'Terminology and Classification in Fundamental Jural Relations'. *The American Law School Review* **4**: 616–23.

Penner, J. and E. Melissaris (2012). *McCoubrey & White's Textbook on Jurisprudence Fifth Edition*. Oxford, Oxford University Press.

Penner, J. E. (1993). 'Nuisance and the Character of the Neighbourhood'. *Journal of Environmental Law* **5**: 1–29.

Penner, J. E. (1996a). 'The 'Bundle of Rights' Picture of Property'. *UCLA Law Review* **43**: 711–820.

Penner, J. E. (1996b). 'Voluntary Obligations and the Scope of the Law of Contract'. *Legal Theory* **2**: 325–57.

Penner, J. E. (1997a). 'The Analysis of Rights'. *Ratio Juris* **10**: 300–15.

Penner, J. E. (1997b). Hohfeldian Use-rights in Property. *Property Problems: From Genes to Pension Funds*. J. W. Harris. London, Kluwer: 164–74.

Penner, J. E. (1997c). *The Idea of Property in Law*. Oxford, Clarendon Press.

Penner, J. E. (2000). Nuisance, the Morality of Neighbourliness, and Environmental Protection. *Environmental Protection and the Common Law*. J. Lowry and R. Edmonds. Oxford, Hart Publishing: 27–49.

Penner, J. E. (2005). 'Decent Burials for Dead Concepts'. *Current Legal Problems* **58**: 313–42.

Penner, J. E. (2006a). Duty and Liability in Respect of Funds. Commercial Law: Perspectives and Practice. J. Lowry and L. Mistelis. London, LexisNexis Butterworths: 207–25.

Penner, J. E. (2006b). 'Ownership, Co-ownership, and the Justification of Property Rights'. *Properties of Law: Essays in Honour of Jim Harris.* T. Endicott, J. Getzler and E. Peel. Oxford, Oxford University Press: 166–88.

Penner, J. E. (2009). 'Property, Community, and the Problem of Distributive Justice'. *Theoretical Inquiries in Law* **10**: 193–216.

Penner, J. E. (2010a). 'Resulting Trusts and Unjust Enrichment: Three Controversies'. *Constructive and Resulting Trusts.* C. Mitchell. Oxford, Hart: 237–66

Penner, J. E. (2010b). 'The State Duty to Support the Poor in Kant's Doctrine of Right'. *British Journal of Politics and International Relations* 12: 88–110.

Penner, J. E. (2011). 'Potentiality, Actuality, and "Stick"-Theory'. *Econ. Journal Watch* **8**: 274–8.

Penner, J. E. (2013). On the Very Idea of Transmissable Rights. *Philosophical Foundations of Property Law.* J. Penner and H. E. Smith. Oxford, Oxford University Press: 244–71.

Penner, J. E. (2014a). Promises, Agreements, and Contracts. *Philosophical Foundations of Contract Law.* G. Klass, G. Letsas, and P. Saprai. Oxford, Oxford University Press: 116–34.

Penner, J. E. (2014b). 'The (True) Nature of a Beneficiary's Equitable Proprietary Interest Under a Trust'. *Canadian Journal of Law and Jurisprudence* **27**: 473–500.

Penner, J. E. (2016). *The Law of Trusts.* Oxford, Oxford University Press.

Penner, J. E. (2018). Rights, Distributed and Undistributed: On the Distributive Justice Implications of Lockean Property Rights, Especially in Land. *Property Theory: Legal and Political Perspectives.* J. Penner and M. Otsuka. Cambridge, Cambridge University Press: 138–60.

Penner, J. E. (2019a) 'As If We Were Strangers: From Social Life to Private Law'. https://papers.ssrn.com/sol3/papers.cfm?abstract_id=3350173.

Penner, J. E. (2019b). *The Law of Trusts, 11th Ed.* Oxford, Oxford University Press.

Penner, J. E. (2020). Don't Crash into Mick Jagger when He is Driving his Rolls Royce: Liability in Damages for Economic Loss Consequent upon a Personal Injury. *Civil Wrongs and Justice in Private Law.* P. B. Miller and J. Oberdiek. Oxford, Oxford University Press: 253–71.

Perry, R. (2009). 'Correlativity'. *Law and Philosophy* **28**: 537–84.

Perry, T. D. (1977). 'A Paradigm Of Philosophy: Hohfeld On Legal Rights'. *American Philosophical Quarterly* **14**: 41–50.

Perry, T. D. (1980). 'Reply in Defense of Hohfeld'. *Philosophical Studies* **37**: 203–9.

Radin, M. (1938). 'A Restatement of Hohfeld'. *Harvard Law Review* **51**: 1141–64.

Rainbolt, G. W. (2006). *The Concept of Rights.* Dordrecht, Springer.

Rawls, J. (1971). *A Theory of Justice.* Cambridge, MA, Harvard University Press.

Rawls, J. (2005). *Political Liberalism, Expanded Edition*. New York, Columbia University Press.

Raz, J. (1983). *The Authority of Law: Essays on Law and Morality*. Oxford, Clarendon Press.

Raz, J. (1984a). 'Legal Rights'. *Oxford Journal of Legal Studies* **4**: 1–21.

Raz, J. (1984b). 'On the Nature of Rights'. *Mind* **93**: 194–214.

Raz, J. (1986). *The Morality of Freedom*. Oxford, Clarendon Press.

Raz, J. (1990). *Practical Reason and Norms*. Oxford, Oxford University Press.

Ripstein, A. (1998). *Equality, Responsibility, and the Law*. Cambridge, Cambridge University Press.

Ripstein, A. (2004). 'Authority and Coercion'. *Philosophy and Public Affairs* **32**: 2–35.

Ripstein, A. (2006a). 'Beyond the Harm Priniciple'. *Philosophy and Public Affairs* **34**: 215–45.

Ripstein, A. (2006b). 'Private Order and Public Justice: Kant and Rawls'. *Virginia Law Review* **92**: 1391–438.

Ripstein, A. (2009). Force and Freedom: Kant's Legal and Political Philosophy. Cambridge MA, Harvard University Press.

Ripstein, A. (2013). Possession and Use. *Philosophical Foundations of Property Law*. J. Penner and H. E. Smith. Oxford, Oxford University Press: 156–81.

Ripstein, A. (2015). 'Means and Ends'. *Jurisprudence* **6**: 1–23.

Ripstein, A. (2016). *Private Wrongs*. Cambridge, MA, Harvard University Press.

Ripstein, A. (2017) 'Property and Authority: How to Tell the Difference'. *Theoretical Inquiries in Law* **18**: 243–68.

Rose, C. M. (1994). *Property and Persuasion: Essays on the History, Theory, and Rhetoric of Ownership*. Boulder, Colorado, Westview Press.

Rousseau, J. J. (1913). *The Social Contract and Discourses*. London, J M Dent & Sons.

Rudden, B. (1987). Economic Theory v. Property Theory: The *Numerus Clausas* Problem. *Oxford Essays in Jurisprudence, Third Series*. J. Eekelaar and J. Bell. Oxford, Oxford University Press: 239–63.

Sage, N. (2012). 'Original Acquisition and Unilateralism: Kant, Hegel, and Corrective Justice'. *Canadian Journal of Law and Jurisprudence* **25**: 119–36.

Sage, N. (2018) Is Original Acquisition Problematic? *Property Theory: Legal and Political Perspectives*. J. Penner and M. Otsuka. Cambridge, Cambridge University Press: 99–120.

Scanlon, T. M. (1998). *What We Owe to Each Other*. Cambridge, MA, Harvard University Press.

Shell, S. M. (1978). 'Kant's Theory of Property'. *Political Theory* **6**: 75–90.

Shiffrin, S. V. (2008). 'Promising, Intimate Relationships, and Conventionalism'. *Philosophical Review* **117**(4): 481–524.

Simmonds, N. E. (1986). *Central Issues in Jurisprudence: Justice, Law and Rights*, Sweet & Maxwell Thomson Reuters.

Simmonds, N. E. (1998). Rights at the Cutting Edge. *A Debate Over Rights*. M. Kramer, N. E. Simmonds, and H. Steiner. Oxford, Oxford University Press: 113–232.

Singer, J. W. (1982). 'The Legal Rights Debate in Analytical Jurisprudence From Bentham to Hohfeld'. *Wisconsin Law Review* **1982**: 975–1059.

Singer, J. W. (1988). 'The Reliance Interest in Property'. *Stanford Law Review* **40**: 611–751.

Singer, J. W. (1991). 'Sovereignty and Property'. *Northwestern University Law Review* **86**: 1–56.

Singer, J. W. (2009). 'Democratic Estates: Property Law in a Free and Democratic Society'. *Cornell Law Review* **94**: 1009–1062.

Smith, H. E. (2002). 'Exclusion Versus Governance: Two Strategies for Delineating Property Rights'. *Journal of Legal Studies* **31**: S543–S487.

Smith, H. E. (2003). 'The Language of Property: Form, Context, and Audience'. *Stanford Law Review* **55**: 1105–1191.

Smith, H. E. (2004a). 'Exclusion and Property Rules in the Law of Nuisance'. *Virginia Law Review* **90**: 965–1049.

Smith, H. E. (2004b). 'Property and Property Rules'. *New York University Law Review* **79**: 1719–1798.

Smith, H. E. (2009a). 'Institutions and Indirectness in Intellectual Property'. *University of Pennsylvania Law Review* **157**: 2083.

Smith, H. E. (2009b). 'Mind the Gap: The Indirect Relation Between Ends and Means in American Property Law'. *Cornell Law Review* **94**: 959–989.

Smith, H. E. (2011). 'Property Is Not Just a Bundle of Rights'. *Econ. Journal Watch* **8**: 279–91.

Smith, H. E. (2012a). 'On the Economy of Concepts in Property'. *University of Pennsylvania Law Review* **160**: 2097.

Smith, H. E. (2012b). 'Property as the Law of Things'. *Harvard Law Review* **125**: 1691–726.

Smith, H. E. (2015). 'The Persistence of System in Property'. *University of Pennsylvania Law Review* **163**: 2055–83.

Smith, L. (2013). 'Scottish Trusts in the Common Law' *Edinburgh Law Review* **17**: 283–313.

Smith, S. A. (2014). Strict Duties and the Rule of Law. *Private Law and the Rule of Law*. L. M. Austin and D. Klimchuk. Oxford, Oxford University Press: 189–206.

Steiner, H. (2013). 'Directed Duties and Inalienable Rights'. *Ethics* **123**: 230–44.

Stern, J. Y. (2018). What is the Right to Exclude and Why Does it Matter? *Property Theory: Legal and Political Perspectives*. J. Penner and M. Otsuka. Cambridge, Cambridge University Press: 38–68.

Stevens, R. (2007). *Torts and Rights*. Oxford, Oxford University Press.

Stone, M. (2011). 'Legal Positivism as an Idea About Morality'. *University of Toronto Law Journal* **61**: 313–41.

Thomson, J. J. (1990). *The Realm of Rights*. Cambridge, Massachusetts, Harvard University Press.

Upham, F. H. (2018). *The Great Property Fallacy: Theory, Reality, and Growth in Developing Countries*. Cambridge, Cambridge University Press.

von Wright, G. H. (1963). *Norm and Action: A Logical Inquiry*. New York, The Humanities Press.

Waldron, J. (1996). 'Kant's Legal Positivism'. *Harvard Law Review* **109**: 1535–66.

Weinrib, E. J. (2002–03). 'Poverty and property rights in Kant's system of rights'. *Notre Dame Law Review* **78**: 795–828.

Weinrib, E. J. (2012). *Corrective Justice*. Oxford, Oxford University Press.

Weinrib, E. J. (2018). 'Ownership, Use, and Exclusivity: The Kantian Approach'. *Ratio Juris* **31**: 123–38.

Weinrib, J. (2008). 'Kant on Citizenship and Universal Independence'. *Australian Journal of Legal Philosophy* **33**: 1–25.

Weinrib, J. (2014). 'Permissive Laws and the Dynamism of Kantian Justice'. *Law and Philosophy* **33**: 105–36.

Wellman, C. (1985). *A Theory of Rights: Persons Under Laws, Institutions, and Morals*. Totowa, New Jersey, Rowman & Allanhead.

Westphal, K. R. (1997). 'Do Kant's Principles Justify Property or Usufruct?' *Jarbuch fur Recht und Ethik/Annual Review of Law and Ethics* **5**: 141–94.

Westphal, K. R. (2016). *How Hume and Kant Reconstruct Natural Law: Justifiying Strict Objectivity without Debating Moral Realism*. Oxford, Oxford University Press.

Williams, H. (1977). 'Kant's Concept of Property'. *Philosophical Quarterly* **27**: 32–40.

Wilson, J. G. (1980). 'Hohfeld: A Reappraisal'. *University of Queensland Law Journal* **11**: 190–204.

Wittgenstein, L. (1958). *Philosophical Investigations*. Oxford, Basil Blackwell.

Index

Note: *For the benefit of digital users, indexed terms that span two pages (e.g., 52–53) may, on occasion, appear on only one of those pages.*

Milton Keynes UK
Ingram Content Group UK Ltd.
UKHW021836301123
433508UK00005B/296